BUSINESS WEEK's Guide to the Best Executive Education Programs

John A. Byrne
Senior Writer, BUSINESS WEEK

Cynthia Greene
with a team of
BUSINESS WEEK Editors

McGraw-Hill, Inc.
New York   St. Louis   San Francisco   Auckland   Bogotá
Caracas   Lisbon   London   Madrid   Mexico   Milan
Montreal   New Delhi   Paris   San Juan   São Paulo
Singapore   Sydney   Tokyo   Toronto

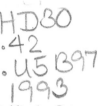

Library of Congress Cataloging-in-Publication Data

Byrne, John A.
   Business week's guide to the best executive education programs /
John A. Byrne, Cynthia Greene with a team of Business week editors.
      p.   cm.
   Includes index.
   ISBN 0-07-009334-2 :   —ISBN 0-07-009335-0 (pbk.) :
   1. Management—Study and teaching (Higher)—United States—
Evaluation.   2. Master of business administration degree—United
States.   3. Business schools—United States—Curricula—Evaluation.
4. Business schools—United States—Faculty—Attitudes.   5. Business
students—United States—Attitudes.   I. Greene, Cynthia.
II. Business week (New York, N.Y.)   III. Title.   IV. Title: Guide to
the best executive education programs.
HD30.42.U5B97   1993
658.4'0071'173—dc20   92-26321
                                                                CIP

1 2 3 4 5 6 7 8 9 0   DOC/DOC   9 8 7 6 5 4 3 2

ISBN   0-07-009334-2   {HC}
ISBN   0-07-009335-0   {PBK}

The sponsoring editor for this book was Theodore Nardin, the editing
supervisor was Barbara B. Toniolo, and the production supervisor
was Suzanne W. Babeuf. It was set in ITC Garamond Light by
McGraw-Hill's Professional Book Group composition unit.

Printed and bound by R. R. Donnelley & Sons Company.

CONTENTS

PREFACE

With previous rankings of the top business schools, BUSINESS WEEK has carved out an influential franchise as *the* No. 1 source on the best in management education. This guidebook is the natural outgrowth of that effort, begun in 1988 with the magazine's first rankings of the nation's best graduate schools of business.

BUSINESS WEEK broke new ground when it expanded its coverage in 1991 to executive education, becoming the first magazine to produce a qualitative ranking of the schools offering nondegree executive education courses and seminars as well as special Executive MBA programs. These programs play an increasing role in training the managers who will soon lead Corporate America. Companies—including many foreign ones—are spending almost $4 billion annually for these efforts at U.S. schools.

To prepare a ranking, BUSINESS WEEK dispatched more than 10,000 surveys to deans, corporations, and participants in 56 programs. The surveys flowed back from every corner of the world—from Australia and China, Kuwait and Germany. The report in the magazine's October 28, 1991 issue immediately became must-reading for every human resources executive and for every ambitious manager on the move.

For this book, the first-ever consumer guide to executive education, BUSINESS WEEK used its consumer satisfaction surveys of managers and corporations as a starting point. Then, the staff interviewed hundreds of students, alumni, recruiters, faculty members, and deans to draw out the strengths and weaknesses of the top schools. The result is a guide that reveals in depth the fascinating findings of our first rankings of executive education programs.

Directing the project was BUSINESS WEEK Senior Writer John A. Byrne, who has been reporting on management education for nearly a decade. Author of *Business Week's Guide to the Best Business Schools*, as well as several other books on business, Byrne initiated the original research and the concept of the magazine cover story as well as the book.

Enlisted to do additional reporting and writing for the guide was Cynthia Greene, a Philadelphia-based freelance writer, who is a former editor of BUSINESS WEEK and the Associated Press. Judi Crowe, assistant editor of information services, greatly assisted in compiling on computer the results of well over 3000 questionnaires from the magazine's several polls. David Leonhardt and Christine Muzyka kept track of many of those responses and also did some reporting work for the project. Monica Roman helped to improve survey response rates from corporate officials. Art Director Malcolm Frouman oversaw the design of the cover. Assistant Managing Editor Mark Morrison supervised the project and edited the guide.

CHAPTER 1

THE RACE TO GET AHEAD

You've worked hard—don't you deserve a summer away from the office grind, thinking the Big Thoughts amidst the ivy-covered brick of some hallowed institution of higher learning? You'll read a few books, sit in on a few lectures, shoot the breeze and knock back a few beers with some other Big Thinkers, then head back to the office, refreshed and ready to continue your climb to the corporate stratosphere.

If this is your idea of what executive education is all about, you'd better think again. Gone are the days when senior managers were rewarded for a career's worth of loyal toil with a college sabbatical on the company tab. Executive programs are no longer a perk for those already inside the executive suite: Nowadays, they're practically essential for survival at every level of the corporate ladder. In most companies, if you're not being tapped for some type of management training, you can consider yourself firmly mired off the fast track.

Indeed, it may well be a sign that you shouldn't wait for the company to tap you on the shoulder for such an experience. These days, companies have become more interested in organizational development and less interested in the personal development of their managers. That means managers need to be more proactive in searching for the right program on their own— whether it's a two-year executive MBA experience that will provide a degree, or simply an update on key skills over a few weeks. In either case, BUSINESS WEEK's guidebook was created to be a roadmap to the best offerings by the best graduate schools of business.

Going back to school offers you more than a chance to cultivate and improve your abilities and skills; it also puts you in touch with new friends and colleagues, linking you into a different network of contacts. But it's not Easy Street. If you are one of the tens of thousands of aspiring chief executives chosen each year to pack their bags for school, you can forget the fantasy of a lazy recess in the groves of academe. True, there's still a taste of the country club in some executive programs. At the Wharton School, for students'

1

midday break, waitresses wheel carts full of freshly baked cookies on linen-lined silver trays through the hallways hung with millions of dollars worth of modern art. At Columbia University's Arden House, executives dine in turn-of-the-century elegance in the wood-panelled, candelabra-lit banquet room gracing the secluded, hilltop mansion that serves as the school's executive retreat. But for the most part, these programs are pure boot camp, with 8 a.m. classes, study groups that meet into the wee hours, and the pressure of measuring up under the scrutiny not only of hard-nosed professors but also of a highly competitive, demanding class of experienced colleagues who are there to get ahead. Don't forget your superiors, who are going to expect that much more from you after spending a hefty sum in tuition and lost hours to send you off to study.

Even though the recession has slowed growth somewhat, companies are spending more and more on employee education. Executive development—in the form of university-based open-enrollment and executive MBA programs; in-house company training; and customized courses taught by business schools, independent learning organizations, and consultants working on commission—now eats up some $12 billion annually from corporate budgets. With slightly more than 25 percent of that amount going to business schools, there's a big attraction to get into the exec-ed game, and more and more schools—roughly 150, at last count—are entering the fray in hopes of capturing a share of the corporate money that enriched Harvard Business School, the field's top player, by nearly $27 million in 1991. After just a decade in exec-ed, Duke University's Fuqua School of Business is already bringing in almost $8 million a year, up 333 percent since 1986. Even the smaller, regional schools are finding a bonanza in management programs: The University of Hawaii's College of Business Administration took in $2.5 million last year, more than doubling its take from five years earlier.

Executive education has been big business for B-schools since World War II, when the federal government called on universities to help train managers to retool factories for the military effort, and then a few years later, in the wake of the war's manpower drain, to help ease the return to civilian life by bringing a new cadre of executives up to speed. Schools like Harvard and Stanford University's Graduate School of Business developed their lengthy, broad-based general management programs with the senior manager in mind, "as a rite of passage for entry into the executive suite," says Morton Galper, dean of Babson College's School of Executive Education. These programs focused heavily on individual development, with the idea that, in an era of devotion to the corporation, what was good for executives would be good for the companies to which they had devoted their careers. In the 1960s, companies expanded this philosophy to include high-potential, mid-level executives, who were dispatched to courses that would prepare them for their eventual accession to the corporate upper echelon.

During the 1980s, however, leading-edge firms such as Xerox and Motorola began to focus on what Galper calls "strategy-driven management development." Managers at all organizational levels attend programs that "reflect the strategic direction and concerns of the organization," Galper says. In other words, companies now want the money they spend on educating their employees to enhance the organization; any benefits to the individual are strictly gravy. "It's not a perk, it's not a reward—it's a statement that the company is expecting them to come back and make a greater contribution," says Maureen Arnott, manager of executive education at Digital Equipment Corp. After all, with worker mobility at an all-time high, who's to say that the vice president who costs you $14,000 to send to the University of Michigan for four weeks won't be working for a rival firm by year's end? "Executive education used to be viewed as a cookie for good performance," says Douglas A. Ready, executive director of the International Consortium for Executive Development Research in Lexington, Massachusetts. "Now, companies demand more relevance. They're saying: 'If I'm going to send $200,000 of corporate property away for several weeks, I want to see a payback.'"

To that end, companies and their employees are becoming increasingly vocal about getting what they want out of B-school executive programs. Exec-ed alumni in general offer upbeat appraisals of the courses they attend. Asked by BUSINESS WEEK in 1991 to rate the return on time and money invested from 0 percent to 100 percent, their responses averaged 81 percent. But there's no shortage of complaints, either. Some managers are surprised by the inconsistent teaching quality at some of the world's most prestigious universities. They gripe about studying outdated cases that seem to have little relevance to today's fast-changing world, many of them recycled versions of the cases they studied 20 years earlier as MBA students. Women and minorities are often shocked to find their classmates still virtually all-male and all-white—except for the growing proportion of foreign participants, who now make up 25 to 50 percent of many schools' flagship general management programs. And those from overseas, as well as the sizable number of Americans working in multinational businesses, are regularly disappointed to discover that much of their study centers on the U.S. operations of U.S. companies.

Even more critical of the B-schools are the corporations that foot the bills for these programs. "They're just too bureaucratic and too slow," says James Baughman, manager of General Electric's Management Development Institute, which devises in-house courses for employees. "The programs are too long. They're not flexible enough. They're too expensive, and they lack action learning [in which executives work on real-world problems to come up with real-world solutions that companies can put to use]." "My perception is that executive education in the universities has been an outgrowth of MBA programs and mirrors the MBA curriculum," says Dick Sethe, manager of ex-

3

ecutive education for AT&T. That may have been fine back when a significant number of managers had no postgraduate education, but these days even entry-level executives are dripping with degrees. Echoes another official from a major user of B-school programs: "We're talking about tens of thousands of dollars for a few days of experience. I feel a righteous indignation to expect high quality."

Many firms have become so indignant about what they're getting from universities that they've begun turning to other sources for executive education. Some look to independent exec-ed providers such as Colorado's Aspen Institute, the Ashridge Management Institute in Great Britain, and the North Carolina-based Center for Creative Leadership. These organizations cater exclusively to working managers, unencumbered by the distractions of undergraduates, MBA and doctoral students, or individual faculty research agendas, to which B-schools must devote time and resources. And corporate human resources officials give these three institutions rave reviews.

Other corporations with the means to do so, such as Motorola and AT&T, run their own in-house programs for employees. Each year, 6000 GE workers attend classes at the company's Crotonville training center in Ossining, New York, with 6000 others put through company-sponsored programs at other sites around the world. Consultants, many of them former business executives or moonlighting university faculty, are hired to teach workers on site. "There's no business school in the world that can deliver the same quality faculty across the whole spectrum of need," says GE's Baughman. "By working with independent faculty, rather than one school, we can mix and match. If the best finance person is from Columbia, and the best marketing person is from IMD (the Switzerland-based International Institute for Management Development), we can put them together as opposed to going to any one of those places."

More importantly, the firms retain complete control over the programs' content and delivery. Schedules can be molded to company needs, to create the least disruption in the workplace; the firm doesn't have to cope with the loss of key personnel for several weeks at a time. And without the proprietary concerns about giving away company secrets in an open-enrollment class rife with potential competitors, participants are free to discuss the problems and solutions that are most pressing to the firm. "We can tailor and customize what we do to increase GE relevance and GE impact," says Baughman. "We can write internal cases and design internal computer-based simulations and outdoor experiences and our own action-learning projects so that they really have payoff for us."

In their own defense, the universities warn that corporations may be taking too short-sighted a view of employee development, since many of the benefits, particularly of a general management program, are intangible ones

4

that may not be apparent for months or even years. When executives go off for up to 11 weeks, as in the case of Harvard's Advanced Management Program, they have time to step back from the daily rush and think about why they do the things they do, comparing notes with other managers from all over the world. The result, at least at first, may simply be a clearer sense of purpose on the job. "Training is spending money to help people do their job today. That's a coping strategy," says George Hollenbeck, a consultant on executive development who has seen the subject from both sides of the coin, as a vice president of human resources for Merrill Lynch and a faculty member at Harvard Business School. "Development is really a building strategy, a growth strategy—investing money in people for the future." Concurs Frank T. Morgan, director of executive education at the University of Virginia's Darden Graduate School of Business Administration: "I think it can be demonstrated that one good decision, especially at the senior management level, pays for the cost of tuition times 1000."

And although program participants may head back to work feeling transformed, full of new plans and renewed vigor, they often encounter resistance to change as the rest of the company continues to do things in the same old way. "When managers get back to their jobs, they face a desk piled with mail and demands from their bosses, and they have no time to exercise anything they've learned," says Margaret Fisher, who heads the Office of Executive Programs at Boston University. "Many times, their bosses don't even know why they've gone."

Nevertheless, the message that corporations are ready for a new approach to executive education has not been lost on the B-schools. "The wake-up call has been ringing for the past three to five years," says the International Consortium's Ready. "The universities have picked up the phone and listened." The result: shorter, more accessible programs that incorporate into their curricula the kinds of issues that companies say they are most concerned about—such as the globalization of business, the rapid pace of organizational change, and continuous quality and productivity improvement—using projects that have immediate applicability back on the job.

To answer company concerns about the length—and consequently the cost in both tuition and time away from the job—of many programs, one school after another has downsized its offerings, especially their longer-term, flagship general management courses. By 1993, the Stanford Executive Program will be honed down from eight weeks to seven; the Program for Senior Executives at MIT's Sloan School of Management from nine to eight; and Cornell University's Executive Development Program from five weeks to four. "Companies are finding it increasingly difficult to send people away for long periods of time," says Peter M. Vantine, director of executive education at Carnegie Mellon University's Graduate School of Industrial Administration, which is shortening its Program for Executives from six weeks to four. "Individuals are increasingly reluctant to spend time away; two-wage-earner families can't go away and leave the burden entirely on the other person."

Chantal Delys, director of executive education at the Graduate School of Business at the University of Texas at Austin, is still more blunt, predicting that even four-week programs will soon prove too much to handle. "These programs are dinosaurs, a breed of the past," she says. "The most precious resource for companies now is their managers' time. People who can leave for four or six weeks aren't necessary." Ronald P. Carter, director of executive development for Merck & Co., agrees: "The right level of person won't go away for two weeks. They don't even take their vacations."

Schools are also looking for ways to personalize their open-enrollment courses. Rather than simply providing general, theoretical information that students must then try to apply to their own companies on their own, many programs are incorporating projects in which participants can work out real-life problems or challenges. "By the time somebody leaves a program, we want them to have an action plan for how to deal with some problem or project they're wrestling with back home," says Mary Anne Devanna, Columbia's director of executive education. Agrees Harry B. Bernhard, associate dean for executive education at Emory Business School: "I want to produce programs that are extremely useful, so when people go back to the office on Monday, they can start applying what they learned."

Other schools, particularly smaller, regional ones, are adopting a niche strategy, choosing one subject area or industry in which to concentrate efforts and become the nation's premier expert. Southern Methodist University's Edwin L. Cox School of Business in Dallas, for example, has cornered the market on exec-ed for the oil and gas industry. Hawaii has taken the lead in programs with an Asian perspective. The University of Tennessee's Management Development Center has established its market by specializing in the quality movement and related issues.

But the most important trend in exec-ed is toward collaborative efforts between the B-schools and their clients. Schools are seeing an ever-growing portion of their revenues coming from custom courses, programs that are commissioned by individual companies for their employees alone. These range from company-specific, massaged versions of open-enrollment programs that are already offered to extensive, intimate relationships between a school and a corporation that result in multiple programs over several years' time. A few holdouts, such as Stanford and MIT, have declined to customize their offerings, citing the drain on resources, the possible blurring of the line between education and consulting, and the desire to maintain academic independence. But even stalwart Harvard is negotiating with a few firms to enter the custom business, and other prestigious universities have dived in headfirst, without hesitation. Half of Wharton's $16 million exec-ed business now comes from such work. "Custom courses are very demanding, but they're a very important dialogue with companies," says Thomas P. Gerrity, dean of Wharton. "In some cases, single-company programs are the most exciting of all because it allows us to do in-company research and brings the company executives here," adds Brandt Allen, the associate dean for executive education at Darden.

A case in point is the relationship between Duke and Johnson & Johnson. In 1988, senior managers turned to the school for help in becoming a "world-class competitor," by making all executives more aware of customer needs and how J&J's operations stacked up against the competition's. For six months, a Duke professor interviewed presidents, vice presidents, and plant managers at 11 J&J companies; focus groups solicited the views of hourly workers; and written surveys helped the corporation's top 200 executives identify key issues. The results were used to create an intensive one-week curriculum on world-class manufacturing. That program's success has led to seven other initiatives with Duke, with some 900 senior and mid-level J&J executives attending the programs since 1989.

Another option that may be more attractive to smaller companies is the idea of the consortium, in which a group of 10 or 12 firms forms a partnership with a university that designs a management course to fit their specifications. It's less demanding for the school than having to come up with a dozen different curricula, and less risky than launching an open-enrollment program, because each company commits to send a fixed number of participants at a set cost for a set time period. For the corporations' part, it's usually less expensive than a company-specific custom course, and the firms still get the benefit of having more control over the course while being able to air their laundry in relative privacy.

Babson College, which pioneered the concept, and Indiana University are two institutions that have enjoyed great success with such partnerships. "We feel that executive education is a valuable learning experience for us as well as the participants," says Babson's Dean Galper. "Every time we dialogue with executives we learn about what's going on inside companies, what we might want to research—it's an important feedback loop to our own education." Brandt Allen of Darden is also looking to the consortium idea for future growth. "Companies see real power in 8 or 10 of them getting together and crafting a program or a series of programs. It gives them a sense of ownership, and they feel they can work with the university and lay out their requirements. Some universities don't want to be dictated to, but having an informed customer tell us what they're doing internally and what they'd like to do on the outside is great. That gives me something to work with."

Taking the idea to an even bigger scale is the International Consortium for Executive Development Research. Formed in 1990, it now consists of

7

some 16 universities and 25 corporations. The companies each put up $25,000 a year to fund research into such topics as how to carry on with executive development in a corporate culture that is undergoing dramatic changes; how to manage a transnational team; and how to define and achieve the so-called "learning organization." "Companies pay the equivalent of sending one executive to one five-week program, and get the benefits of $300,000 to $400,000 worth of customer-focused research," claims Ready.

Despite the many innovations in executive education, however, there is still room for the traditional, university-based open-enrollment general management program. There is no other arena in which executives can find such enriching, broadening contacts with managers from other companies, other industries, and even other countries. Here is where you will find the most objective information about management, unfiltered through any corporate lens, based on the best, most up-to-date research available. The truly leading-edge companies in executive development, such as IBM and AT&T, recognize that fact, and take advantage of all the many forms of exec-ed out there in the marketplace. AT&T, for example, has two in-house management programs aimed at two different executive levels; participates in several consortia, including those at Babson and the International Consortium for Executive Development Research; commissions custom programs from a number of institutions; and counts itself among the biggest users of open-enrollment general management programs at such top-ranked schools as the University of Michigan's School of Business, Duke, Northwestern University's Kellogg Graduate School of Management, and Darden. "We send 800 people a year to programs, half internal and half external," says Dick Sethe, AT&T's manager of executive education. "We try to blend."

HOW TO GET IN
ON THE ACTION

With all the hassles of trying to get away from home and office for a few weeks, the prospect of putting in grueling 18-hour days while you're at school, and the heavy load of catchup work you know will be facing you when you return, you might be tempted to pass on the chance to attend an executive program. It sure sounds like more trouble than it's worth.

But consider these comments from executives recently in general management programs at top-rated schools across the country:

It was one of the most fulfilling and rewarding experiences of my career.

The program has dramatically changed my life and, as a result, my way of thinking and doing. The eight weeks have been the most beneficial in my entire life.

My executive education experience recharged my energy level and gave me a new outlook on my current job and future opportunities.

It was the most stimulating experience in my entire career.

I can now count as friends and colleagues people from Thailand, Holland, Finland, and India. These folks stretched my perception of myself and others dramatically.

The executive program was the most satisfying experience I have had over the last 15 years.

Subsequent to the program, I was more relaxed, more human, and more effective. My responsibility doubled, I earned a seven-figure equity payment, and I became president of a company... all within a year.

Not everyone who attends an executive program will end up at the helm of his or her company in just a few months, of course. But the zeal with which many executives describe the effects of exec-ed on their way of doing business hints at just how important it can be to attend the right program, at the right school, at the right time in your career.

First, there's the credential you'll be able to add to your résumé. For a manager whose previous educational credits are lackluster—particularly for those who don't have an MBA—here's a chance to be able to say you've attended a name-brand, top-notch university. And if the cachet of being an Ivy League or Big 10 alum doesn't attract you, don't forget the thousands of other upwardly mobile executives who will gladly boast of their time at Harvard, or Wharton, or Stanford when promotion time rolls around. What with the abundance of competition, the lack of such a credential can hurt you as much as its presence can help. Attending an executive program is like taking out an insurance policy that guarantees you're on the cutting edge of developments in management practice.

Then there's the unique opportunity for networking that a good-quality executive program affords you. Where else can you not only meet several dozen of the corporate best and brightest from all over the world, but also get to know them intimately as you eat, sleep, and labor together for a few intense weeks? It's like joining an exclusive club: Many of the top schools have active alumni organizations that help you maintain the associations you make during the program for years to come. It's not at all unusual to hear of job opportunities, business partnerships, and even lifelong friendships that have grown out of these programs. One executive who attended Harvard's Advanced Management Program in 1989 finds he now has a global web of contacts he can turn to for advice and camaraderie: "We've gotten together on occasion in different cities when traveling, and we'll pick up the phone and call each other as well," he says. "I was on a trip recently and ran into a colleague in the Geneva airport." Affirms another executive who attended Duke's Advanced Management Program, "My classmates provided a rich array of backgrounds and professional experiences. Their views and paradigms were extremely interesting, and I interact with over 30 percent of these individuals on a continuing basis."

Executive programs also provide a rare chance to step back from the day-to-day routine, even if just for a week or two, and reassess yourself—your way of dealing with people, your achievements to date, and your goals for the future. In fact, personal growth is one of the biggest benefits cited by managers who extol the virtues of exec-ed. An executive program may lead to a promotion, a raise, better working conditions, or it may not—leaving its value in the way it broadens your horizons. "The educational experience and the extended absence from the office has allowed me and my managers to alter our day-to-day focus and interrelationships. Now I focus much more on the longer-term, broader corporate issues and strategic matters, leaving the day-to-day operational and administrative matters to them," says one corporate vice president who attended the Stanford Executive Program. "It also gave me an opportunity to refocus my personal and work objectives. Letting go of my managers and the detail has allowed me to reduce my workaholic tendencies and devote more time to my mental and physical health and my family, while at the same time giving my employer more high-quality executive time."

Even if you're convinced of the value of executive education, however, the vast array of programs, with such a wide range of subjects, time frames, and price tags, can be bewildering. Time was—and still is, in the case of some companies—that the corporate human resources department took the matter out of your hands, deciding who to send and where to send them. Employees had little input, and often the choice was simply a matter of a worker achieving a certain status in the company and the CEO having some long-time connection with the school. But in the current economy, with executive development budgets tightening, the corporate psychology has changed. Firms are taking a much harder look at how exec-ed money is spent, and they want to see concrete organizational results, not just a single worker's personal development. Managers have to be much more proactive in seeking out continuing educational possibilities that will develop their own skills and satisfy the company's needs, as well as lobbying their superiors to foot the bill.

So how do you pick the best program? And once you've chosen one, how do you convince your company to let you attend?

What is important to remember is that no single program will be "best" for everyone. Several factors will help you determine what will be best for you, however. First is the stage of your career: How long have you been working—five years? Ten? Twenty? How broad-based is your experience—have you spent your entire career in the narrow confines of one function, like accounting or marketing? Or have you moved through several departments and taken on more general corporate responsibilities? Are you on the verge of being promoted to a new supervisory level? Or poised to make the leap from vice president to head of the company?

Next, consider the program's content. Will it help you perform better in your current job? Or will it help you reach out to a new area of expertise, increasing your value to your firm as a multitalented executive? Will it give you the skills or perspective for a position to which you aspire—or for which the company has already tapped you? Perhaps your firm has recently entered the international marketplace, or wants to do so—a course that focuses on doing business globally might be in order. Or a merger is in the works— maybe a course with a strong emphasis on managing cultural change would be beneficial.

Then there are the logistical considerations. How much does the program cost? Can your firm afford it? How much time will you have to spend away from the office? Your family? Is the traveling distance prohibitive, as it may be with a European location?

After all these factors have been taken into account, you may still find that as many as a dozen different programs could fill the bill for you. That's where school quality comes in. BUSINESS WEEK hopes to take most of the guesswork out of comparing institutions through this guidebook. Based on surveys of past participants, B-school deans, and corporate customers, we have for the first time compiled a ranking of the best schools for executive education. Even here, however, a caveat is in order: The schools at the top of the list may be weaker in your one particular area of interest than one lower in the rankings. By reading through our extensively researched profiles of each one, you should be able to judge whether a school's strengths match your own.

There's still the not-so-small matter of persuading your company to write the tuition check and give you the time off to attend your program of choice. It's usually best to work first through your immediate supervisor, and then through the corporate human resource department, presenting evidence that your participation in the program will produce concrete organizational improvements: project work that can be used on the job, contacts with professors who are researching areas of interest to the company, or even a more general cost-benefit breakdown that shows how easily the tuition cost can be offset by the better decision making or more efficient operations you hope to bring back from the program. "To convince companies to send them, executives should research what's available and see whether content matches what they need to do their job better—or a job they may have in the foreseeable future," advises Frank Morgan, Darden executive education director. "Then do a cost-benefit analysis to show how the organization would be impacted financially."

One last word of advice: The field of executive education is changing almost as rapidly as the business world the B-schools examine. Especially now, programs are in a state of flux, changing formats, adding or dropping content, disappearing altogether in favor of new, more current offerings. Since corporate budgets tend to plan attendance several cycles in advance, keep tabs on the program you choose to be sure it will still offer what you're looking for by the time you enroll. But, then, keeping up with the whirlwind is what got you on the fast track to begin with, isn't it?

CHAPTER 3

RANKING THE BEST

Who offers the best executive education programs in the country? That all depends on who you ask. The executives who participate in these programs gave the best reviews to the University of Virginia. The corporations that foot the tuition bills give the nod to the University of Michigan. Business-school exec-ed directors vote for Northwestern University. And opinions about individual schools may career wildly from one end of the spectrum to the other. While corporations placed France's INSEAD, the only non-U.S. school on the list, way up at No. 2, the response from the managers who actually attended was far less enthusiastic, with a lukewarm ranking of No. 22. North Carolina, the fifth favorite among consumers, lagged at No. 16 in the survey of companies.

The reason for the disparity? Students, their employers, and the schools themselves are largely looking for different things from executive education. The corporate sponsors, naturally, want to see a tangible return on their sizable investment of time, talent, and money—that is, immediate operational changes once the employee is back in the office. The executives, on the other hand, are more interested in personal growth and a fulfilling educational experience, which may or may not be readily apparent on the job. And the schools hope to serve both masters while gaining in prestige, boosting revenues, and exerting some influence on the workings of corporate America.

Moreover, a school that garners rave reviews for its general management programs may do only a lackluster job in more functional areas such as finance or marketing. So overall rankings of a school's executive education offerings can only go so far in helping you to decide what business school is best for you. Still, objective ratings are an important start in the search for the best. They can help to steer you toward the top-quality programs and guide you away from the losers. Managers won't find this information anywhere else because BUSINESS WEEK's comparative ranking is the first and only one of its kind in executive education.

A Guide to the Rankings and What They Mean

What school tops the chart in nondegree programs? The answer may surprise you. Based on extensive surveys of participants and corporations, the University of Michigan's School of Business is No. 1 in executive education, capturing the top spot among corporations and earning the third-best grades from executives who have attended its programs. Among other surprises yielded by our research: Some of the traditional, elite B-schools, such as Harvard, Columbia, and Wharton, were passed over in favor of Virginia, Northwestern, Duke, and Stanford. What makes for a powerhouse MBA program does not necessarily lead to excellence in executive education. The results of our study:

BUSINESS WEEK's **Top Twenty Executive Education Programs**

BW overall ranking	Consumer ranking	Corporate ranking	Revenues, 1990–1991 (millions)	Partici-pants, 1990–1991	No. of programs
1. Michigan	3	1	$16.7	5529	54
2. Virginia	1	3	8.1	1750	28
3. Northwestern	2	7	9.8	3000	43
4. Duke	9	4	7.8	2500	29
5. Stanford	4	9	7.0	590	8
6. Harvard	13	5	26.8	1900	18
7. Pennsylvania	11	8	16.0	4700	60
8. Columbia	17	6	7.5	1180	14
9. INSEAD	22	2	20.0	2700	75
10. UNC	5	16	3.4	1706	43
11. Penn State	16	10	4.0	1034	22
12. MIT	15	11	9.0	674	18
13. Tennessee	10	14	6.0	1600	30
14. UCLA	6	21	3.0	1300	12
15. Carnegie Mellon	7	22	1.9	310	4
16. Dartmouth	12	18	1.4	264	9
17. Cornell	18	13	1.4	350	11
18. Babson	14	19	2.7	893	20
19. SMU	8	23	2.4	3603	71
20. Indiana	19	15	1.5	510	18

To formulate the rankings, BUSINESS WEEK targeted the schools' two key markets: the executive alumni of the school's flagship program and the corporate customers of these schools. The consumer poll was mailed to 3456 managers who attended the flagship programs of 26 respected schools, chosen by an earlier survey to B-school directors. A total of 1567, or 45 percent, responded, assessing the quality of such characteristics as teaching, curriculum, classmates, and facilities at their schools. The poll of corporations was sent to officers in charge of management development. Of 346, some 144, or 42 percent, replied. Both results were then combined to create an overall ranking of the best of the roughly 150 schools offering exec-ed programs.

The rankings were designed to be of value both to the executive who would like to attend a management program and to the employers who are considering sending one or more of their staff members. Companies and employees gain the most when they choose programs that are carefully matched to their individual needs. Since content, duration, cost, and intended audience vary considerably from one school to the next, BUSINESS WEEK's survey findings can be used to evaluate the factors that matter most to you. Would you prefer to listen to lectures or spend most of your time working on group projects? Is it more important that your teachers are considered at the leading edge in their fields, or that their schedules provide enough flexibility to make them available outside class time? Do you mind spending a few weeks in a college dorm, or is a more luxurious style of accommodation essential? The following graphs will give you clues about these and other particulars. Keep in mind, however, that all 25 of the schools included on the graphs are well-respected institutions, and that for some questions, the top and bottom scores are not that far apart. Also remember that BUSINESS WEEK surveyed the users of the multi-week general management flagship programs, not those who attended shorter, functional courses. Because these experiences are commonly the flagship programs, you can bet that the participants receive the best a business school can offer. The competition is indeed tough.

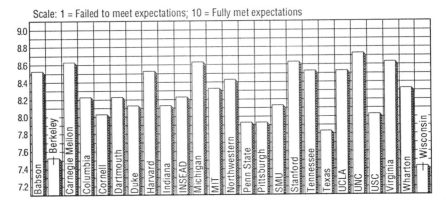

1. To what extent did your executive education experience fulfill or fail to meet your expectations of what a good program should be?

Business executives who enroll in executive education programs are a savvy bunch: You don't get to be a high-level manager in a top-flight organization otherwise. So, through their own research and word-of-mouth reports, most participants know pretty well what to expect before they arrive on campus—and our survey shows that, by and large, those expectations are fulfilled. North Carolina, Carnegie Mellon, Michigan, Stanford, and Virginia shone in this category; Wisconsin and Berkeley ranked lowest.

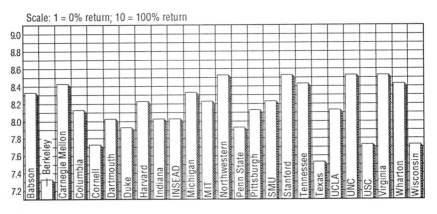

2. Do you believe your program was worth its cost in time and tuition?

Executive education is not cheap. Companies not only have to lay out several thousand dollars for tuition, room, board, and transportation, but also must absorb the cost of losing a key employee for a number of weeks. And the higher the fees and the more time spent on a program, the bigger the return on investment managers and their employers will expect. Which schools were deemed most worthwhile? Northwestern, Stanford, North Carolina, and Virginia. Those who attended Berkeley, Texas, USC, and Wisconsin were least satisfied.

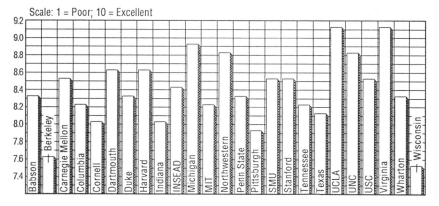

Scale: 1 = Poor; 10 = Excellent

3. How would you rate the quality of the teaching in the program?

Among the qualities cited as making for stellar teaching in an executive program were presenting up-to-date information; being well-organized, to avoid wasting any of the program's compressed time; and recognizing that the students were experienced business executives, not college sophomores. Even the highest-ranked schools drew some complaints about the uneven quality of teaching, and with only a handful of faculty members involved over the short time span of most programs, one clunker can sour the entire experience. The teaching at UCLA and Virginia got the highest marks; participants at Berkeley, Pittsburgh, and Wisconsin felt a little remedial work was needed.

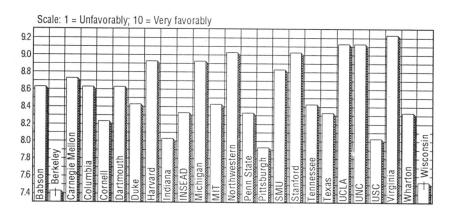

Scale: 1 = Unfavorably; 10 = Very favorably

4. Overall, how did the teachers in your executive education program compare with others you have had in the past?

Executive education consumers are a tough audience for professors. Not only are they an experienced, worldly group, they are by and large a well-schooled one as well, with alumni of some of the world's most prestigious colleges and graduate schools represented. So their standards for teaching are high. Most impressed by the executive program faculty were those who attended Virginia, North Carolina, and UCLA. At the bottom of the chart? Berkeley, Pittsburgh, and Wisconsin.

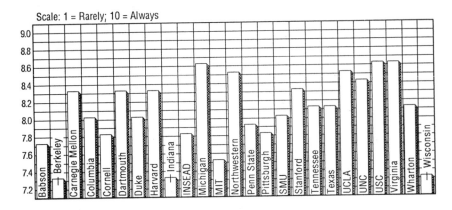

Scale: 1 = Rarely; 10 = Always

5. Did you have the feeling that your teachers were at the leading edge of knowledge in their fields?

This is a fine line to walk. Schools that rely heavily on outside consultants can end up with teachers who have a lot of hands-on know-how, but haven't a clue about up-to-the-minute theoretical business thinking. On the other hand, too many ivory-tower professors without current real-world experience can result in a lot of academic babble with little relevance to what's happening in today's business arena. Participants felt the best balance between theory and pragmatism was struck at Michigan, USC, and Virginia; Berkeley, Indiana, and Wisconsin lagged in this area.

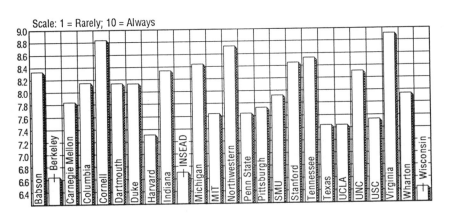

Scale: 1 = Rarely; 10 = Always

6. Was the faculty available for informal discussion when classes were not in session?

Faculty excellence counts for more if the instructors are easily accessible, particularly since so much of the learning in executive education takes place outside the lecture hall. Unfortunately, professors face multiple demands on their time, with graduate-school courses to teach, corporate clients to consult, and their own ongoing research. Some of the best schools solve this problem by assigning faculty exclusively to executive programs, at least while they're in session. Participants at Virginia, Cornell, and Northwestern believe their teachers were highly accessible. Berkeley, INSEAD, and Wisconsin drew criticism in this department.

18

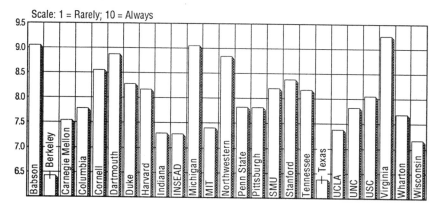

Scale: 1 = Rarely; 10 = Always

7. To what extent were faculty aware of the material other faculty members would cover?

In programs of such short duration, repetition can be a fatal time-waster. And no student is more critical of wasted time than a business executive who's spending several weeks away from job and family and whose company is spending big bucks on the experience. Additionally, when faculty members are abreast of what's happening in other classrooms, they can better relate their own material to the program's grand design. The faculty intercommunication at Babson, Michigan, and Virginia drew top honors; Berkeley and Texas ranked lowest.

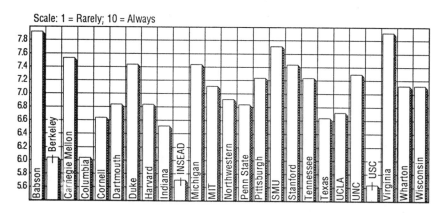

Scale: 1 = Rarely; 10 = Always

8. How curious were the members of the faculty about you and your knowledge?

While it isn't easy for instructors to get to know every student during a course that lasts just a few weeks, some schools try harder than others to personalize the process. After all, the managers themselves are a wonderful educational resource, bringing years of knowledge and experience that can be shared with classmates. And if professors know what their students know, they can shape the curriculum to play to strengths and bolster weaknesses. With respect to the personal touch, Babson and Virginia drew praise; INSEAD and USC drew fire.

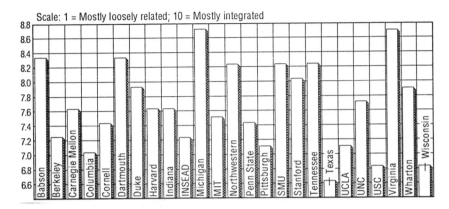

Scale: 1 = Mostly loosely related; 10 = Mostly integrated

9. To what extent was the coursework integrated, as opposed to being taught as a cluster of loosely related topics?

A corporate department doesn't work in a vacuum, with finance under one bell jar, marketing under another, and production under yet another. In fact, that's why many executives come to these programs—to learn how to put all the pieces of the puzzle together. For general management programs, in particular, one of the keys to success is integrating the disparate subjects of study into a cohesive body of knowledge that managers can use later on the job. Michigan and Virginia garnered kudos for their coordination of subject matter; Texas, USC, and Wisconsin scored poorly.

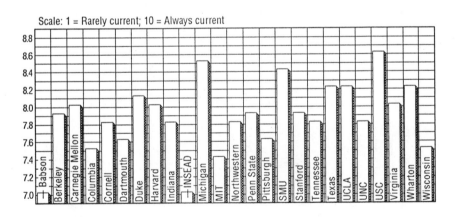

Scale: 1 = Rarely current; 10 = Always current

10. How current was the material/research presented in class for discussion and review?

In any scholarly pursuit, outdated study material is useless. But in business nowadays, it's hard to keep up with the whirlwind pace of change: Some case studies from as recently as the 1980s are already obsolete. Michigan, SMU, and USC were judged best at staying on the cutting edge; Babson and INSEAD drew up the rear.

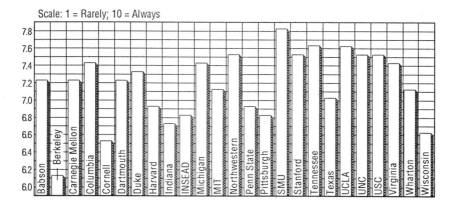

11. Was the material you learned directly useful in your work?

Judging by the responses to this question, this is one area in which consumers feel executive education falls short—no school scored really well here. While part of the blame can be placed on balky corporate bureaucracies that are reluctant to embrace change, it is incumbent on the executive programs to find ways to make what they're teaching both relevant and practically applicable. SMU, Tennessee, and UCLA were the leaders here; Berkeley, Cornell, and Wisconsin fell shortest of the mark.

Scale: 1 = Just barely; 10 = Very useful

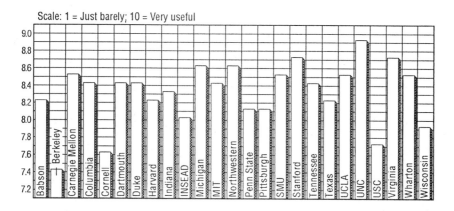

12. Do you believe the material you learned will be or has been useful to your personal long-term development?

Whether or not what they learned could be used on the job, most executives felt they personally benefitted from attending one of these programs. Many said that came simply from having a few weeks to step away from the daily grind and consider the big picture for a change. Others noted the unique networking opportunity of being thrown together with an international mix of managers from a wide range of businesses. Whatever the reason, participants at UNC, Stanford, and Virginia felt they personally had gained the most from the experience; those at Berkeley and Cornell felt they had gained the least.

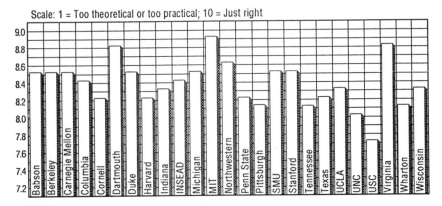

Scale: 1 = Too theoretical or too practical; 10 = Just right

13. Was there an appropriate balance between theory and practical application of theory?

While graduate B-schools are often criticized for placing too little emphasis on the real world, managers seem to be looking for the opposite from executive education. After all, participants are already operating out in the great beyond, so a respite in the realm of the theoretical may be a welcome departure. While no school was accused of being overly oriented to theory, MIT, Dartmouth, and Virginia were closest to striking the perfect balance.

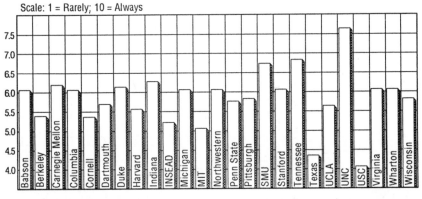

Scale: 1 = Rarely; 10 = Always

14. Were you given assignments or projects that had some linkage to your own full-time job?

Respondents across the board were unimpressed by the executive programs' attempts to relate the curriculum to their individual on-the-job needs. While several schools recently have begun to include this aspect in their programs, it remains a sore point for consumers who felt that, considering the commitment of time and money, they should be bringing something concrete back to the workplace. UNC stood head and shoulders above the rest in attempting to relate projects to participants' real-life issues. The weakest in this area? Texas and USC.

22

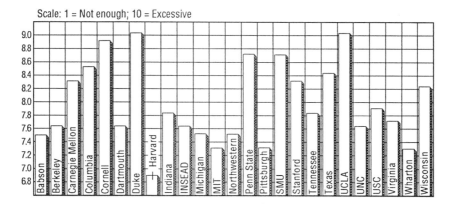

Scale: 1 = Not enough; 10 = Excessive

15. Was the amount of assigned work and reading so excessive that it impeded learning?

Many programs drew complaints for trying to cram too much information into too little time. It was the rare consumer who felt he or she wasn't worked hard enough. Some participants thought the schools deliberately delivered a staggering workload in order to impress or intimidate them. The danger here is that information overload can turn a lively, thought-provoking learning experience into pure drudgery. "Slavedriver" awards went to Cornell, Duke, and UCLA, while Harvard students felt they got off relatively easy.

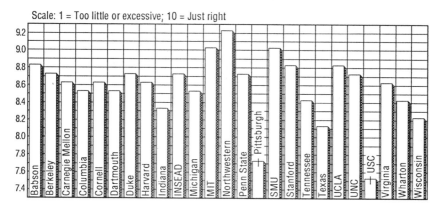

Scale: 1 = Too little or excessive; 10 = Just right

16. To what extent were analytical skills stressed in the curriculum?

Teaching analytical skills is rightly emphasized by many schools, since they allow managers to apply what they've learned to a variety of unfamiliar and unexpected situations that may arise on the job. But stressing analysis to the exclusion of other important material is undesirable. Northwestern, MIT, and SMU struck the best balance. Pittsburgh and USC fell a bit short on this score.

Scale: 1 = Too little or excessive emphasis; 10 = Just right

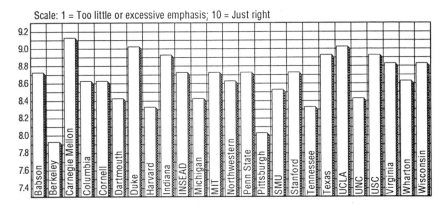

17. To what extent were interpersonal skills stressed in the curriculum?

Unlike the typical MBA candidate, students come to executive education with a good deal of experience in interpersonal relations. That doesn't necessarily mean they excel at it; in fact, companies are known to send employees to these programs precisely in the hope of improving human relations skills. No school fared badly on this question, though managers believed that Carnegie Mellon, Duke, and UCLA did the best job. This was less true at Berkeley and Pittsburgh.

Scale: 1 = Not enough; 10 = Many ways

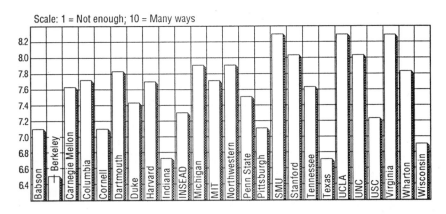

18. Were you given new ways of thinking or approaching problems that will serve you well over the long haul?

Taking a sabbatical from the office to concentrate on the big picture, in the company of like-minded managers on leave, should be the ideal environment for fostering innovative thinking. One of the biggest reasons managers clamor to attend executive programs is so they can take off the blinders that inevitably develop day-to-day on the job and open their eyes to new ways to solve their workplace problems. SMU, UCLA, and Virginia received high marks for cultivating innovative approaches; Berkeley, Indiana, and Texas were found lacking here.

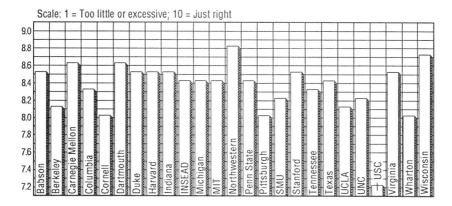

Scale: 1 = Too little or excessive; 10 = Just right

19. To what extent did the school pay attention to insuring that students could relate to one another on a professional level?

One executive education director noted that formulating the makeup of a management class was like putting together the ultimate dinner party: Invitees must be able to find common ground for conversation, but you don't want to fill your table exclusively with nuclear physicists either. Those who attend executive programs already have the obvious in common—they're all executives—but there are ways to spice up the mix, by seeking out a diverse range of businesses, a geographic cross-section, and varying levels of experience and organizational clout. Judging from our survey, Northwestern puts together great dinner parties; USC could work on its guest lists.

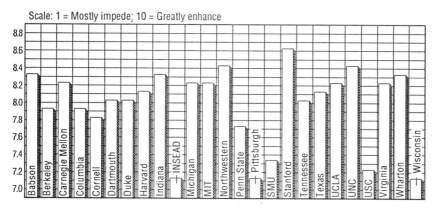

Scale: 1 = Mostly impede; 10 = Greatly enhance

20. Did the caliber of your classmates impede or enhance the learning process?

Some of the highest praise in our survey went not to the faculty or facilities, but to the other participants. Frequent mention was made of how much the executives learned from their classmates, and how many lasting relationships resulted. At the same time, some managers were dissatisfied with their peers. One student with a marked lack of knowledge or experience can drag the entire class down to his or her level; too many heading straight from the airport to the golf course can kill a program that's heavily dependent on group input. Stanford won top honors for the consistently high quality of its students; the classes at INSEAD, Pittsburgh, and Wisconsin were deemed more uneven.

25

Scale: 1 = Too much lecture or group interaction; 10 = Just right

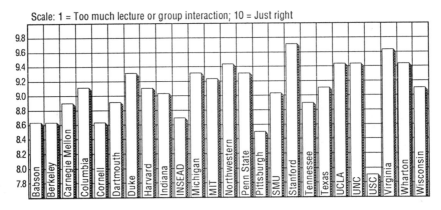

21. How would you rate the balance between lectures and group interaction?

Many programs are organized around small-group activities, including study groups, leadership workshops, and computer simulation teams. The idea is to let executives learn from one another as well as from the professor. But consumers want to hear business education's brightest stars as well. Which schools create the best balance? Stanford and Virginia. On the other end of the scale is USC.

Scale: 1 = Not at all; 10 = Absolutely

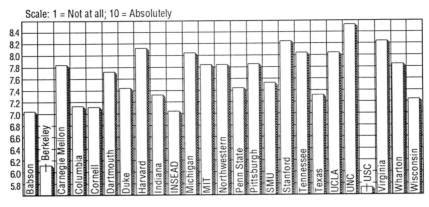

22. Will you be able to shoulder greater responsibility as a direct result of the program?

Often one of the main goals in sending an employee to an executive program, particularly a general course, is to expand his or her managerial realm from a narrowly defined function, such as accounting or marketing, to a broader supervisory role. A curriculum that integrates a wide range of functional skills and strengthens leadership is solid preparation for taking on more responsibility. Respondents from UNC, Stanford, and Virginia were ready to take on the world following their programs. Those from USC and Berkeley felt their programs were only marginally beneficial in this area.

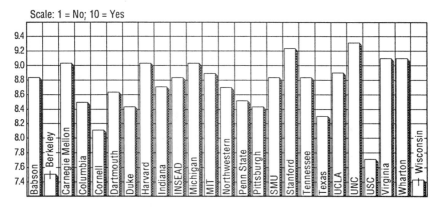

Scale: 1 = No; 10 = Yes

23. Would you urge a friend to take the same executive education program at the school?

It's one thing to regale your boss with tales of the substantial benefits you gained from the program for which your company just shelled out a few grand; it's another to recommend that a buddy follow your lead in spending several hard-working weeks away from home. Let's just say that the latter requires a somewhat higher degree of satisfaction. While the programs overall scored well, Stanford and UNC really shone here. Executives who attended Wisconsin, Berkeley, and USC were less likely to send their friends along.

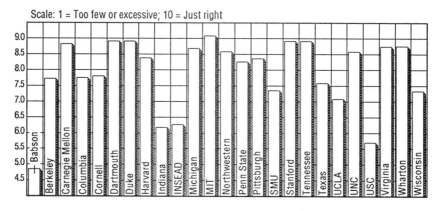

Scale: 1 = Too few or excessive; 10 = Just right

24. Did the school offer enough opportunities to allow your spouse to better understand the demands of the program on your time?

Almost every general management program of extended duration now has some type of program for spouses. The intensity can vary widely, however, from a one- or two-day kaffeeklatsch for spouses who are too often assumed to be bored homemakers to a substantive presentation that is practically a miniversion of the full program. Among the best-received spousal programs were those at MIT, Dartmouth, Duke, Stanford, and Tennessee. Husbands and wives gave Babson and USC thumbs down.

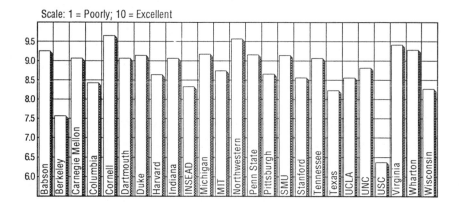

Scale: 1 = Poorly; 10 = Excellent

25. If you needed help with logistical matters such as room and board, how well did the school respond?

Little things do mean a lot. If a CEO needs access to a fax machine, or an oversubscribed program requires extra bedroom space at a nearby hotel, there shouldn't be a major hassle—particularly not at these prices. The typical executive consumer is accustomed to a high level of service on the job and will expect no less on campus. Cornell and Northwestern were rated best at keeping the housekeeping distractions to a minimum. Berkeley and USC clearly need some work in this department.

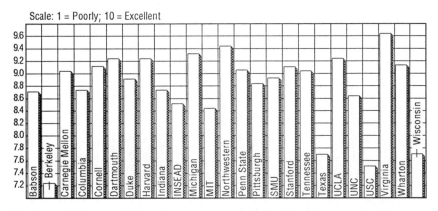

Scale: 1 = Poorly; 10 = Excellent

26. Overall, how well was the program organized?

It almost goes without saying that a good manager is an organized manager; organizational skills are a basic job requirement. Similarly, a good management program is an organized one. The curriculum should be well thought-out and current; the faculty should be at the top of their games; necessary supplies and equipment, such as computers, should be readily available; and the basic human needs of food and shelter should be attended to with a minimum of fuss. Virginia and Northwestern received the highest scores for their overall organization, while Berkeley and USC could stand some improvement.

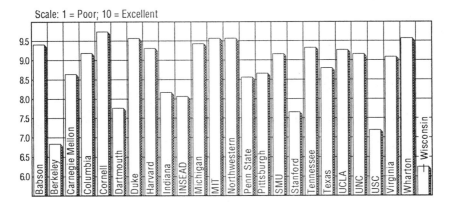

Scale: 1 = Poor; 10 = Excellent

27. How would you rate the facilities?

At the prices charged by most executive education programs, managers have a right to expect more than a garret for sleeping, dorm-style shared showers, and fish sticks on the menu. Obviously, senior-level corporate managers are used to a more luxurious standard of accommodation than the average graduate student. Some schools have recognized this fact, laying out millions of dollars to construct hotel-quality, state-of-the-art executive centers. Others simply offer the same living quarters MBA candidates use. Rave reviews went to the facilities at Cornell, Duke, MIT, Northwestern, and Wharton. The accommodations at Berkeley and Wisconsin received a sound drubbing.

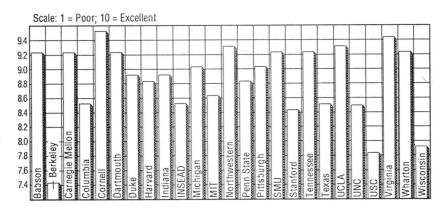

Scale: 1 = Poor; 10 = Excellent

28. How would you rate the quality of the business school's support staff assigned to the executive education program?

The support work for an executive program begins long before the students set foot on campus. Applications and acceptances must be processed, registration and payment completed, travel arrangements made, and accommodations set up. The work continues throughout the course of the program as a multitude of needs arise. The support staff can color the entire experience one way or the other, by making things run seamlessly or by letting nuisances turn into major obstacles. The staffs at Cornell and Virginia got A's for their effort. Those at Berkeley and USC coasted by with C's.

29

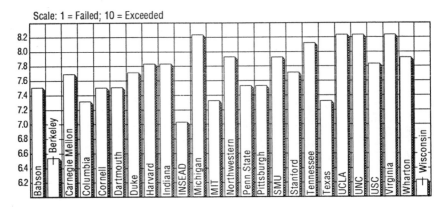

Scale: 1 = Failed; 10 = Exceeded

29. To what extent did the program live up to the expectations raised by the business school's promotional materials?

Executive education is big business, and few schools are loath to use a little sales razzle-dazzle in promoting their programs. Slick, four-color brochures sing the praises of faculty and campus, complete with alumni testimonials. So it's pretty hard for reality to exceed the hype in most cases. Nevertheless, consumers at Michigan, UCLA, UNC, and Virginia were pleasantly surprised by what they got from their programs. Those at Wisconsin, Berkeley, and INSEAD were more likely to be disappointed.

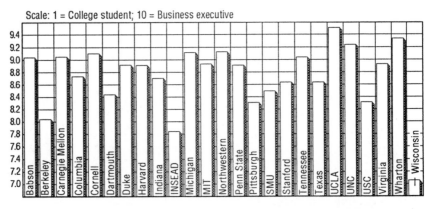

Scale: 1 = College student; 10 = Business executive

30. Overall, did you have the feeling that you were "treated like a college student in a vacant dorm" or "treated like a business executive"?

Just because executives are willing to spend a few weeks back in the classroom doesn't mean they're longing to relive the undergraduate experience. (There's a reason people go to school while they're still young enough to withstand the Spartan lifestyle and grueling workload.) Corporate managers expect to be treated as colleagues, not college freshmen, and the results of our survey show that most schools understand that fact. UCLA and Wharton go farthest out of their way to make sure their student-executives are handled with kid gloves; INSEAD and Wisconsin are less careful than the rest.

CHAPTER 4

THE TOP TWENTY B-SCHOOLS IN EXECUTIVE EDUCATION

The executive programs on BUSINESS WEEK's Top 20 list represent the world's best in management training. But finding the school with the highest rating isn't all there is to choosing the program that's right for you. There are a vast array of educational opportunities out there, and careful research can turn two or three weeks away from the office into a pivotal career move—instead of a waste of time.

Each of our profiles starts with a snapshot view of the school that tells you something about the breadth of its executive education offerings, its standing in the polls, and its experience and growth in the field. Does a school run dozens of different programs, or concentrate its efforts on just a few? Schools with many programs tend to be versatile and rich in resources, but those with a small number may be able to devote more time and attention to both the individual program and the individual student. How many managers does a school run through its executive education offerings each year? A large number can signal popularity, but may mean you'll feel lost in the shuffle.

We then present an in-depth description of the school's flagship general management course. Where there are often superficial similarities—most target senior-level executives—these programs can differ tremendously in such important areas as length, cost, curriculum, faculty, size of class, and facilities. Each boasts its own style and culture, strengths and weaknesses. This is followed by capsule profiles of the most notable programs offered by each school in functional fields. Each school has carved out a niche in these key areas. Corporate human resources directors, for example, think Harvard is best in general management; Northwestern in marketing; Wharton in finance; Michigan in human resources; Virginia in leadership; and Tennessee in quality.

Leaders in Key Areas

Indeed, BUSINESS WEEK asked corporate human resources officials to name the schools that did the best jobs in specific areas. Here's what they said:

General Management	*Human Resources*
1. Harvard	1. Michigan
2. Stanford	2. Cornell
3. Virginia	3. Virginia
4. Northwestern	4. Duke
5. Michigan	5. Penn State

Marketing	*Finance*
1. Northwestern	1. Pennsylvania
2. Columbia	2. Stanford
3. Harvard	3. Michigan
4. Virginia	4. Columbia
5. Pennsylvania	5. Harvard

Manufacturing	*Strategy*
1. Harvard	1. Michigan
2. Michigan	2. MIT
3. Virginia	3. Columbia
4. MIT	4. Harvard
5. Northwestern	5. Pennsylvania

Information Systems	*R&D/Technology*
1. MIT	1. MIT
2. Harvard	2. Carnegie Mellon
3. Pennsylvania	3. Stanford

Global Business	*Quality*
1. INSEAD	1. Tennessee
2. Harvard	2. Northwestern
3. Pennsylvania	
4. Columbia	

Finally, virtually all the courses profiled here are public programs to which any company or individual can apply for admittance. Not included are custom programs commissioned by a company for its managers alone. Custom courses have been included in counting the number of programs a school offers. Duke, Michigan, and INSEAD are recognized as leaders in this fast-growing field of executive education.

1. University of Michigan

School of Business
700 East University
Ann Arbor, Michigan 48109

Corporate ranking: 1	*Consumer ranking*: 3
Number of programs: 54	*Number of programs in 1986*: 45
1990–1991 participants: 5529	*Years in executive education*: 38
Annual revenues: $16.7 million	*Change since 1986*: 165 percent

Contact: Thomas Kinnear, senior associate dean, 313-763-4233; Ann Walton, director of executive education, 313-763-6402

The Executive Program

"Have you heard the story about the two Californians on a camping trip?" asks C.K. Prahalad, Michigan's guru on global competitiveness. "One woke up in his tent and said to the other, 'There's a grizzly bear out there! I better get my jogging shoes.' 'You think you can outrun a bear?' asks the other. 'That's not the point. I only have to out-run you.'"

Prahalad delivers the line with the élan of a first-class comic. The crowd of managers in The Executive Program (TEP) roars. The professor's point about global competition sinks in, and he resumes a witty, provocative lecture. He paces the floor, working the auditorium as if it were a stage, climbing steps, calling managers by name, challenging them with questions. One of a core of six permanently assigned faculty members to TEP, Prahalad is one of many reasons why Michigan stands out in exec-ed. One wag jokes that Michigan's program should be renamed "CK and the Pips." (Says one participant: "C.K. was clearly the star of the show." Adds another, "He alone was worth the price of admission.")

While Prahalad may be the most well-known and widely praised, however, he's just one of an exceptional crew who know how to please. All six practically live and breathe the program, sitting in on one another's sessions, teaching joint classes, and making themselves readily available to students in and out of the classroom. Dennis Severance's segment on computers is also singled out for its pragmatic approach in using technology as a strategic tool for business.

Prahalad, Severance, and the rest of the core faculty—B-school Dean Joe White, Ray Reilly, Tom Kinnear, and David Ulrich—were hand-picked from the business school staff, in part because of their ability to relate to executives and their respect for real-world experience. "They were as interested in learning from us as we were from them," says Mike McCaffrey, president of DePuy, Inc., a 1990 participant. Professors also use their ongoing consulting for such companies as AT&T, Eastman Kodak, and Philips to make academic theory more relevant. "In class, I try to personalize lessons from my consulting experience," says Prahalad. "The long-term scorecard for me is not how well we are rated in the classroom, but whether we're having an impact on changing the way companies compete globally."

Indeed, if general management programs had theme songs, Michigan's would be "We Are the World." Its goal: to turn out businesspeople who can compete successfully in a global marketplace. The international spirit is apparent from the moment executives arrive on the Ann Arbor campus from such far-flung locations as Chile, the Philippines, India, and Finland. In fact, as many as one-quarter to one-third of the 50 or so students who attend each session (the four-week course is held twice a year, beginning in September and in May) are from outside the United States. And this worldwide perspective is underscored by the school's proximity to Detroit and the auto industry's obsessive concern with overseas competition.

Michigan won top honors overall in our survey, with the No. 1 ranking from corporations—which have the most to gain from a successful exec-ed experience and the most to lose from a poorly run program. In Michigan's case, employers believe they see a tangible return on their investment of money, time, and talent, particularly in the form of new ideas their managers can use directly on the job. Ulrich talks about the use of "customer training" as a new marketing tool, getting managers to share their companies' "best practices." Reilly drums up interest in what he calls "value-based supplier relationships" to gain a competitive edge. "These people want results," says Professor F. Brian Talbot, who directs one of the school's shorter, functional programs. "They hope to take away one or two big-impact ideas. And that's what we deliver."

The school's flagship program, TEP, reviews the basic functional skills executives need to operate in the upper echelons of a large corporation—the five key segments of study include corporate strategy, financial analysis and economics, strategic marketing, human resource management, and information technology. Michigan, however, prides itself on integrating these segments into a cohesive plan of attack. Indeed, that's one of the program's strongest selling points, eliciting applause from many of the surveyed participants. "This is the general manager's agenda—thinking about how to integrate the functional areas," says Ann Walton, director of executive education. "Our faculty works together to do just that."

With all this emphasis on a global perspective, it is not surprising that the program draws its participants almost exclusively from large, multinational corporations. Competition for space in the program is relatively fierce, with only 60 to 70 percent of those who apply accepted. The typical student is 42 years old and makes $110,000 to $120,000 a year; about 70 percent of each class is made up of senior corporate managers, with the rest gleaned from upper-middle management ranks. Although Michigan attracts an international clientele, it has had less luck in luring women and minorities, which each represent only about 5 percent of the average class.

Michigan's ascendance to the top is no overnight success story. The School of Business entered the executive-education market in its infancy, offering its first program back in 1954, around the time most of the top B-schools were testing the waters in this area. And its commitment to exec-ed has grown steadily over the past four decades: In 1990–1991, Michigan drew 5529 participants to its programs, significantly more than any other school. One source of appeal is the first-rate facilities. Classes are held and participants housed in Michigan's Executive Education Center, built in 1984 at a cost of $15 million. It's a far cry from what participants had to put up with in the 1970s when Michigan sent managers to local hotels and a rented sorority house on Washtenaw Avenue. Now, amphitheater classrooms, study lounges, and computers are housed in one building; next door is a seven-story, hotel-style residence hall, with 96 single rooms with baths, a 24-hour front desk, concierge, and next-day laundry services. The dining room, which serves breakfast and lunch buffets and sit-down, full-course dinners, receives accolades for its excellent cuisine (from the swordfish to the double-chocolate cake served with cappucino or espresso). Cost for the program is $14,000, including tuition, room, board, and supplies—about average for programs of similar duration.

Michigan crams in 78 class sessions in four weeks, rather than the longer spans opted for by such prestigious competitors as Stanford and Harvard. The limited time frame means that the workload is heavy, with evening and Saturday study sessions, late-night reading, and little freedom for recreation and exploration. Nevertheless, managers express satisfaction with the month-long duration, with several noting that it would have been difficult to keep up the intense pace for a longer period and a hardship to spend more time away from their jobs and families. Michigan also offers a supervised fitness program throughout the course, and a three-day Partners' Program during the final week, with spouses invited to lectures by the core faculty—including, of course, the entertaining Prahalad.

Organizations sending most participants: General Motors; AT&T; Eastman Kodak; Thomson Consumer Electronics; Philips International

Other Programs of Note

Advanced Human Resources Executive Program: No school offers a more highly regarded series of HR programs than Michigan. This one explores the dual role of the senior human resources executive—as a member of the corporate management team and as leader of the human resources function. Led by Professor J. Wayne Brockbank. Designed for senior-level human resources executives with organization-wide responsibility and those expected to achieve such a position in three to five years. Two weeks; held annually, in November; 30 students per session; $8000, including tuition, room, board, and supplies; by application only.

Human Resources Executive Program: Examines state-of-the-art human resources techniques and how the link between personnel and corporate strategy can affect an organization. Led by Professor David Ulrich, who has consulted with such corporate heavyweights as Amoco, General Electric, Digital Equipment, and MCI. Intended for corporate or divisional-level personnel directors with general policy-making responsibilities. Two weeks; held twice a year, in October and April; 35–40 students per session; $7600, including tuition, room, board, and supplies; by application only.

Management of Managers: Some companies use this series of programs for most of their development of management talent. Emphasizes interpersonal, administrative, and conceptual skills needed by those who manage other managers. Led by Professor Kim Cameron. The key program is most beneficial to mid-level managers with at least eight years' experience, though there are two other versions: a three-day session for newly-appointed managers and a five-day program for those with four to eight years experience. Five days; held monthly throughout the year; 30–35 students per session; $3750, including tuition, room, board, and supplies; open enrollment.

Manufacturing Executive Program: Explores the contribution of manufacturing to corporate strategy, particularly how specific manufacturing capabilities can be translated into competitive advantages. Led by Professor F. Brian Talbot. Open to

35

senior-line managers in manufacturing with at least 10 years' experience, including division managers, vice presidents of manufacturing, and plant managers. Two weeks; held twice a year, in October and May; 25 students per session; $7600, including tuition, room, board, and supplies; by application only.

Global Leadership Program: An annual five-week exercise in building multicultural teams, with executives from the United States, Europe, and Asia. It's a labor of love for the indefatigable Noel Tichy, the professor who helped General Electric Co. CEO Jack Welch revamp the company's highly regarded Management Development Institute at Crotonville. See Chapter 6, The Ten Most Innovative Programs.

Understanding and Implementing Activity-Based Costing: An immersion course on the basics of activity-based costing that even includes a "how to" segment. Led by James S. Reece, accounting professor, and David D. Galley, manager of General Motors' program. Intended for staff specialists and functional managers such as controllers, plant and pricing managers, marketing directors. One week; held twice a year, in March and July; 30 students per session; $2800, including tuition, room, board, and supplies; open enrollment.

Organizations sending most participants: General Motors; AT&T; Amoco; Pepsico; IBM

Michigan Consumers Sound Off

Michigan and everything connected to it was excellent. There was rigor and recreation, application and theory, individual and group work, cutting-edge and common sense. The professors were totally integrated in their approach, yet stood alone as individuals with strong opinions on their areas of influence. We definitely were treated as professionals in class when we challenged theories or positions held dear by staff.
—**Corporate Vice President**

*Facilities and the vicinity were really first-class, but the intense homework impacted participants' availability to enjoy them. The evening reading assignments were entirely too much—several participants actually got ill, run down and exhausted.—**Engineering Manager***

*The blend of executives from around the world was very valuable in understanding different business cultures, problems, perspectives. This will be very valuable in my career.—**District Manager***

*One of the greatest benefits of the program was the interaction of the participants. It was a break from concentrating just on your own industry and company. For most of us, it was the first time we had spent a month away from our offices and outside of our industries. This I found to be enlightening and refreshing.—**Vice President for International Sales and Marketing***

The director should be more selective about who is admitted into the program. I feel that if a $14,000 check is attached with the application form, admission is automatic.—President

The five basic areas covered—finance, information management, international competition, human relations, and marketing—are presented and discussed as a cohesive whole, rather than as individual, unrelated abstractions. This adds a reality to the program that is very valuable—that's the way these things must function in an ongoing business.
—Corporate Director

Too many case studies and not enough time to really get into them. Felt like we were in a "case-study marathon."—Chief Operating Officer

Outstanding, exceedingly well-coordinated academic program. Professors each knew what the others were teaching, and instruction constantly referenced points made in earlier lectures. The final synopsis tied all the disciplines together. I wish my graduate school had developed such a comprehensive program.—U.S. Navy Captain

This experience far exceeded my expectations. The amount of work done is overwhelming at first, but it is nicely integrated over the term of the program. Our company is sending two people to each Executive Program over the next five years or so, and we've also contracted with the program director to host a series of seminars on our premises in coming years. Much of the thought and many of the exercises will be brought back to our staff to allow everyone an opportunity to step back and think intellectually about the job and the work!—President, Insurance Company

I consider myself fairly jaded about these sorts of programs, but I was extremely surprised to find the program at Michigan so well integrated and thought-provoking. My own thinking and job performance has been expanded and improved as a direct result of the program. Besides, Ann Arbor is a wonderful place to spend some time.
—Corporate Planning Manager

The post-course follow-up has been excellent. I still feel like I'm part of the program. The staff keeps in touch, and there's good networking potential with managers at comparable levels from other companies. I have had the opportunity on several occasions to call upon classmates to resolve problems or get assistance.—Logistics Director

Although there was no one else from my industry in attendance, it was heartening to find how my company relates to other industries in terms of management, personnel policies, motivation, structure, global competitiveness, etc. Overall, it's a good course for the right level of attendant.
—Director

2. University of Virginia

Darden Graduate School of Business Administration
P.O. Box 6550
Charlottesville, Virginia 22906

Corporate ranking: 3	*Consumer ranking*: 1
Number of programs: 28	*Number of programs in 1986*: 20
1990–1991 participants: 1750	*Years in executive education*: 38
Annual revenues: $8.1 million	*Change since 1986*: 76 percent

Contact: Frank T. Morgan, director of executive education, 804-924-4847

The Executive Program

For managers ready to shed their suits, roll up their sleeves, and really get their hands dirty, the Darden School's Executive Program offers the perfect opportunity. During the six-week course, participants spend a day in the Charlottesville woods, puzzling out such problems as how to get a bunch of middle-aged, not necessarily athletic executives to climb over a 14-foot wall within a specified amount of time—and before competing teams can do so. You'll definitely work up a sweat. And since your teammates may include a petite, 5-foot-tall woman or a hefty, 250-pound man, trying to figure a way to climb that wall may be a tall order.

What does scaling a stockade have to do with corporate management? Everything, according to Frank T. Morgan, Darden's director of executive education. "These are really problem-solving exercises using the outdoors as a vehicle," says Morgan. "If you want to get over that wall, your team must function together. Naturally, leadership and team-building occurs." At Darden, strengthening collaborative skills is considered a prerequisite for success in management.

The Executive Program (TEP) does cover the basics: About 25 percent of the course is devoted to functional review, with equal amounts of time spent on globalization and strategy. But group learning is central to the teaching method here. Lecture time is kept to a minimum. Computer simulations and competitions figure prominently in the schedule. And while the curriculum's major emphasis is still on case study, it gets a fresh twist through what is called the "learning team" system, in which small, rotating groups of executives, carefully chosen for a diverse mix of business types, job experience, and geographical representation, are required to study and discuss cases together. This idiosyncratic, hands-on approach wins hands-down approval from the people who are perhaps in the best position to judge its effectiveness: No other general management program won so much praise from past participants.

All this group learning and self-teaching doesn't mean the professors are sitting around doing nothing, however—in fact, Darden also garnered the top reviews for the quality of its teaching. A core of eight professors, chosen from the B-school faculty, is assigned as a team to TEP for at least a year; during each session of the program, which is held annually beginning in June, they devote all their time to nothing but the program—even venturing onto the basketball court for games with managers. (The instructors always play with their shirts off.) "The faculty commitment is to exercise with them, have dinner with them, and to sit in on classes they don't teach," says Darden School Dean John W. Rosenblum. "The people who teach in the program have an emotional and intellectual attachment to the endeavor that goes beyond anything I've ever experienced in education."

That assessment is supported by both executives and the corporations which send them. Says a plant manager from a major U.S. company: "The program was thorough, global, penetrating, and taught by professionals who care about the customer! It was the most stimulating experience of my entire career." One reason for those great reviews has to do with how closely the faculty works with one another and the group. "What we do one day builds on the next," says Brandt Allen, one of the school's most gifted teachers, who has taught in the program for 15 years. "In some of the other programs, there is a dancing bear format. You get great bears, but each day it's a new bear and once the dance is over, it goes home. We're here all the time with the possible exception of one day a week for personal consulting, but that's it."

By any measure, the TEP faculty is an exceptional group. All are active consultants, and over half serve on corporate boards. Every one of them holds a Ph.D., yet most are also MBAs with real-world business experience, including the former president of a family-owned business. Two of the eight have lived and worked in other countries. The current leader is Alan R. Beckenstein, a Darden professor for two decades. Beckenstein, once a full-time management consultant and an expert in industry economics, teaches the global environment segment. Other team members include Allen, Jay Bourgeois, Dick Brownlee, Christopher Gale, Bob Harris, Alec Horniman, and Bob Landel. There's also a trio of TEP fellows. The 1991 group included David Simon, chief operating officer of British Petroleum, who told about the transformation of his company into a team-based organization; Mitch Willey, a Washington lawyer, who spoke on negotiating business deals in Central and Eastern Europe; and Ruhi Ramazani, a Middle Eastern expert, who offered his perspectives on that volatile region of the world. "Half of what we do is educate people in current practice, whether finance or leadership," says Allen. "Second, by the choice of topics and the outsiders who come in, we attempt to raise for them the challenges of tomorrow." In 1992, for example, Darden added a three-day program on environmental management that was jointly planned by the National Geographic Society and the Conservation Fund. The well-received session featured a day in Washington, D.C., with meetings between the group and well-known scientists and regulators.

Classes at Virginia are broken into two sections of about 50 managers. Those sections are further pared down into learning teams of five or six people, allowing for intimate exchanges with new colleagues from other companies. The program is consistently oversubscribed, with nearly twice the applications as there are spaces available. The typical participant is a 43-year-old senior manager who makes over $100,000 a year; three-quarters of each class comes from large businesses, but managers of medium-sized firms make up 20 percent, and there is even some room for small-business executives. About 10 percent of each class is female, a more sizable number than most general management courses. Indeed, many women managers delivered unsolicited praise for its nonsexist orientation—in sharp contrast to those who have studied in Harvard and Stanford's programs.

Typically, about a quarter of the students hail from overseas, and officials stress their commitment to the study of the international marketplace in the curriculum; nevertheless, a number of participants noted that globalization was one of the program's weaker points. "Many of the foreign students, from India, Taiwan, etc., told me they did not feel part of the exercises, and even during the lectures were not drawn out for comments," says one alumnus. "The majority of the participants were Americans with little exposure to operations outside the United States. The case studies were equally predominantly U.S.-based," adds another. Darden apparently took that criticism to heart. In 1992, foreign enrollment hit a new high at 37 percent of the class from 20 countries outside the United States. The school also brought in Andrei Manoukovsky, dean of a business school in Russia, as a TEP fellow. And it began to negotiate with senior executives in Asia and Europe to come aboard as TEP fellows and executives-in-residence for 1993.

Virginia joined the exec-ed bandwagon early on, in 1954, and its commitment is apparent both from the number of different programs offered—28, with more being added all the time—and from Sponsors Hall, the $6 million executive center built in 1979. Located across the street from the Darden School (where classes are held), the executive dormitory is as group-oriented as the rest of the program, with participants paired up in two-bedroom apartments with shared bath, kitchen, and living quarters. Most meals are served in the Sponsors Hall dining room, but regular social dinners, including picnics and cookouts, are held during each session.

In keeping with Darden's holistic approach to management training, TEP boasts one of the most elaborate spousal programs around. Dubbed "The Sixth Week," partners are invited to spend the entire final week of the program listening to lectures and case studies presented by faculty, taking educational tours of the history-rich countryside near Charlottesville, and trying to gain an understanding of what their spouses have been through for the previous five weeks. Couples are given rooms at an inn near campus, rather than at the executive dormitory, and are treated to a dinner/dance at the closing. All these extras keep the fees a bit on the pricey side—$19,000, including tuition, room, board, supplies, and Sixth Week activities and accommodations. But BUSINESS WEEK'S survey shows that participants overwhelmingly agree: It's well worth the cost.

Organizations sending most participants: AT&T; IBM; General Motors; Philip Morris; Ciba-Geigy

Other Programs of Note

Managing Critical Resources: A two-week examination of business functional areas, their interaction with one another, and the problems that span traditional functional boundaries. Emphasis is on intensive small-group study and discussion of cases. For further details, see Chapter 6, The Ten Most Innovative Programs.

Young Managers' Program: Designed to improve the functional planning, team-building, and leadership skills of emerging young executives, with an emphasis on operating in new and unfamiliar situations. Led by Professor Sherwood Frey, who consistently earns rave reviews from MBAs for his teaching style. Intended for high-potential specialty managers who have been targeted for greater responsibility. Three weeks; held twice a year, in spring and fall; 32 students per session; $8900, including tuition, room, board, and supplies; open enrollment (group discount available).

Sales Management and Marketing Strategy: Offers sales managers ways to improve sales force effectiveness, including how to develop and motivate successful salespeople. Led by Professors Derek Newton, one of Darden's best teachers, and Neil Borden, Jr. Intended for sales and marketing managers and their support staff, as well as generalists. One week; held six times throughout the year; 30 students per session; $3400, including tuition, room, board, and supplies; open enrollment (group discount available).

Financial Management for Nonfinancial Managers: Provides nonfinancial managers with the skills needed to understand annual reports, financial ratios, and budgets, showing how such financial information can be used in managerial decision making. Led by Professor C. Ray Smith. Intended for managers in marketing, sales, manufacturing, and engineering, and newly appointed general managers from these areas. One week; held three times a year, in winter, spring, and fall; 35 students per session; $3400, including tuition, room, board, and supplies; open enrollment (group discount available).

Creating the Future: The Challenge of Transformational Leadership: A "think-tank" seminar designed to encourage executives to confront business issues from fresh perspectives, particularly as part of an effective management team, in the face of today's fast-changing environment. Led by Associate Professor Jack Weber. Intended for CEOs, COOs, division presidents, general managers, senior line executives, and growth business owners; the participation of entire management teams is encouraged. One week; held twice a year, in March and June; 25 students per session; $3200, including tuition, room, board, and supplies; open enrollment (group discount available).

Creating the High-Performance Workplace: Explores the concept of superior productivity and offers ideas in quality management practices and motivational techniques to get better results. Designed for all managers concerned with performance improvement. One week; held three times a year, beginning in February, September, and November; 30 students per session; $3400, including tuition, room, board, and supplies; open enrollment (group discount available).

Organizations sending most participants: AT&T; IBM; Bell Atlantic; Eastman Kodak; Philip Morris

Darden Consumers Sound Off

The Executive Program taught me the value of learning—again. The total experience was so well-managed that it was obvious that Darden really "walks what it talks." They paid great attention to my needs in education, accommodations, and personal needs, but they pushed me very hard to learn.—Vice President for Sales

Overall, the Darden program was excellent. However, while many of the participants were executive management-caliber, some did not have the experience that should be a prerequisite for an executive development program, and a few appeared to be near the end of their careers.—Assistant Controller

41

The faculty was extremely accessible and willing to spend whatever time and energy necessary to assure participants got as much out of the program as they chose. While at times the workload appeared overwhelming, it proved manageable.—**Vice President of Credit and Operations**

As a female executive, it is refreshing to realize just how much gender was not an issue—in spite of the very small number of female participants. I would attribute that result to the fact that fundamental to the program are two particularly important values—inclusion and respect. There is no room for discrimination, exclusion, or minimization.—**Finance Program Manager**

As an international executive with extensive experience in several countries, I felt the lack of other internationally-minded participants. The majority of the participants were Americans with little exposure to operations outside the United States. Also, the case studies were equally predominantly U.S.-based.—**Vice-Director**

One-fourth of our class of 80+ were from other countries. These folks stretched my perception of self and others dramatically. I can now count as friends and colleagues people from Thailand, Holland, Finland, and India.—**National Publishing Director**

The program fostered an attitude of "I'll show you what I know" on the part of the participants, rather than one of "I'm here to learn." A lot of showboating took place at the expense of other participants.—**Labor Union Administrative Assistant/Director**

The Executive Program was a demonstration in excellence—practical, theoretical, current knowledge in an environment that brings out your best and demonstrates daily the value of effective teamwork.
—**Area Manager**

When you showed up at the school to get your room assignments and books, the support staff knew your name without looking it up and immediately made you feel welcome. The program ran without a hitch. I do not remember one instance where the school failed to get a class or social event off on time without great results.—**Manager**

The professors obviously enjoyed what they were doing. Their enthusiasm was contagious. They excelled in getting the most out of participants. It was an enjoyable experience, but a tiring one as well. It's hard to spend six weeks in such a concentrated program of study, but I'm not sorry I did.—**Assistant Director**

3. Northwestern University

Kellogg Graduate School of Management
2169 Sheridan Road
Evanston, Illinois 60208

Corporate ranking: 7   *Consumer ranking*: 2
Number of programs: 43   *Number of programs in 1986*: 42
1990–1991 participants: 3000   *Years in executive education*: 36
Annual revenues: $9.8 million   *Change since 1986*: 105 percent

Contact: Nancy Hartigan, associate dean and director of executive education, 708-864-9270

Advanced Executive Program

When Robert Gerrish, program manager for the Boeing Commercial Airplane Group, enrolled in Kellogg's AEP, he was hoping the professors would be able to bring their case studies to life. He got his wish, in spades. After spending much of the four weeks studying U.S. Gypsum's fresh triumph over a hostile takeover attempt, Gerrish found himself face to face with both the chairman and chief financial officer of the mining and manufacturing giant, explaining how he believed Gypsum should deal with its subsequent debt load.

It's this high standard of currency and grounding in the real world that gained Kellogg's executive programs the No. 1 ranking among B-school deans and the second-highest rating from past participants. For each session of the program, which is held twice a year, beginning in February and in June, the faculty devises a spanking new case study based on a company that has made recent headlines, then invites the firm's top officials to hear the students' findings and recommendations. "The fact that they could bring in these high-level executives was very impressive," says Gerrish. Managers say that knowing their course work will be of use to an actual company motivates them to work harder and take the program more seriously than they might otherwise. In fact, AEP is so popular among its student-executives that it boasts its own alumni group, which meets annually for a three-day mini-session either in the United States or in Europe.

Among corporate exec-ed customers, however, Kellogg is a little like Rodney Dangerfield. The school that has long dazzled corporate recruiters of MBAs isn't getting the same amount of respect in executive education. In our company survey, Northwestern earned seventh place. It's not for lack of trying that Kellogg remains relatively unrecognized by corporations: The fast-growing school boasts 43 different management programs, one of the biggest and most diverse offerings of any university. And just as it shined up the image of its now-top-ranked MBA program a few years back, Kellogg is tackling its lower executive profile head on. Having almost doubled its exec-ed capacity since 1986, the school plans to boost it 50 percent further by the summer of 1993.

While Northwestern has been a player in the executive education game for more than three decades, the school began to pursue the discipline earnestly in the late 1970s, when Dean Donald P. Jacobs promoted the idea of building a large, modern on-campus facility exclusively for managers. A skeptical university president told him the building would probably end up becoming an undergraduate dorm within two years. Jacobs forged ahead anyway, proving his boss wrong in the process. The $15 million James L. Allen Center opened in 1979, taking full advantage of its picturesque site on the shores of Lake Michigan just north of Chicago.

Every year, it hosts more than 3000 executives. The center offers 100 private bedrooms with baths, study lounges, classrooms for both large and small groups, over 50 personal computers, and two glass-walled, lakeside dining rooms whose cuisine earns pretty good reviews. Indeed, the atrium dining area features a chef in whites and a toque who whips up made-to-order omelets for breakfast. Any complaints? Hurry to the Johnson Wax Dining Room where Dean Jacobs is nearly a permanent fixture for lunch and dinner at a corner table next to Windover, a modern bronze sculpture.

Make no mistake: a stay at the Allen Center is generally no-frills living. A typical bedroom is 9-by-12, with a double bed, a clock radio, two chairs, and a small desk. There are neither televisions nor computers in these rooms. The expansion plans call for adding 50 more bedrooms, a 200-seat forum, and even more study space to the center. The extra space isn't likely to increase the number of AEP spots available—the current head count is a maximum of 60 per session—but instead will enable Kellogg to offer an even wider range of programs and custom courses. (Company-specific courses already account for 45 percent of the school's exec-ed business.)

The Advanced Executive Program takes a three-pronged approach to the study of general management. First, students examine the current worldwide social, political, and economic environment as it affects business operations, covering such topics as the balance of payments, ethical considerations for multinational companies, and communication with the Japanese. A second segment is devoted to review of the basic managerial functions, including finance, marketing, organizational behavior, and strategic planning.

Then the seven core faculty members permanently assigned to the program— among the most popular are course director Robert Duncan and Dean Jacobs—team-teach the integrative case study written for the session. Author of two business books on corporate change, Duncan is a consulting virtuoso. He's worked with a Who's Who of clients, including the American Bankers Association, Clorox, 3M, General Motors, IBM, and Peat Marwick. For five years, Duncan also served as university provost at Northwestern. Along with the other members of the team, Duncan delves into many other smaller cases to show how environmental and functional disciplines intersect in the real world. Outside speakers, including the chief executives of such companies as Hartmarx, Commonwealth Edison, and R.R. Donnelley, supplement the lectures by the faculty.

One disappointment: Managers gain no exposure to Kellogg superstar Philip Kotler, whose expertise in marketing has made him the school's most visible faculty member. Moreover, the heavy emphasis on case study bothered some participants, who groused that they would like to see more informal classroom interchanges among managers. "I figured we did nearly 50 cases in the four weeks," says one alumnus. "After a while, some of the cases just blur together." Nevertheless, the faculty receives high marks, with one or two exceptions, for its blend of theory and pragmatism.

While the program does include global issues, and more than one-third of the average class comes from outside the United States, Kellogg places less emphasis on the international than, for example, Michigan, so applicants who are particularly keen on exploring that aspect of management should be forewarned before forking over the $13,000 for tuition, room, board, and supplies. The typical AEP participant is a 42-year-old senior executive with general management or cross-functional responsibilities at a large corporation, earning a hefty $155,000 with some 20 years' business experience under the belt. Women and minorities each make up about 5 percent of the average class.

AEP's workload is not light: Expect a full eight hours a day in class, three to four more hours of small-group work, reading in the evening, and even some Saturday sessions. But participants say they had enough time to socialize, over a cup of coffee or glass of wine in the comfortable Allen Center lounges and during field trips to such locations as the Chicago Board of Trade. A spouse program is offered during the final three days of the course.

Organizations sending most participants: AT&T; Eastman Kodak; Ford; IBM; Hoechst

Other Programs of Note

Executive Development Program: Aims to prepare participants for higher-level management by increasing their understanding of accounting, finance, marketing, organization behavior, and human resource management. Led by Nancy Hartigan, director of Kellogg's executive education efforts. Designed for managers with senior-level potential and 10 or more years of work experience, as well as entrepreneurs and small-business owners. Three weeks; held three times a year, in May, July, and October; 60 students per session; $10,200, including tuition, room, board, and supplies; by application.

Business-to-Business Marketing Strategy: Covers the latest developments in strategic marketing planning, product targeting, communications, distribution management, and pricing, in both industrial and service fields. Led by Professor Richard Clewett, a Kellogg veteran who has consulted with Procter & Gamble and W. R. Grace. Marketing heavyweight Kotler also does a session in this course. Intended for division-level managers, product managers, and marketing managers in medium and large firms, as well as presidents and vice presidents of marketing in smaller firms. One week; held twice a year, in April and September; 70 students per session; $3700, including tuition, room, board, and supplies; open enrollment.

Merger Week: An intensive study of mergers and acquisitions, including strategy and planning for a merger; financial analysis; accounting and tax aspects; and the process of search, pricing, negotiation, and post-merger integration. Led by Professor Alfred Rappaport, a well-known consultant with his own firm, Alcar Group Inc. Designed for managers involved in corporate development, strategic planning, marketing planning, or anyone responsible for corporate growth. One week; held twice a year, in April and September; 50 students per session (more if interest warrants); $4200, including tuition, room, board, and supplies; open enrollment.

Creating World-Class Quality: Co-sponsored with corporate quality leader Motorola Inc., the seminar boasts speakers and case studies from Malcolm Baldrige award winners. Some say it could be mistaken for a "how to" course on how to win a Baldrige. That's hardly true, though the seminar has featured a lecture on the award's selection criteria by the Commerce Department official who directs the award. The idea for the course came from former Motorola Chairman Robert Galvin who helped the company capture a Baldrige in 1988. Led by Professor Eithan Zemel, an academic with a background in math who also co-heads Kellogg's Master's of Management in Manufacturing program. Five days; held twice a year, in January and June; 60 students per session; $3250, including tuition, room, board, and supplies; open enrollment.

Organizations sending most participants: AT&T; Unocal; Citicorp; Union Carbide; Dow Chemical

Kellogg Consumers Sound Off

Excellent program with group interaction by an international student body made for a very interesting and diverse, yet consensus, approach to problem solving. The discussions and varying viewpoints were all-inclusive and allowed us to see the situations through many eyes. I enjoyed and benefited from this program immensely.—**Marketing Director**

I had an MBA prior to attending Kellogg's Advanced Executive Program. The Kellogg experience validated my graduate degree by providing 33 percent of the contact hours of my 60-hour MBA program and did it with the professors who wrote the textbooks and articles that I studied at another university. Kellogg is fabulous!—**Manager**

There is a great tension between the need to convey information to executives and their need to discuss what they do or do not understand about that information. If Kellogg errs, it is on the side of conveying information and not allowing us to interact in the classroom.—**Executive Director**

I felt as though the school used its best and brightest faculty members to teach the Advanced Executive Program. The course is well-suited to an executive at a senior level in a functional specialty who is being prepared for or who has been identified as having the potential for a position in general management.—**Assistant Treasurer**

Unlike several graduate business schools and executive education programs I have been exposed to, the faculty at Northwestern's Kellogg School are not eggheads promoting esoteric academic theories. Rather, they are most pragmatic and blend real business experience with teaching of current management issues.—**Corporate Planning Director**

I felt that the lectures and written material were excellent, but could have been done in two to three weeks instead of four. Lecturers tried to allow

classes to be only participative, and the result was that 90 percent of the time the discussion veered off on a tangent. Also, the case study method wasted too much time.—Chairman and Managing Director

There was too much material with no prioritization or ranking of usefulness.—Senior Vice President

*The skillful development of lecture material and evening projects work toward a final project, where a real company was used as a case study, was extremely well planned. To have the senior officers of that company present to listen and provide feedback to your analysis was masterful.
—Program Manager*

During the last of the four weeks, much time was devoted to bringing in spouses, and the intensity of the program plummeted. This was a severe disappointment.—General Manager

The program was great for me in several ways. It confirmed that I was on the right track in a number of things I was doing. It gave me the opportunity to meet a group of international executives to discuss our similarities and differences. It gave me a list of peers with whom to discuss some things I am planning to do, possible things to watch out for and be concerned about.—Executive Director

Nothing revolutionary came out of this course as far as I was concerned. However, the learning allowed evolutionary growth which actually increased when I returned to my job. You soon realize how the learning and interaction in the program enable you to do things better after completing the course.—Group Managing Director

A majority of the first week was devoted to managing organizational change and to organizational culture. At the time, I had the opportunity to hear my classmates tell of their personal experiences in this area with regard to mergers and acquisitions. However, I had no idea that I would have an immediate opportunity to utilize their experiences only a week after finishing the program. Upon my return to the office, my company was merged with another and over the next 18 months, I was very much involved in the integration process.—Vice President, Strategic Operations

4. Duke University

Fuqua School of Business
Durham, North Carolina 27706

Corporate ranking: 4	*Consumer ranking*: 9
Number of programs: 29	*Number of programs in 1986*: 23
1990–1991 participants: 2500	*Years in executive education*: 10
Annual revenues: $7.8 million	*Change since 1986*: 333 percent

Contact: Jean G. Hauser, acting director of executive education, 919-660-6346

Advanced Management Program

You can sum up Fuqua's executive-education philosophy this way: Give the customer what he or she wants. Perhaps more than at any other school, the folks at Fuqua, the field's fastest-growing newcomer since launching its first exec-ed program a decade ago, bend over backwards to accommodate consumers in every conceivable way. For example, Fuqua's four-week AMP is held three times a year, with three different schedules. You can sign up for four consecutive weeks in late spring. Or you can spend two weeks on campus in August and return for the second two weeks in October. Or you can attend one week of classes a month during February, March, April, and May. If all these choices remind you of a menu at a fast-food joint, you're not far wrong: The exec-ed center at Duke is named for R. David Thomas, founder of Wendy's International (yes, that same, jolly, people-pleasing "Dave" you see in the restaurant's TV commercials).

Fuqua's flexible, diverse bill of fare has paid off. Its executive programs ranked fourth overall among corporations, though it was No. 1 in custom programs for single companies, such as Johnson & Johnson, Eli Lilly, and Ford (two-thirds of its nearly $8 million in annual exec-ed revenues comes from company-specific courses). The Advanced Management Program, with a price tag of $12,500 per manager, is consistently oversubscribed. Its 55 available slots per session are snapped up quickly. In keeping with Fuqua's "keep the customer satisfied" outlook, however, relatively few applicants are rejected outright because the school works closely with corporations to steer inappropriate candidates into other programs.

Fuqua's flagship management program has succeeded where many other top schools have tried and failed by attracting significant numbers of female managers. At Duke, women account for an unheard-of 30 percent of some split-session classes. (More typically, only 5 percent of the managers in flagship general management programs at the Top 20 universities are women.) Warren Baunach, Fuqua's former director of exec-ed, says he saw female enrollment skyrocket from around 10 percent soon after the divided program was first offered in 1989. "My wife explains it this way," Baunach chuckles. "Most working women hold down two jobs—one in the office and one at home—and they simply can't be away from home that long."

When you arrive on campus, it's hard not to be impressed by the university and the Research Triangle Park Area. Duke is one of four major universities in the triangle of Durham, Chapel Hill, and Raleigh. The mild climate, the rural yet progressive environment, and the modern-looking business school aim to charm. It's a 10-minute walk to the Gothic-looking Duke Chapel, the heart of the university campus. For some, that's a welcome diversion from the fast pace of the program.

The "customer-driven" mentality is reflected in AMP's curriculum, which is oriented toward strategy and marketing and places less emphasis on the basic functions than many general management courses. (For managers with weak backgrounds in finance, AMP offers self-evaluative tests, preparatory reading assignments, and an optional tutorial on the subject the weekend before the program begins.) While some participants complain that production and manufacturing receive short shrift, others applaud the in-depth exploration of what they believe to be more useful topics, such as corporate culture, negotiation skills, management styles, decision making as a strategic tool, and leadership. The latter culminates in a day of outdoor exercises known as "low ropes" and "high ropes," which strike fear in the hearts (and stomachs) of acrophobes. It includes maneuvers such as freefalling 100 feet by cable and climbing by rope ladder from treetop to treetop in the piney North Carolina woods. (Although the segment is optional, 95 percent of students participate.)

While the program touches on globalization, it is not a major thrust, and just 15 percent of the average class (or even fewer in the split sessions) hail from overseas, as compared with the 25 to 30 percent foreign students in the managerial programs at Michigan, Virginia, and Northwestern. The typical AMP student is in his or her late 40s, has upwards of 20 years' business experience, and makes over $150,000 a year at a major American corporation (although some 10 percent of each class hails from the armed services).

AMP's teaching staff consists almost entirely of Fuqua faculty, ably led by Professor Dan Laughhunn, a gray-haired veteran of the school. Laughhunn, an expert in the telecommunications business, has taught in executive development programs for such companies as IBM, New York Telephone, and Bell Canada. Along with Professor John Forsyth, who also serves as a faculty leader, the core group is joined by an occasional visiting professor from another university, and computer-simulation games are run by an outside firm. While participants were largely satisfied by the quality of teaching here, several commented that the faculty seemed to lack solid real-world experience and suggested bringing in a few guest-lecturing CEOs to fill in the gaps. Another criticism voiced with alarming regularity among participants concerned AMP's dearth of cutting-edge, up-to-the-minute case studies. "The reality is that for a business case to make the curriculum, it's too old to be relevant in the fast-paced business world of today. You do 15-year-old cases on Philip Morris when Nabisco is in the news. They talk about an up and coming company in a business case that is already an institution. They need more relevance to today's issues," complained one manager. Out of date or not, the assigned readings come fast and furious here, with past participants rating the workload among the heaviest of the Top 20 general management courses. Be prepared to bust your chops trying to keep up.

Yet, generally, participants didn't seem to mind the workload, in part because they were treated royally by the school. Much of the credit for the customer-friendly focus at Duke goes to Baunach, who was lured away in late June of 1992 by the University of North Carolina's B-school. With years of experience behind him at AT&T and General Foods, Baunach knew how to please busy executives. Jean G. Hauser, who as assistant dean has worked closely with companies on tailored programs, has assumed his job on an acting basis.

While there are areas of AMP that still need fine-tuning, one aspect that got rave reviews was the Thomas Center. Linked to the main business school building by a bridge across a ravine, it's a state-of-the-art facility on a beautifully landscaped, wooded campus site. It's also authentic hotel-style living, as it is managed by Marriott Corp. Opened in May of 1989, the center boasts 113 resident rooms with queen-size beds and executive-size desks, two 64-person classrooms with the latest audiovisual equipment, guest lounges with snack-laden kitchenettes for those late-night study sessions, a fitness center with exercise machines and sauna, and a much-admired dining room ("I had hoped to shed a few excess pounds while attending the program—a vain fantasy, as it turned out!" wrote one alumnus). If the way to a student's heart is through her stomach, Fuqua is definitely on the right track—Dave Thomas would be proud.

Organizations sending most participants: AT&T; John Hancock; DEC; Polaroid; Travelers

Other Programs of Note

Program for Manager Development: A mini-AMP for general management newcomers, focusing on leadership preparation; the integration of such functional areas as marketing, manufacturing, human resources, technology, R&D, and finance; strategy; global competitiveness; and government regulation. Led by faculty members Wesley Magat and Robert Reinheimer. Intended for upper- and mid-level managers with potential for greater responsibility. Two weeks; held four times a year, with consecutive two-week sessions in January, April, and September, and a split session with one week in July and one in August; 55 students; $6800, including tuition, room, board, and supplies; by application.

Strategic Marketing Program: Explores how companies can become customer-driven, by integrating functions to meet customer needs, building on core competencies, and keeping strategies realistic. Led by Associate Professor Robert Reinheimer. Designed for functional managers who need to increase their knowledge of marketing, and newly appointed marketing managers. Two weeks; held annually, in late spring; 35 students; $6600, including tuition, room, board, and supplies; by application.

Competitive Strategies in the Telecommunications Industry: No school beats Duke when it comes to this industry-specific program. It explains how deregulation, new technology, changing markets, and increased competition affect telecommunications companies' strategy and profitability. Led by Professor James Vander Weide. Intended for mid-level executives at operating telephone companies, equipment manufacturers, cellular phone companies, cable TV firms, and major telecommunications users. One week; held twice a year, in spring and fall; 35–45 students; $3600, including tuition, room, board, and supplies; by application.

Executive Program for Corporate Counsel: Designed to introduce corporate attorneys to the technology, language, and functions of other disciplines inside their companies, with a review of economics, finance, strategy, marketing, human resources, and the impact of technology, regulation, and competition. This highly rated program is led by Associate Professor Robert Reinheimer; a joint program with the American Corporate Counsel Association. Intended for corporate counsel with at least five years' experience. A split two-week session held annually, with one week in late winter and another in early spring; 35–45 students; $6900 ($6600 for ACCA members), all inclusive; by application.

Organizations sending most participants: AT&T; Xerox; NYNEX; Bell South; IBM

Fuqua Consumers Sound Off

It is difficult to find negatives about the Advanced Management Program. The program was thoughtfully planned and unfailingly well-executed. The faculty was highly qualified, uniformly well-prepared, and intensely interested in the viewpoints of the executives expressed during group discussions. In my judgment, the tuition is well justified by the experience.
—General Counsel and Secretary

The case studies used were dated—late 1970s, early to mid-1980s. The biggest failure was the lack of current trends and areas of the issues being addressed. I guess the program was adequate, but I was not challenged intellectually nor required to reach for any "lofty" principles. I would call the program middle of the road, not a "head and shoulders" course.
—Systems Acquisition Director

There was not enough time to digest the material. They were in such a rush to cover the allotted material that it did not allow for in-depth discussions. As a result, topics were given only surface coverage.
—Business Manager

The problem with any executive education program is the different levels of knowledge and experience of the participants. The Advanced Management Program does the best job I have seen in balancing this problem, with a world-class curriculum. **—General Manager**

I was exceptionally pleased with the way the faculty drew upon the knowledge and experience of the participants, and the quality of the participants themselves. The faculty had a unique knack of drawing out group discussions that helped support and illustrate the concepts they were presenting. **—Comptroller**

Too many people from the same company—class was 20 percent government and 10 percent Navy officers. This reduced the variety and richness of the discussion. In short, I got a feeling that this was a money-making endeavor, not a learning endeavor. **—Program Manager**

Production/manufacturing needs to be emphasized. Session in this area was too general, weak. **—Vice President**

The overall quality of Duke's facilities is superior. The administrative staff was congenial, accessible, very sensitive to meeting the needs of its cus-

tomers. The amount of time committed to actual program work was aggressive but well-managed, and enough time and resources were made available for recreational activities.—**Field Vice President**

The greatest benefit I received from attending this program was the realization that I could "run with the big dogs." My class included a large number of high-level people from a wide range of businesses. I was relatively early in my management career, yet I felt my grasp of the material was as good as any. I was gratified to be chosen for a leadership role in some of the team assignments. This experience gave me more confidence in my judgment and has allowed me to be more effective at my job. —**Manager**

It was one of the most significant personal and professional experiences of my life. The subject matter of the program challenged and broadened my perspectives and is directly germaine to my professional responsibilities. The concepts I learned have been extremely useful in such assignments as making capital spending decisions, customer and labor negotiations, strategic planning assignments, and altering my leadership style. —**Division Manager**

I have initiated numerous projects at work since I completed the program. They have resulted in significant improvements, enhancing the quality of service in our company, promoting employee empowerment, and increasing managerial effectiveness. I left Duke with an education that I will share with everyone I come in contact with. My wish for my company is that it would send all 150 senior executives to Fuqua. I believe there would be a profound and immediate competitive advantage in exposing the company's key executives to the wisdom in Duke's superior educational package.—**Group Director**

5. Stanford University

Graduate School of Business
Stanford, California 94305

Corporate ranking: 9
Number of programs: 8
1990–1991 participants: 590
Annual revenues: $7.0 million

Consumer ranking: 4
Number of programs in 1986: 8
Years in executive education: 42
Change since 1986: 35 percent

Contact: James E. Howell, director of executive education, 415-723-4141

Stanford Executive Program

Get up at the crack of dawn for some exercise with your buddies. Pull on your button-down shirt and chinos and head off to class for a few hours of high-powered thinking. Take a break from your afternoon studies to play soccer with the cafeteria workers. Catch dinner at the campus mess hall. Head back to your sparsely furnished dorm room for some heavy-duty late-night reading, periodically punctuated by a friendly academic debate with one of your neighbors. When Friday night rolls around, *party hearty*! Take part in a beer-chugging relay, spoof the professors in a musical-comedy revue, or laugh your head off when some of the boys put on a ballet in drag.

Sounds like a college fraternity brother's dream schedule—or a capsule description of the Stanford Executive Program. If your fondest memories are of your years as an undergrad (or if you've always wanted to relive those days in a new and improved version), SEP is right up your alley—a sort of mini-MBA in an idyllic campus setting, with a whole lot of fun thrown in as a bonus. Indeed, the program is right up a lot of executives' alleys. Again and again, past participants bubbled over with enthusiasm. Stanford received top marks for its return on investment of time and money (albeit a sizable investment, at seven weeks and $25,200), for its high-caliber student body, and for the level of growth, both personally and on the job, that managers felt resulted from attending the experience. Managers here resoundingly affirmed that they would recommend the program to a friend (only the University of North Carolina rated a higher level of satisfaction).

So what accounts for this zeal? It certainly isn't the kid-glove treatment students receive. There's no secluded, multimillion-dollar executive center at Stanford. Managers are put up in undergraduate dormitories, with their picturesque Spanish architecture but decidedly ascetic accommodations. "It's a shock to people—the inside looks like a medieval nunnery," notes Doug McIntyre, who attended SEP in 1989. You don't have to fight over who takes the top bunk. Everyone at least gets a single room, but you still have to share a bath. Meals are served at the university dining hall; lectures are held in the regular Graduate School of Business classrooms. There's no special core faculty for the program; professors are rotated in from the B-school staff, with the occasional one-shot visitor (almost always a Stanford alum) thrown in. The class is not small: Between 180 and 190 managers swarm into Palo Alto for the annual summer session, although participants are broken up into smaller working groups of about 60.

What you do get is a rigorous, traditional review of the management basics. Stanford is not a trendy place; it prefers to do a few things, and do them well. Its foray into exec-ed is intentionally limited—the school offers just eight different programs (the same eight it offered five years ago) and no single-company, custom courses. Stanford is making a few concessions to current fashion in its mainstream executive program. For one thing, there's a growing emphasis on international business and strategic management. More importantly, beginning in the summer of 1992, the program will be shortened from eight weeks to seven to satisfy the demands of customers.

"The pressures on executives today involve a range of issues, from globalization of the economy to regulation to family pressures," says Bruce McKern, program director. So for senior executives, time is at a premium now more than ever. Just because the program is shorter, however, doesn't mean you'll be getting off easy. "If anything," adds McKern, "the program will become even more intense as a result of having to fit in more in a shorter elapsed time." Rather than eliminate anything, Stanford will hold classes on Saturday mornings, which were previously free for independent reading and group study.

The program will continue to devote one area of study to factors external to corporations: the economy, the economies of developing countries, business-government relations, and ethics. The drill of functional skills includes accounting, quantitative analysis, managerial psychology, organizational behavior, finance, and marketing. And the integrative segments, which bring everything together, encompass strategy, planning, and analysis; manufacturing strategy; and managing the total enterprise.

Overall, the teaching quality received good marks, with a few caveats: The finance and accounting courses, taught in recent sessions by Jim Van Horne and Chuck Horngren, were singled out as top-flight; the marketing segments, on the other hand, were criticized as too elementary and out-of-date. Outside speakers are brought in occasionally to supplement the faculty, and while some managers groused that there seemed to be a requirement that speakers have some Stanford connection, the school can attract the likes of former Secretary of State George P. Shultz for a question-and-answer session on world politics.

You also get to spend two months in the company of an experienced, well-educated peer group, which contributes bountifully to the learning process. The typical participant, a 45-year-old senior executive from a medium- to large-size company, with at least 15 years of business experience; two-thirds have graduate degrees, and about half are from outside the United States. There's a wealth of expertise here, and SEP is not shy about taking advantage of it. In one recent session, a student who was an expert on corporate foreign exchange joined with a professor to speak on the subject; a group of executives with fresh experience in mergers and acquisitions gave a presentation; and the European participants put together a seminar on the European Community and the Continent's business outlook for the 1990s. Evening study groups, which are regularly scrambled for diversity's sake, provoke lively discussions of the next day's assignments. "I got as much on a personal level from my peers as I got in the curriculum level from the faculty," remarks one manager.

Sustaining a high level of academic intensity for seven long weeks requires some R&R, and the SEP crowd plays as hard as it works. Northern California's glorious summer climate and spectacular scenery encourages a plethora of outdoor activities, from the daily 6:15 a.m. exercise session to weekend bike rides to San Francisco, sailing on the Bay, and tours of wine country and Yosemite National Park. Student-organized outings are popular, including golf and tennis tournaments and a class "Olympiad" with events like frisbee throwing and sack racing. Near the program's beginning, participants choose a social chairman to oversee the planning of elaborate Friday-night theme parties, complete with appropriate food, drink, and costumes—Mexican Night, Swiss Night, Asian Night, French Night. A couple of years back, for example, "Colonial Night" featured an aborigine dance routine choreographed by an Australian participant and performed with great ineptitude by a bunch of bewigged, middle-aged executives who unwisely flaunted their pot bellies above their grass skirts. Participants even put together their own yearbook and, following a short spouse program the final week, attend a "graduation" ceremony complete with robes and certificates.

Unfortunately, there is one big drawback to the SEP "fraternity": Like its undergraduate models, it is made up almost exclusively of white males. While few general management programs break the corporate glass-ceiling limit of more than 5 percent women, Stanford barely manages to draw a pitiful 3 percent, as one participant after another pointed out in our survey. "The SEP 1991 class included just six women, which all of us (male and female alike) felt was an embarrassment. It was a somewhat lonely experience being in such a minority for such a long time, isolated from family and friends," one alumna commented. And while James E. Howell, director of executive education, says the school keeps no record of minority involvement, people of color are represented even more poorly than women—in one class of 200, there were no black and two Hispanic participants, despite the internationally diverse makeup. As one (male) alum succinctly put it, "Who are these guys, and why are they living in the 1950s?" The upshot is that executives who don't fit the Stanford mold may not feel comfortable there, a fact that all the excellent academics and raucous camaraderie in the world can't hide.

Organizations sending most participants: Hewlett-Packard; Monsanto; Amoco; AT&T; Unilever

Other Programs of Note

Executive Program in Organizational Change: Designed to help senior executives develop better ways to recognize the need for change within their organizations and more productive strategies and techniques for responding to that need. Emphasis on small-group interaction with other participants. Led by Professor Jerry I. Porras, who worked for Lockheed and General Electric before joining academia. Intended for high-level executives, including CEOs and managers of autonomous major divisions of large organizations, with at least 10 years' management experience. Two weeks; held annually, in early summer; 42 students per session; $9500, including tuition, room, board, and supplies; by application.

Executive Program for Smaller Companies: Focuses on general management problems confronting independently owned firms with 50 to 1000 employees, with an examination of corporate strategy, marketing, finance, and human resources. Led by Lecturer John R. Berthold, a former brand manager at Procter & Gamble who has also managed a few small companies of his own. Intended for senior executives over

35 years of age in small- to medium-sized businesses (mainly chief executives and those reporting directly to the CEO). Two weeks; held annually, in July; 130 students per session; $8400, including tuition, room, board, and supplies; by application.

Marketing Management: A Strategic Perspective: Probes marketing from a total-organization viewpoint, with an eye toward increasing understanding of how marketing fits into overall corporate strategy, with an emphasis on the marketing environment of the future. Led by Professor David B. Montgomery, a Stanford veteran of over 20 years. Intended for senior managers with 10 years' experience. Two weeks; held annually, in August; 68 students per session; $8400, including tuition, room, board, and supplies; by application.

Financial Management Program: Offers an analysis of financial policies for decision making and concepts relating to securities markets, blending traditional corporate finance with modern economic advances in such areas as valuation, operation of markets, options, hedging, capital structure, financial forecasting, and diversification. Led by Professors George G.C. Parker and Paul Pfleiderer. Designed for executives with overall financial responsibilities for their organizations, including chief financial officers, treasurers, controllers and senior general managers who have financial staff reporting to them. Two weeks; held annually, in early summer; 60 students per session; $8400, including tuition, room, board, and supplies; by application.

Organizations sending most participants: AT&T; Hewlett-Packard; IBM; Northern Telecom; Monsanto

Stanford Consumers Sound Off

*Outstanding atmosphere, camaraderie, practically-oriented lecturers, strongly engaged and understanding professors—a unique occasion for any executive to recover from his or her own problems and to enjoy another world.—**Executive Vice President/Chief Financial Officer***

*The formal teaching varied from the excellent to quite mediocre. All teachers were technically competent, but some did not pitch their presentations to mature, experienced managers and were more geared to undergraduate or MBA teaching.—**Industrial Relations Director***

*I gained at least as much from the other attendees as from the professors. Half of our 190+ members were from outside the United States. It took several weeks to drop our guards and really open up to one another. But when we did, the insights were penetrating and lasting.—**President***

The business school administration and executive program director displayed an appalling lack of sensitivity to the issue of women in business and spouses (primarily female). The course contained no material specifically addressing the issue; the faculty were ill-prepared to discuss the issues raised by a female work force; the spouse program assumed the majority were either stay-at-homes or had low-level-responsibility jobs. No lecturers were female, and the only guest lecturer (female) who spoke on women in the work force was arranged because of pressure from the women who were attending the course. —**Senior Vice President**

The Palo Alto climate and Northern California sightseeing were a distinct plus and allowed for much physical exercise. —**Division President**

Accommodation was way below the standard of what may reasonably be expected for lodging senior executives, each paying $25,000 for an eight-week program. No air conditioning in California in July and August! —**Managing Director**

The inclusion of current events in the program through special sessions is good. George Shultz, an expert on the Soviet Union and a Chinese scholar familiar with events leading to the Communist crackdown, brought world events or trends to life for us. —**Product Development Manager**

The excellence of the program is partly based on the variety of countries, businesses, and activities represented, and the high level of the participants. The program's organization was excellent, the professors were all highly qualified, and in general, I consider it an A-1 program. —**Executive Vice President**

6. Harvard University

Harvard Business School
Soldiers Field
Boston, Massachusetts 02163

Corporate ranking: 5
Number of programs: 18
1990–1991 enrollment: 1900
Annual revenues: $26.8 million

Consumer ranking: 13
Number of programs in 1986: 12
Years in executive education: 49
Change since 1986: 51 percent

Contact: Jay Lorsch, senior associate dean and chairman of executive education programs, 617-495-6413

Advanced Management Program

In 1989, David Ellis had been president of Lafayette College for more than 10 years, a most successful decade. He had guided the Pennsylvania institution through a major capital campaign, raising over $100 million during his tenure. He had overseen the construction of a student center building and watched with satisfaction as a computer network wired its way across the hilltop campus. But he was feeling restless. The school was pushing to start another big fund drive, and at age 53, Ellis knew it was time to choose whether he'd stay at Lafayette until retirement, or seek out a new challenge before his time ran out. With this weighty decision hanging over his head, he packed his bags for Boston and Harvard's Advanced Management Program. For 11 weeks, he picked the brains of his professors and scores of classmates: "Every Sunday night, I thought through what I might like to do," he recalls. When he returned to Lafayette, he began drawing up his resignation letter.

Not every alumnus has such a dramatic story to tell, but many people do describe their exec-ed experiences at Harvard as pivotal, galvanizing episodes in their careers. While partly due to the cachet that the Harvard imprimatur seems to bring to all of academia, there is something special about the general management courses here. Since the 1940s, when AMP was established to prepare managers and their factories for the war effort, Harvard has been the field's leader, widely admired and copied. After all, this is the biggest, richest, most prestigious B-school in the country—the school that invented the case study. Companies rate the school's general management courses best in the United States. If executive education were a corporation, Harvard would definitely be chairman of the board, and AMP would be the showcase product.

But in recent years, the chairman has begun to age. As other B-schools have come to see exec-ed as a key to boosting their reputations—and filling their pocketbooks—Harvard's market share eroded from 13 percent in 1986 to 5 percent today, among the Top 20 schools. AMP participants and sponsoring companies alike have begun complaining that the commitment of nearly three months of time, at a cost that will top $31,000 by the fall of 1992, is simply too great. And the school is finding it increasingly difficult to fill 160 openings twice a year (the program is offered in both spring and fall). What many perceive as Harvard's inflexible attitude doesn't help matters: While competitors like Stanford and MIT are scrambling to shorten their flagship programs to meet corporate demands, "We're refusing to buckle under," says Jay Lorsch, chairman of Harvard's executive education programs. "Other schools purport to be doing the same thing in 3 weeks that we do in 11 weeks, but we think we deliver a superior product. It's our mission to convince the companies that they need to make this commitment."

But even Harvard has to keep its customers satisfied, and changes are beginning to creep into the exec-ed lineup. Although the current offering of 9- to 12-week general management courses and 1- to 2-week specialized courses seems unlikely to change much, the school has begun holding brief, 2- to 3-day workshops for CEOs on such topics as retailing, agribusiness, and corporate governance. Harvard is also negotiating with a handful of major corporations to move into the custom-program market, which for many B-schools is the most lucrative, fastest-growing business. "We're going through a major evaluation," says Lorsch. "We want to be more proactive than we may have been in the last few years."

AMP may also be headed for a sea change. Professor Earl Sasser, who is taking over as faculty chairman of the program in the fall of 1992 following a stint chairing the MBA staff, believes that for AMP to remain competitive, "Companies need to see more value—and soon after their people get back." So Sasser is proposing that by fall 1993, the program begin guiding participants in individual assessments of how their companies can reach maximum performance levels. Assuming he can convince the rest of the faculty to go along with him, he envisions a self-study guide devised by the faculty that will allow each executive to establish a benchmark for world-class performance for his or her firm, and then devise an agenda for change in order to reach that benchmark. Lectures, group study, joint teaching projects, computer work, and input by students with particular areas of expertise would all contribute to the process.

Sasser's plans would substantially change the face of a program that has always held case method as king, and it's a safe bet that you won't hear any complaints about a reduction in the massive volume of assigned reading. "There was a universal feeling that the cases were written more with the idea of being appreciated by another academician, as opposed to a businessperson," says one alum. (Apparently students haven't felt compelled to complete every word, anyway: In our participants' survey, Harvard surprisingly ranked lowest of the Top 20 schools in terms of workload.) The current course structure is organized very much according to function, with separate classes in general management; business, government, and the international economy; industry and competitive analysis; leadership; corporate financial management; financial management and accounting; marketing management; information, organization, and control systems; and operations strategy. It will likely be revamped to allow more emphasis on trendier material, such as corporate renewal and global competition. "It would be much more cross-functional than functional," says Sasser.

Whatever modifications are in store for the curriculum, much of what you learn will be influenced to a large extent by the interests of AMP's superstar core faculty, culled from the B-school's 200 professors, many of them well-known through their consulting and publishing efforts. While the lineup is due for some turnover as Sasser begins his term as chairman, previous classes have been able to hear the insights of strategy guru Michael E. Porter; global finance wizard Samuel L. Hayes III, whose recent book *Investment Banking: A Tale of Three Cities* examined the securities markets of New York, London, and Tokyo; Robert S. Kaplan, the nation's foremost expert on management accounting; John P. Kotter, leadership guru and author of several seminal books on organizational behavior; and quality expert David Garvin, who leads a full-day computer exercise based on the Baldrige Award. Then again, you might come across a professor like the one who spent nearly half a class discussing whether a new CEO should arrive by limousine or helicopter the first day in order to send the appropriate message through the corporate ranks. And many participants complain that faculty members' myriad obligations, including MBA courses, their own research and writing, and consulting, make it impossible to be truly accessible to a class the size of the AMP's. Indeed, some executives say their exposure to Michael Porter was limited to an informal gathering at a reception (meaning he spent no time at all in the classroom). Sasser says he thinks the new format would free up the teaching staff to give students more individual attention.

One of AMP's strengths has always been its elite participant list, drawn from the highest echelons of the biggest companies in the nation. That has been changing in recent years, however, because many brand-name American corporations simply can't afford to give up a top executive for 11 weeks. To offset the decline in business from such "academy" companies, Harvard has been enrolling fewer vice presidents and more managers from mid-sized companies. The school also has significantly enlarged foreign participation. Non-U.S. students now make up 50 percent of every class, up from only 25 percent a decade ago. Harvard has done less well in attracting women executives, who usually still can be counted on the fingers of one hand in each session. Women, even more than men, find that 11 weeks is an almost impossibly long time to be away from home: "Contrary to the stories we heard, no one got divorced when they returned home—as far as I am aware," one participant reports.

The sense of isolation is assuaged largely by your "can group," fellow residents of an eight-bedroom suite with a large, shared living room in Baker Hall, the exec-ed dorm. (Before Baker was built in the 1960s, the only shared space was the communal bathroom, hence the terminology.) Although each resident nowadays has a private lavatory, the accommodations are anything but plush. "The bedrooms are about the size of a cheap stateroom on a cruise ship, and the bunks are rock-hard," laughs William Van Brunt, general counsel for the food operations at General Mills, who attended AMP in 1989. The arrangement encourages you to spend a lot of time in the company of your can mates, who are selected with an eye toward diversity of nationality, industry, and function: Among Van Brunt's can were a Japanese banker, a British engineer, an Argentine finance and marketing manager, an American retailing manager, a Malaysian general manager, and a U.S. government attorney. They become your study partners in the wee hours of the morning—MBA students have been known to call the campus police to quiet down a 2 a.m. AMP study-session-turned-party—and, often, friends for life. "We've gotten together on occasion in other cities while traveling, or we'll pick up the phone and call each other," says Van Brunt.

It's that kind of lasting effect that AMP Chairman Sasser doesn't want to tamper with. "This program has an impact on students as they come through," he says. "We don't want to lose that." Just ask David Ellis: Within a year after leaving Lafayette, he came back to Massachusetts for good, as director of the Museum of Science in Cambridge—just across the Charles River from the B-school he says helped him change his life.

Other Programs of Note

International Senior Management Program: Focuses on business in an international context, with more than 90 percent of participants from outside the United

States; examines such general management topics as marketing, international trade, operations structure and strategy, finance, and organizational behavior, with an eye toward maintaining competitiveness in a fast-changing global environment. Led by Professor Christopher A. Bartlett. Intended for top-level executives of multinational and non-U.S. companies. Nine weeks; held annually, beginning in May; 100 students per session; $29,500, including tuition, room, most meals, and supplies (weekend and holiday meals, spouse program, $150 health insurance fee, and $500 class association fee are extra); by application.

Program for Management Development: A 12-week course to prepare functional executives for general management positions, this program's extensive computerization and use of "electronic cases" may be the wave of the future in management training. For further details, see Chapter 6, The Ten Most Innovative Programs.

Owner/President Management Program: A management-training course exclusively for owners of mid-sized firms who are also chief executives, focusing on expanding managerial skills to meet the demands of growing, increasingly complex enterprises. Study topics include planning and strategy, goal setting and policy formulation, risks and rewards of business growth, profitability, and transition to more formal management methods. Led by Professor Martin Marshall. Intended for owner/chief executives of companies with $5 million to $100 million in sales who have at least 10 years' experience. Nine weeks; held over the course of three years, in three-week units each year, with the first unit beginning in May; 120 students per session; $10,400 per unit, including tuition, room, board, and supplies; by application.

Achieving Breakthrough Service: Seeks to improve skills in analyzing target markets, positioning service concepts, refining operating strategies, and developing service delivery systems. Led by Associate Professor Leonard A. Schlesinger. Intended for executives of multi-location service organizations, either general managers or senior managers of service operations, marketing, or human resources. One week; held annually, in January; 70 students per session; $6400, including tuition, room, board, and supplies; by application.

Managing the Information Services Resource: Focuses on managing, evaluating, and planning the growth of information systems, with an emphasis on critical management issues. Led by Professor F. Warren McFarlan, one of the charter members of the so-called Cambridge Mafia of information gurus. He also brings in Richard Nolan, another member of the group whose consulting firm of Nolan, Norton has established itself as a key player in the info biz. Intended for management information systems managers and the senior executives to whom they report. Two weeks; held annually in July; 110 students per session; $7875, including tuition, room, board, and supplies; by application.

Harvard Consumers Sound Off

Harvard Business School was every bit as good as its reputation and course fees lead one to expect. Our company has sent numerous representatives to business schools; none has convinced me that their experiences could surpass those I was privileged to have at Harvard.—**General Manager**

Some of the professors were absolutely excellent; conversely, some appeared to be on the scrap heap. I don't think that we consistently were given the best people available.—**Vice President**

The international mix of the class members brought a worldwide business and cultural experience through interaction, which was extremely valuable for exposure and networking.—**Director of Instrumentation**

Superb facilities, great academic theoreticians, practical application, high-caliber associates and fellow students from around the world. The program was one of the richest experiences of my life.—**Government Director**

Overkill on cases—was it intended to crack participants up in the first few weeks? In the middle section of the program, there was a slavish adherence to the Harvard case study blackboard technique: drag out the obvious, suppress personal experience, adhere to the timetable. I feel that my classmates had a great deal to offer, but were often prevented by the program or certain members of the faculty.—**Director of Operations**

The major area for improvement revolves around the international aspects of the case studies. These are primarily related to U.S. operations or U.S.-owned groups. The program would be enriched if considerably more effort was devoted to case studies in Europe and the Far East.
—**Development Director**

The program was excellent but too long. Time away from my job definitely affected the performance of my business unit.—**President**

7. University of Pennsylvania

Wharton School
255 S. 38th St.
Philadelphia, Pennsylvania 19104

Corporate ranking: 8   *Consumer ranking*: 11
Number of programs: 60   *Number of programs in 1986*: 42
1990–1991 participants: 4700   *Years in executive education*: 40
Annual revenues: $16.0 million   *Change since 1986*: 181 percent

Contact: Robert E. Mittelstaedt, Jr., vice dean, 215-898-4560

Advanced Management Program

When you walk into the Steinberg Conference Center, home to Wharton's aggressive efforts in executive education, you might have to double-check the sign in front to be sure you're in the right place. The plush, $25 million facility, built in 1987 as that decade's opulence reached its crescendo, could easily be mistaken for a museum of modern art. The lobby fairly bursts with oil paintings, lithographs, engravings, and sculptures. Heading down a corridor to class, you might stumble upon a Miro aquatint or a Warhol silkscreen. As you sit down for lunch in the dining room, you'll be surrounded by nineteenth-century Burmese tapestries. When you kick off your shoes for an informal study session in one of the student lounges, you might look up to find a series of Salvador Dali's surreal lithographs staring back at you. In this richly appointed environment, waitresses wheel carts of midday treats—freshly baked cookies in silver trays on white linen—down the hallways outside the modern classrooms.

Like alum Saul Steinberg, the flashy corporate raider who is the center's namesake and major benefactor, Wharton likes to think big, even though it is a relative newcomer to the big time executive education business. The school only began to offer its flagship Advanced Management Program in 1988—45 years after Harvard launched the granddaddy of AMP experiences. So Wharton aimed to be different, radically different. At Wharton, AMP is a management-training course, a mini-review of the humanities, and a trip to the psychiatrist's couch, all rolled up in one. Like the center's extensive contemporary art collection, the B-school's Advanced Management Program may not be everyone's cup of tea—but it's sure to leave an impression.

Take, for example, its "Human Dimension" segment. Before arriving on campus, managers are asked to get half a dozen of their subordinates, peers, and superiors at work to evaluate their personalities and their ability to relate to others on the job. At the same time, students come up with their own self-profiles. During the five-week program, a psychiatrist observes participants in the classroom and out, getting to know them at social events, mealtimes, and study sessions. Then, as AMP draws to a close, each executive meets privately with the doctor to receive counseling on how to improve his or her interpersonal relations and become more effective leaders. "They told us things you need to know about yourself that normally only your spouse would tell you," notes George W. Morriss, chief financial officer of Connecticut-based People's Bank, who attended the program in 1990. "It was fairly traumatic."

The program's focus evolved in this direction, says Robert E. Mittelstaedt, Jr., vice

63

dean of executive education, because Wharton believes this is what managers need most. "In many executives, it's the interpersonal skills that are lacking," he says. "An effort is made here to evaluate where they are and where they are going." Another aspect of the Human Dimension is its use of material from the arts and sciences to supplement the usual management fare. As each week comes to a close, time is allocated to readings and discussions of American slave songs, or the immigrant experience, or the Civil War, led by University of Pennsylvania faculty specializing in anthropology, history, or English literature. A morning might be spent in the university art museum; an afternoon excursion might take the class to Philadelphia's historical sites. The curriculum goes with the flow; if managers decide they'd like to delve into events in the Persian Gulf, for example (as Morriss's class did), AMP's director, Paul Kleindorfer, will arrange to have an appropriate expert from Penn's vast stable of talent come in and give a talk. The bearded Kleindorfer is quite an expert himself, having consulted on manufacturing policy for such companies as DuPont, IBM, and Lear Aircraft. In short, this program is definitely not the place to go for a review of the rudimentary executive functions: the basics of marketing, finance, and management are covered only in relation to such themes as globalization, enhancing shareholder value, and boosting employee production.

AMP's approach to team-building is equally distinctive—Morriss described it as "analogous to one of those dances where the boys and girls start out on opposite sides of the auditorium, then wander around trying to find a partner." After a couple of introductory get-togethers during the program's first few days, the 45 class members are put into a room and told that each is to find for a partner the person most dissimilar to him- or herself, in terms of background and personality. With over half the participants from foreign locations as disparate as Russia, Israel, and Switzerland (about 5 percent are women and 10 percent minorities), and with backgrounds ranging from investment banking and government to medicine and the nonprofit sector, some pretty odd couples can result. Then each pair is told to find another pair, until the group is broken up into teams that resemble a mini United Nations. These teams stay in place throughout the program for group projects, simulations, and study sessions, and many managers say that after the initial cultural and language barriers are overcome, the close interaction with such diverse colleagues is one of AMP's highlights, complementing the globalization segment nicely.

A pair of capstone projects quickly get the teams into the nitty gritty of business life. In one, each manager must assess his or her company's competitive position in global markets. The project requires participants to call back to their offices for information to plug into an analytical framework devised by Professor Howard V. Perlmutter, an expert in global corporate strategy. A manager's group then selects the best presentation to be made to the entire class at the end of the program. The other assignment calls for each participant to explore a joint alliance with a company represented by another participant in the program. These make-believe deals also are presented to the entire class, although on at least one occasion a group refused to make a presentation. The reason? The managers wanted to pursue their venture for real after the program ended and didn't want the proposal to leak out.

Unlike executive programs at many other schools, which seek to stabilize their core faculties, AMP intentionally rotates its teaching staff among the sizable Wharton community (it has to be big, what with the school's mammoth MBA program and whopping 60 different exec-ed offerings). You sometimes need a scorecard to keep track of the players. The director's post changes every two years: Kleindorfer took over in 1992 from William F. Hamilton, who remains involved with the program. Some 25 percent of AMP's core faculty is drawn from outside the university—from other schools, consulting firms, and corporations. While officials cite striving for freshness as the main reason behind the ever-changing professorial slate, managers believe that the teaching quality suffers as a result, ranking Wharton in the bottom half of the exec-ed Top 20 in that key arena.

What it lacks in sheer teaching quality, Wharton certainly makes up for in the attention devoted to the amenities. The quality of the food surprises many, especially one of the house favorites: rolled stuffed flank steak with horseradish cream. Every dinner comes complete with a table of killer desserts and a bottle of fine wine. Outside the second-floor dining room, neat stacks of the latest newspapers—*The Philadelphia Enquirer, The New York Times, The Wall Street Journal,* and *The Financial Times of London*—are piled on a table for participants. Even the recycling bins in the center are made of mahogany with brass nameplates.

For quiet study, there's a small, secluded library on the first floor. For beer and sports on a big-screen television, there's an evening lounge and bar on the fifth floor that features a view of the city and the Wharton quad. The fifth floor also features a fitness center equipped with a couple of Airdynes, a Concept II rowing machine, a treadmill, a bench press, and sauna. A block away, you have access to an Olympic-sized swimming pool as well as squash and tennis courts in the university gym. Every seven or eight guest rooms has access to a case study room with a TV, VCR, personal computer and printer, a conference table, and small kitchenette.

Despite the program's idiosyncracies, however, plenty of executives are eager to win a spot in one of its sessions, held three times a year in spring, summer, and fall. The typical participant is 45 to 47 years old, making $200,000 a year as a senior line or functional manager. Mittelstaedt says the program receives up to double the number of applications it can take. Just be prepared: When you sign up for Wharton's AMP, you're in for something more than a little different.

Organizations sending most participants: Digital Equipment; Petroleos de Venezuela; British Airways; AMR; Eastman Kodak

Other Programs of Note

The International Forum: A trio of four-day seminars on global strategic issues for chief executives of companies in Europe, Asia, and the Americas, held in the United States, Belgium, and Japan. Uses guest lectures by foreign business, government, and cultural leaders. For further details, see Chapter 6, The Ten Most Innovative Programs.

Executive Development Program: Guides functional managers through the transition to general management, with an exploration of finance, marketing, and operations, but focusing on leadership and human relations. Each participant returns to work with a plan of action regarding a current problem perceived at her or his own company. Led by Professor Ross A. Webber, a former Eastman Kodak engineer and consultant to Texaco. Intended for functional specialists moving into generalist positions. Two weeks; held twice a year, in late fall and early summer; $7900, including tuition, room, board, and supplies; 40–45 students per session; by application.

Finance and Accounting for the Nonfinancial Manager: No school beats Wharton when it comes to finance. This basic course is one of Wharton's biggest moneymakers. It provides a basic grounding in finance and accounting, including how to read and understand financial statements, cash-flow, and investment data. Led by Associate Professor Peter H. Knutson, a former Arthur Andersen accountant who has consulted with Mellon Bank, Fidelcor, and CoreStates Financial. Intended for general managers, nonfinancial functional managers, or those with new financial responsibilities. Five days; held six times throughout the year; $3950, including tuition, room, and board; 40–50 students per session; by application.

Advanced Industrial Marketing Strategy: Explores marketing in businesses that service other businesses (rather than individual consumers), with a focus on the impact of strategic marketing and finance decisions on the overall company. Led by Professor David J. Reibstein, one of the school's top teachers. Intended for product and marketing managers in business-to-business firms. Two weeks; held twice a year, in spring and fall; $8100, including tuition, room, and board; 40–50 students per session; by application.

Organizations sending most participants: AT&T; NYNEX; General Motors; Johnson & Johnson; Bell Atlantic

Wharton Consumers Sound Off

*Right subject matter—stressed interpersonal skills, leadership, globalization, and ethics, all subjects sorely lacking in American business today.—**General Services Director***

*The Human Dimension module was a feature of the Wharton program which attracted me to the course in the first place. The relevance of this module provoked some debate amongst the participants. For me, it was cleverly integrated with the other topics, and left me at the end of the program with a far better intuitive appreciation of the degree to which everything we do has a cause and effect.—**Attorney***

*Human Dimension studies could have been cut short and speeded up, as most of us were familiar with the initial offerings.—**Chief Executive Officer***

*Perhaps the most unique facet of Wharton's program is emphasis on the total executive, to the point that they include the social sciences, history, anthropology, and English literature in the curriculum. Even a personal consultation with a doctor of psychiatry was provided. A great experience! —**Assistant Vice President***

*The program is particularly strong in the area of globalization. The faculty and readings were carefully selected to support this, and the class was multi-national and multi-cultural. Overall, an excellent learning experience.—**Corporate Telecommunications Manager***

66

*There was significantly greater emphasis on globalization than I antici- pated. I sensed that many of the professors were using this program as both a sounding board and launch pad to exploit their globalization business consulting practices.—**President***

*Wharton has zeroed in on two key areas which make it a very attractive venue. First, the five-week program is the appropriate time frame for today's executive. Second, their commitment to bringing in experts from other major competitive institutions and government to supplement their own well-qualified staff speaks highly of their professional ethics in estab- lishing a top-notch management program.—**Chief Executive Officer***

*The school strove to include people from a wide diversity of cultures and locations and succeeded admirably. The principal result was a broad range of opinions, particularly on management techniques and interper- sonal relations. While only slightly familiar with other such programs, I believe Wharton devoted a particularly large amount of time and effort to the psychological and human relations facets of managing. I found these extremely rewarding.—**Chairman and CEO***

*Wharton's focus on a large portion of foreign students significantly en- riched the learning experience by exposing all of us to so many divergent opinions. One of the benefits that resulted is that I am very comfortable dealing with multiple opinions on a single issue. There are a lot of right answers. As they taught us at Wharton: "You've got to be able to accept increasing ambiguity and manage it."—**President***

*The small size of the class and the mix of the participants were important positive factors in the educational process. My class had 33 executives from Europe, Asia, and America from varied industries. All were senior managers with more than 20 years of experience each. The five-week ex- perience was most beneficial to me not through the analytical knowledge gained but because it broadened my perspective and ability to look at things from many other angles.—**Chairman***

8. Columbia University

Columbia Business School
324 Uris Hall
New York, New York 10027

Corporate ranking: 6	*Consumer ranking*: 17
Number of programs: 14	*Number of programs in 1986*: 14
1990–1991 participants: 1180	*Years in executive education*: 42
Annual revenues: $7.5 million	*Change since 1986*: 64 percent

Contact: Mary Anne Devanna, director of executive education, 212-854-3405

Executive Program in Business Administration

Think of Columbia, and you think of New York in all its glory and squalor—crowded subways and gleaming skyscrapers, street hustlers and world-class department stores, the homeless and the glitterati, an exhilarating whirlwind. But when it comes to Columbia's executive education programs, you'd better think again: You'd be hard-pressed to find a more decidedly nonurban experience.

First off, you won't be in the Big Apple at all; you're headed 50 miles up the Hudson River to Arden House, the magnificent hilltop mansion that has housed the school's executive programs since shortly after their inception 42 years ago. The former family estate of statesman W. Averell Harriman, the gracious, turn-of-the-century stone building boasts wood-panelled living and dining rooms, guest rooms and lounges with panoramic river views, plus state-of-the-art audiovisual and computer equipment. The isolated property, with its outdoor pool, gymnasium, and exercise room, and miles of scenic trails through the woods, is the picture of serenity. A rarefied atmosphere, indeed, for a school whose hallmark has always been city grit.

Columbia does tend to handle its exec-ed students with kid gloves. The school works hard to serve its corporate customers, with Executive Education Director Mary Anne Devanna spending much of her time either on the road or on the phone. "I do 100 company calls a year, talk to 100 management development people, and I barely scratch the surface," she says. While Columbia hasn't ventured very far into custom courses (which account for only 12 percent of revenues), the open-enrollment programs are continually being updated to meet corporate needs. Firms are encouraged to send teams of executives to study together, and the school enjoys a large percentage of repeat business, with companies like California-based PSE&G enrolling two or three managers a shot in recent sessions of the "Creating the Customer-Oriented Firm" program. The extra effort has paid off: Our corporate survey ranked Columbia's business school sixth.

The school's flagship general management course, the Executive Program in Business Administration, has also seen some changes due to customer demands; it was shortened from six to four weeks in 1983, for example. Offered twice a year, in June and August, this is a program for seasoned managers. Two-thirds of the participants are senior-level executives of billion-dollar companies, and there is no time devoted to functional review. In fact, if candidates have any doubts about their competence in a given area, they'll be asked to test themselves ahead of time and either attend a one-week refresher course or do extra readings to get up to snuff.

Bypassing the basics allows the four-week course to focus intensively on the bigger-picture management topics of strategy formulation and implementation, people skills, and change management. Cutting-edge issues play an important role in the curriculum, which in recent years has meant an emphasis on restructuring, downsizing, intracompany entrepreneurship, and globalization. A hefty 40 percent of each class of 60 to 70 students is from outside the United States, providing an international dimension to discussions.

Small-group case study and lectures dominate the teaching method, though each manager also prepares a personal case project. Executives are asked to take real issues they're dealing with on the job and write up their own cases, which are then presented to a small group of classmates for comment and advice (managers can choose their own groups for proprietary reasons). Participants not only have something tangible to take back to the office, but also get a crash course in group dynamics.

However, while Columbia is concentrating on keeping companies happy, the participants themselves say they'd like to get a bigger share of the school's attention. Their discontent shows up in the school's consumer ranking of seventeenth in our survey. Many of the complaints involve EPBA's lack of intensity. In keeping with the school's special treatment of executives, managers are not subjected to the MBA-style frantic pace and rah-rah rivalries, but it seems that a lot of them are looking for exactly that. "I don't really feel that we worked or were worked very hard," says one recent alum. "I was prepared to put in long hours and work intensively, but it wasn't required." Adds Christian K. Pechmann, an insurance company branch manager, who attended the program in 1989: "It was a casual and cooperative effort—the leaders didn't charge the groups to compete actively. This gave a certain amount of comfort and safety to members, but didn't necessarily make the product better."

The faculty's level of enthusiasm also came under fire. Managers generally found the staff to be extremely knowledgeable but distant, uninvolved, and lacking in teamwork. "Academic ego gets in the way of good lecturing at times," says Pechmann. "Pontification doesn't work in the outside world." There were, of course, some major exceptions among the 15 to 20 faculty members who teach in the program. Singled out for praise, for example, are academic director, E. Kirby Warren, a Columbia mainstay for more than three decades, who specializes in organizational management; leadership maven, Donald C. Hambrick; and a distinguished lineup of guest speakers culled from Columbia's first-rate New York corporate connections. John O. Whitney, former president of the Pathmark division of Supermarkets General, also wins plaudits for his insights into business turnarounds. Oklahoma-born Whitney, dubbed the "Cash Flow Cowboy" by his MBA students, looks like a character out of an old Western movie—only he's even more entertaining in the classroom.

Columbia's "grown-up" attitude carries over into the program's social arena as well. You're not going to find students heading out to the local tavern for shots, beers, and storytelling. For one thing, there are no taverns to be found near the secluded property. Instead, it's cocktails and dinner in the elegant dining room, then a history lecture or chamber-music performance. The idea of fun here is to listen to a Columbia professor lecture on demographics one evening, then tour lower Manhattan on Saturday morning to get a firsthand look at changing urban life. Weekend activities run more toward excursions to Broadway plays than sack races and theme nights—so maybe you will get a taste of the city after all.

Organizations sending most participants: AT&T; Digital Equipment; IBM; Maersk; Ciba-Geigy

Other Programs of Note

Executive Program in International Management: One of the first programs for international executives, designed to strengthen the skills of managers in multinational firms in the areas of strategy formulation, functional management, human resources, and the international environment. Class makeup is 30 to 40 percent American, 60 to 70 percent foreign. Led by Professor Donald E. Sexton, a Columbia teacher for over 25 years. Intended for senior general managers, country managers, or high-potential functional managers of multinational organizations. Four weeks; annually, in October; 60 students; $14,500, including tuition, room, board, and supplies; by application.

Marketing Management Program: Columbia gains strong marks from corporate HR officers for its marketing offerings. This one examines market problems from a whole-company perspective, including strategy, finance, and sales. Led by faculty members William K. Brandt, James Mac Hulbert, and Donald E. Sexton. Intended for senior and mid-level managers with significant policy-making experience; about 75 percent are marketing managers, but generalists and those in other functions may benefit. One week; held five times annually in New York, once at a conference center in Lake Como, Italy, and once at a hotel in Santa Barbara, California; 50–75 students; $4250 (fees for California and Italy sessions are slightly higher); by application.

Creating the Customer-Oriented Firm: Explores how companies can improve or acquire the characteristics essential to being customer-responsive, with individual consultation available. Led by Professor James Mac Hulbert, a marketing expert and consultant on Columbia's faculty since 1969. Designed for CEOs, division managers, senior functional managers, and human-resources executives of medium- to large-size corporations. One week; held annually, in spring; 25 students; $4750, including tuition, room, board, and supplies; by application.

Managing Strategic Innovation and Change: Focuses on how to maintain current performance while introducing new products, services, technologies, and production processes. Led by Professor Michael L. Tushman, who has also taught at Cornell, MIT, and Berkeley. Intended for all kinds of managers who work in rapidly changing environments. One week; held twice annually, in late spring in New York and in early summer in Lake Como, Italy; 45 students; $4250 in New York, including tuition, room, board, and supplies; $3500 in Italy, not including room and board; by application.

Achieving the Sustainable Turnaround: Examines ways to boost performance in companies falling short of their potential, including the elimination of nonproductive operations and the streamlining of other operations and finances, with focus on preventing management and financial crises rather than reacting to them. Led by Professor John O. Whitney, the most popular teacher in the school's MBA program. Intended for top managers of manufacturing and service companies; teams of three to five managers from the same company are encouraged to attend together. One week; held annually, in May; 35 students; $4250, including tuition, room, board, and supplies; by application.

Managing Cultural Diversity: Explores how corporations can incorporate and effectively manage employees from diverse cultures, with an examination of prejudice and discrimination, the different concepts of achievement among such groups as Hispanics, African-Americans, Asian-Americans, women, and white male Americans, and techniques both to make managers more comfortable with diversity and multicultural employees more comfortable within the organization. For further details, see Chapter 6, The Ten Most Innovative Programs.

Organizations sending most participants: AT&T; DuPont; American Cyanamid; Milliken; NYNEX

Columbia Consumers Sound Off

Program was well-organized and structured (relevant material in appropriate doses). Good balance between classroom, workshop, academic, practical, and social components.—**Group Executive**

Not worth the time and expense in investment.—**Vice President**

An executive training program of one month or more represents a substantial commitment by the company to the participant/employee. The programs must be structured and focused carefully to balance a breadth of subject matter with a well-chosen participant profile. A curriculum too broadly drawn and a widely divergent group of participants, based on experience (and) industry background, leads to an ineffective program. Columbia's program was very close to being too ambitious.
—**Branch Manager**

Never again will I have the marvelous opportunity to interact on both a personal as well as professional level with such a diverse group of business professionals from around the world.—**Operations Manager**

The case-study format was good, but most were old situations that had little in common with modern business practices and/or technology and changing human-resources factors. At least a smattering of new cases would have lent more practical enrichment.—**Regional Insurance Manager**

The course had one weakness, the result of a reduction to four weeks. Finance was not covered adequately.—**General Manager**

Lecturers were mainly experienced and well-educated top-level "turn-around guys" or consultants, with examples at real companies. Very charismatic lecturers. Excellent experience.—**Managing Director**

I feel I did gain something from this program—in relationship to how I am viewed by my company. It's almost as if the rough edges have been smoothed out, and I've acquired a little more polish and a little more jargon for my vocabulary. Do I feel more successful, for having completed this program? No. Would I do it again if the opportunity arises? Yes.—**Vice President**

Possibly the greatest value of this program comes from the relationships formed with other executives. I have since met with my classmates in locations all over the world—Japan, Australia, and New Zealand.—**Vice President**

Living in a third-world country, I found the exposure to business issues in the program fascinating and exciting. At times, though, there was an overemphasis on the Japanese thought/system which seemed irrelevant to my world (and sometimes American needs). Still, it was just what I needed!—**Sales and Marketing Director**

The four-week program covered many critical topics for success in today's business world. But it also contained too many basic management subject matters. It would have been an even better two-week program.—**Senior Vice President**

The program did not teach or ingrain particular skills or increase specific capabilities. However, it did update the participants in key management styles, techniques, and perspectives that have become a part of the basis for future decision making. Looking back on the experience, it was worthwhile and beneficial on a long-term basis.—**Director**

9. Institut Européen d'Administration des Affaires (INSEAD)

Boulevard de Constance
F-77305
Fontainebleau, France

Corporate ranking: 2
Number of programs: 75
1990–1991 participants: 2700
Annual revenues: $20.0 million

Consumer ranking: 22
Number of programs in 1986: 59
Years in executive education: 23
Change since 1986: 182 percent

Contact: Leon M. Selig, director of executive education, 33-1-60-72-40-00; Carol Grayson, regional coordinator, 212-418-6579

Advanced Management Program

Never has there been as much interest in international business as there is today. As U.S. companies rapidly globalize their markets or find themselves increasingly pinched by competitors from overseas, many are looking for a truly international education for their executives, one that can quickly familiarize them with foreign business cultures and climates. That's where the Institut Européen d'Administration des Affaires, or INSEAD for short, steps in. Although it has offered executive education programs for more than two decades, it's only in recent years that the French school, widely considered the best graduate school of business in Europe, has attracted a burgeoning audience of corporate admirers in the United States. Indeed, INSEAD is the only non-U.S. school to make the Top 20, garnering a No. 2 ranking from companies surveyed by BUSINESS WEEK and surpassing such traditional B-school giants as Harvard, Stanford, and MIT.

Again and again, corporations cite INSEAD's European locale, its multinational faculty (the school's 80 resident professors hail from 22 different countries), and its unique class makeup of just 5 percent Americans (who find themselves outnumbered for a change by British, French, German, Swiss, Scandinavian, and Asian participants) as their reasons for favoring the school. "Our international mix simply can't be found anywhere else," boasts Carol Grayson, INSEAD's New York-based regional coordinator. The school's four-week Advanced Management Program aims to capitalize on this strength, bringing a global perspective to a broad review of such management basics as accounting, operations, marketing, information technology, finance, economics, strategy, and organizational behavior.

So in theory, INSEAD's general management training should be ideal for the multinational executive. However, at least for now, the theory apparently outstrips the reality. Actual AMP participants diverge sharply from the companies' view of the program's merits, handing the school a lackluster rating of twenty-second in our survey. Complaints center around the uneven quality of teaching, the heavy reliance on Harvard case studies (which was exactly what many students were hoping to escape by crossing the Atlantic), the failure to take advantage of participants' experience and expertise, and even the facilities and support staff, which many felt need some polishing.

Lured to the school by its reputation for cultivating a more global flavor, many managers then found the program to be too American in focus. "I wanted something different, something with an international flavor, but in hindsight, that did not turn out to be the case," says Amnon J. Golan, director of the World Bank's Economic Development Institute in Washington, who attended INSEAD's flagship program in 1989. "I felt that if I went to Harvard or Stanford, I would get a heavy dose of American thinking. But in spite of the fact that INSEAD was European, it was weighted heavily toward American companies or U.S. companies operating overseas. There were fewer Americans, but in teaching case studies, it was a textbook American business school." Perhaps that should come as no surprise because since its inception, INSEAD closely modeled its management experience after Harvard's Advanced Management Program, and nearly half the faculty is Harvard-educated. It was also a joint venture with Stanford that added executive education programs to the school, which was founded in 1959 by local businesspersons and the Paris Chamber of Commerce.

Even so, INSEAD officials are taking the criticism to heart. Over AMP's next few sessions, which are held in English three times a year (winter, summer, and fall), you will see changes in many of these areas, says Leon M. Selig, director of executive education. "I said to the faculty, 'You guys think you're pretty good, but participant ratings show we're not the best in the world.' That's helped to shake people up." The first step: to assign a permanent core faculty that will meet regularly to coordinate curriculum and address complaints. The program's staff had been drawn on an ad hoc basis from the school's MBA faculty with a boost from a revolving band of visiting professors, mainly from the United States.

Selig expects AMP to move away from its devotion to Harvard cases, by getting the school's researchers to crank out new cases and by handing participants more independent projects. "There will also be a change in the level of faculty input and participants' roles," adds Selig, addressing two major points of criticism by participants—that the professors, while on the whole competent and sometimes brilliant, spend too much time up on the podium, aloof and uninvolved with their students; and that the program fails to mine the wealth of knowledge and diverse experience brought to the table by the executives themselves. When BUSINESS WEEK asked INSEAD participants how curious the faculty was about them and the knowledge they brought to the classroom, the school ranked twenty-fifth out of 26 schools surveyed.

That's a shame, because with its relatively small class size of 40, AMP is fertile ground for meaningful international interchange. Trying to capture that experience in classroom debates and discussions are marketing whiz Jean-Claude Larreche, Finance Professor Herwig Langohr, and organizational behavior experts Manfred Kets de Vries and Fernando Bartolome.

Unfortunately, they will have to battle a program setup that doesn't lend itself to the development of a great deal of camaraderie. Most managers' stay on campus is adequate, but by no means luxurious (the cost is included in the program fee of approximately $16,150, which may fluctuate slightly with the exchange rate). Though the school is housed in modern steel and glass buildings, every three dorm rooms share a lavatory. No wonder some choose, for an extra $30 to $70 a day, to stay at one of the charming hotels in the picturesque town of Fontainebleau, at the edge of the Fontainebleau forest some 34 miles south of Paris. The 17-acre wooded campus was once the private hunting ground of French kings. Socializing tends to be informal and low-key, consisting largely of small study groups heading out to a local restaurant for a typically French evening of eating and conversation. During the one long weekend break, most of the European managers head home while the rest scramble to cram in a little sightseeing or visiting.

But executives don't come to INSEAD for the fun and games. They come for a solid, general overview of management fundamentals, offered in an international setting. The student profile won't change. AMP will continue to cater to 40-ish general managers or top functional managers at major corporations who make around $150,000 a year. (In fact, participants are sometimes surprised at how much they do have in common: Joseph J. Lavin, president of Dallas-based Zoecon Corp., a subsidiary of the Swiss pharmaceutical giant Sandoz, says that his study group included a Scot, a Briton, an Austrian, a German, and a Frenchman. Yet, he and another student had a mutual friend.) And AMP's basic agenda will remain the same, despite the facelift the program is currently undergoing. The challenge for INSEAD will come in making sure the program can better satisfy managers without changing what companies find so appealing.

Organizations sending most participants: Ciba-Geigy; ICI; Hewlett-Packard; Digital Equipment; BAS

Other Programs of Note

International Executive Program: The corporations polled by BUSINESS WEEK rated INSEAD No. 1 when it came to offering the top programs in global business. This program is one of the school's best. Prepares participants for broader organizational responsibilities and more effective operation in a global marketplace, reviewing basic functions and highlighting financial analysis and negotiation techniques. Led by Professors James Teboul and Daniel Muzyka. Intended for high-level functional managers in large multinational corporations, general managers in medium-sized firms, and entrepreneurs. Seven weeks; held twice a year, beginning in late winter and fall; 50–90 students per session; about $17,500, including tuition, supplies, and lunch, plus an additional charge of between $78 and $148 a day for room and breakfast; by application.

Young Managers Program: Focuses on developing skills in organizational behavior, marketing, finance, operations management, and strategy, as well as the integration of these disciplines. Led by Professor Claude Viallet. Designed for managers with five years' experience and strong track records in their functional areas who have been targeted for promotion. Three weeks; held three times a year, beginning in winter, late spring, and late summer; 90 students per session in winter and late summer, 45 students in late spring; about $9670, including tuition, supplies, and lunch, plus an additional charge of between $78 and $148 a day for room and breakfast; by application.

European Marketing Program: Explores marketing in the current environment, with special segments on marketing strategies either for consumer goods and services or industry. Led by Professor Reinhard Angelmar. Intended for sales and marketing managers and senior general executives with marketing oversight responsibility. Three weeks; held twice a year, in spring and summer; 35–65 students per session; about $9670, including tuition, supplies, and lunch, plus an additional charge of between $78 and $148 a day for room and breakfast; by application.

Management of People: Examines human resources management in relation to today's changing strategic and organizational needs of corporations, particularly international firms. Led by Professor Paul Evans. Intended for general and senior line managers with human resources responsibilities, personnel managers in company-wide policymaking positions, and newly appointed personnel managers in international corporations. Nine days; held annually in May; 35 students per session; about $6170, including tuition, supplies, and lunch, plus an additional charge of between $78 and $148 a day for room and breakfast; by application.

Managing the Multinational Enterprise: INSEAD's most senior general management program, examining ways multinational companies can gain or maintain a competitive advantage through financial, technical, and human resources management on a global basis. Led by Associate Professor Sumantra Ghoshal. Intended for international line executives, including chief executives, division executives with worldwide responsibilities for a business line, and regional and country managers; senior functional staff with international responsibilities; and senior members of government institutions. Two weeks; held annually, in early summer; 35 students per session; about $10,840, including tuition, supplies, and lunch, plus an additional charge of between $78 and $148 a day for room and breakfast; by application.

Organizations sending most participants: Ciba-Geigy; ICI; Hewlett-Packard; Digital Equipment; BAS

INSEAD Consumers Sound Off

My only significant criticism was the poor balance of case studies: Too many were processed too superficially. Otherwise an excellent program with a significant block devoted to the impact of work/career on family and personal life.—**Managing Director**

The program I attended did a great job of highlighting the multitude of changes that will impact corporations and enterprises now and into the foreseeable future. However, ways to transform organizations to meet this challenge were not adequately addressed.—**Human Resources Director**

During the program there was widespread dissatisfaction with one faculty member dealing with a major segment. This dissatisfaction stopped just short of a major walkout and was certainly widely commented upon in the feedback questionnaire. Amazingly, the school appears to have learned nothing from the feedback, as subsequent programs still have the same faculty member handling this segment, with similar levels of dissatisfaction being encountered and expressed.—**General Manager**

From participants in other programs, I learned that INSEAD covers about the same material in four weeks that they do in three months. INSEAD is

packing a lot of learning into four weeks with little spare time for recreation, etc. I preferred it that way.—Vice President for Sales

Some parts of the course—marketing and behavioral work—were excellent. Production was dull, and strategy very mixed. Insufficient effort was made to update material and to use the experience and skills of an impressive bunch of participants as part of the learning experience.—Manager

The one big disappointment was the quality of the accommodations. I did not expect the Oriental Hotel, but notable deficiencies were: three bedrooms sharing a lavatory; no quiet communal area; constantly being stampeded by MBA students; barely adequate dining facilities; no worthwhile fitness facilities; no dining facilities on weekends, a big problem for those who could not go home during the month.—Divisional Director

This is a tough program. It forces the participant to sustain his or her concentration for a long (average 12 hours a day) period. There was so much to learn, but this was somewhat unfortunate because there was hardly any time to socialize outside the course with other participants. Yet, it was refreshing to spend four weeks away from work and to reflect in a campus environment where you are allowed to make "mistakes" and to learn from them. The quality of interaction was very good all around—between faculty and participants and peers.—Managing Director

The program was acceptable and certain areas, such as finance, economics, and marketing, were excellent. But the course failed to utilize the broad professional knowledge of the students to interact. With a little work, it could be outstanding.—Vice President

*I had also attended Stanford Executive Program a number of years earlier. I found the teaching at Stanford conceptually and technically better by far, except for the European aspect for which INSEAD is the best.
—Director*

I wanted to attend a program at a school which (a) had an international perspective and (b) could relate to dramatic changes taking place in business. For these reasons, I felt a European school would be better than a U.S. one. My requirements were mostly satisfied. We criticized the school for using too many Harvard case studies. I also felt that insufficient time was spent studying and discussing service industries.—Controller

10. University of North Carolina

Kenan-Flagler Business School
Executive Education, Kenan Center
CB# 3445
Chapel Hill, North Carolina 27599

Corporate ranking: 16	*Consumer ranking*: 5
Number of programs: 43	*Number of programs in 1986*: 29
1990–1991 enrollment: 1706	*Years in executive education*: 50
Annual revenues: $3.4 million	*Change since 1986*: 115 percent

Contact: Warren Baunach, associate dean and director of executive education, 919-962-0327

The Executive Program

This top-rated business school has a slight problem. It isn't that executives are unhappy with Chapel Hill's Executive Program: Students adore the management experience. Indeed, managers rated the quality of teaching ahead of the likes of Harvard, Stanford, and Wharton; in terms of payback, they award the flagship executive program the highest marks of any school in the country. Managers who attend TEP report that it has immediate applications on the job, that they were able to take on more responsibility as a result, and that they experienced significant personal growth in the process.

They're particularly enthusiastic about the confidential long-range strategic plan each student draws up for his or her own real-life employer, in one-on-one consultation with a B-school faculty member. Quite a few of these plans jump off the drawing board and into action when managers return to the office, the way the Golden Corral restaurant chain took its president's 1989 TEP project and turned it into a redesign of the chain's steakhouses. Within months, the first spanking new dining room, more than doubled in size, and sporting a streamlined salad bar, buffet, and bakery, opened its doors a few miles north of bucolic Chapel Hill, and B-school officials were treated to a celebratory chow-down to thank them for their help.

So what's the problem? Despite the consumer accolades and the fact that UNC was one of the first universities in the country to get into executive education, many corporations seem to scarcely know the school exists, rating it sixteenth of our Top 20. The B-school attracts almost no foreign managers and only a small percentage of executives from major, nationwide companies, drawing most of its students from North Carolina-based firms with fewer than 10,000 employees. It's as if the school were doomed to live in the long shadow cast by Duke's exec-ed powerhouse, just 15 miles up the road.

But the Tarheels have decided to put their money where their mouths are. Following the advice the school likes to give ailing corporations, Barry Roberts, associate dean for executive education, and staff have drawn up their own long-range plan to address the weaknesses, both real and perceived, in the university's general management programs. A 42-member outside advisory board—drawn from alumni, corporate human resources managers, and officials from companies whose business the school would like to attract—will be reviewing the plan before it is phased into operation during 1993. "We're not proud," jokes Roberts. "We'll take help from wherever we can find it."

He's not kidding. One of the first things the school did was to steal away from Duke its highly regarded director of executive education, Warren Baunach. Baunach, who has years of real-world business experience behind him, having worked at AT&T and General Foods, joined North Carolina in late June of 1992.

The upshot: a complete revamping of both the mainstream Executive Program and the school's Young Executives Institute to make them more customer-friendly. The pool of prospective students will be divided according to experience levels and needs among three different general management courses. A new, two-week program is being developed for functional managers who lack MBAs, with an emphasis on review of the basic business functions. At the same time, a four-week course, which will probably retain the name "TEP," will be offered to young executives and new general managers. It will assume a working knowledge of the fundamentals and focus on integrating the functional disciplines. A third, two-week program, targeting experienced, senior-level executives, will explore corporate strategy and the external factors companies face. Class sizes for all three will remain at about 50. "Our programs were very much oriented toward small companies, where one person did everything," Roberts explains. "Now we'll be more oriented toward functional managers. We also found that our curriculum had started at too low a level for many upper-level people," who will now be able to choose a course that skips the basics they may not need.

While the new formats are not scheduled to go into operation until 1993, some changes in TEP will already be evident in the fall of 1992. The course has been shortened from six weeks to four and will be held one week a month between late August and early December—a format similar to the one introduced at Duke by Baunach. While some managers like the program spaced out this way so they don't have to be away from home and office for too long a stretch, this has also been the source of some problems. "The split format is good for regional companies, but it doesn't work at all for national and international companies," says Roberts. "It's just too expensive to keep coming back and forth." The new version will offer both the divided schedule and a month-long, consecutive program. Long-range plans will not be included in the unbroken course, however, because the time span simply isn't long enough to accommodate the necessary amount of work.

One thing that won't change is the superb quality of the teaching—a major reason why this school does so well in BUSINESS WEEK's rankings of MBA programs. Many of the same faces will be appearing behind the lectern in the revamped program. Bringing a global and technological slant to his lectures on operations management is William A. Fischer, a former Dravo Corp. engineer and globetrotter who also teaches at the highly regarded Institute for Management Development in Lausanne, Switzerland. There's also Jay E. Klompmaker, a consultant to such firms as Ciba-Geigy, Eli Lilly, Northern Telecom, and IBM, who brings a bundle of energy to his sessions on marketing, and John J. Pringle, a former vice president for NCNB Corp. and a Rand Corp. cost analyst, in finance. Pringle also teaches at IMD.

Another thing that won't change is the facilities. They're comfortable, but hardly fancy. Classes are held on campus at the Kenan Center, the school's handsome brick exec-ed building. Students are housed in downtown Chapel Hill at the antiquated Carolina Inn, a university-run hotel sorely in need of a facelift. It's a bit of a trek from one to the other, so van transportation is provided for those who don't feel up to the hike. Currently, fees for TEP—which will likely change before the new programs are introduced—total $11,000, including tuition, room, a two-day spouses program, graduation, and most meals, which are served at the inn. The food is good and plentiful. "It was kind of a contradiction," laughs Kenneth R. Hyde, Jr., chief operating officer of Hackney Brothers Inc., a North Carolina-based manufacturer of refrigerated truck bodies. "They offered you this optional morning class in fitness and health, then they stuffed you at meals."

Although a lengthier program in residence might alter the mood, right now TEP is not a particularly chummy, colleague-bonding experience. While students are assigned to review assignments in small groups before the morning and afternoon classes, there are no major organized group projects or evening study sessions. "Our class did not develop much camaraderie, because after dinner, everybody went their own way," says Hyde. "It might have been better to devote night time to study groups, instead of taking away from class time for review during the day. It often seemed the professors were rushing and didn't have time to finish what they'd started." Social activities are low-key and minimal, with weekly get-togethers for a barbecue, cocktails at a professor's house, or golfing at one of the area's many fine courses. But with most students driving in on Monday morning and taking off on Friday afternoon, the team-building and leadership segments central to other programs are missing at UNC.

Organizations sending most participants: Northern Telecom; RJR Nabisco; Bell Northern Research; Wachovia; IBM

Other Programs of Note

Young Executives Institute: Designed to broaden young executives' functional skills and prepare them for general management, with emphasis on policy development, decision making, communications, negotiations, and marketing. Led by Associate Professor Linda C. Bowen, a former Peat Marwick senior accountant with several teaching awards to her credit. Intended for managers with five years' experience at the functional level who are targeted for top management. Four weeks; held once a year, in one-week sessions between January and May; 50 students per session; $9000, including tuition, room, board, supplies, and graduation; by application.

Program for Technology Managers: Designed to expand technological managers' business skills so they can understand broader organizational functions and goals and better communicate with nontechnological managers, through the study of management control and measurements, finance, human resources, strategy, marketing, ethics, and the environment. Intended for first-line or middle managers of such technologies as computer systems, engineering, laboratory and clinical research, environmental science, and productivity. Two weeks; held twice annually, either consecutively in July or in five three-day sessions between February and May; 35 students per session; $5245, including tuition, supplies, and most meals; lodging at a nearby inn costs an additional $1050; by application.

Seminar for Technology Managers: Sponsored jointly with the Swiss Federal Institute of Technology and held at a conference center in Ascona, Switzerland, the seminar explores how to manage people and operations in technology-driven international companies. Intended for specialists with technical backgrounds and responsibility for managing the creation and implementation of technology and innovation, as well as general managers who supervise them. One week; held twice a year, in January and September; 25–30 students per session; $3100, including tuition, supplies, and some meals; by application.

Consortium Program for Global Executives: A joint offering with schools in Europe and Japan, this program invites six or seven companies per session to participate in three one-week seminars on three continents over a year's time. The goal: to spark intensive interaction between diverse corporate cultures so executives may better understand one another's operating styles, markets, and strategies. IMD in Lausanne, Switzerland, and InterMan/Japan and Sophia University in Japan developed the program with North Carolina. In a recent session, meeting between March 1992 and April 1993, some 30 senior executives are attending from such companies as Digital Equipment, DuPont, Asea Brown Boveri, Fiat, KF Industries, and Nordic Construction. Led by UNC Professor William Fischer and IMD Professor Fred Neubauer. Future participants, schedules, and costs can be negotiated with program director Anne Montgomery, 919-962-3119.

Organizations sending most participants: Glaxo; Sonoco Products; Bahlsen; AT&T; GE Capital Mortgage

North Carolina Consumers Sound Off

The program was very good. You felt as though you were brought up to date on the latest business techniques, backed up by academic theory. The program was balanced—i.e., marketing, economics, finance, accounting, manufacturing, long-term strategic planning, etc.—and helped to round out participants by educating them in areas outside of their normal disciplines.—Senior Vice President

The overall experience was invaluable. Reviewing current business techniques and strategies while still managing your business offers an excellent opportunity to question a lot of practices now being used in running your business.—Operations Manager

The major focus at UNC was on the business plan. For me, this was very worthwhile, as I needed to prepare a formal business plan for my company.—Vice President and Treasurer

There was too much in-depth study. We would find ourselves in class listening to professors and two or three students discussing something way over the other 40 students' heads.—Senior Vice President

Format of one week of classes per month was practical. Duties at the office and home did not suffer too badly, and continuity of the program was maintained.—President and Treasurer

I would have preferred to see a better balance between service industries and manufacturing. It seemed that most of the lectures and case studies were manufacturing-oriented. **—Senior Vice President, Human Resources**

The interest which the faculty seemed to have in each student was the most surprising part of the program. The general consensus of our class was amazement that every professor was outstanding. **—Nonprofit Executive Vice President**

I also attended a two-week program in corporate finance at the Harvard Business School and would rate this program at UNC-Chapel Hill as first class. It was also well-rounded, focusing on personal skills as much as analytical skills. **—Senior Vice President**

As a Swiss native, it was positive and refreshing to see that you have business schools in the United States that act and work to prepare students for the international marketplace. **—President**

The major impact to my personal career is that the executive program made me actually think again. After years of management programming and practice, members of an executive program are required to use a different part of their brain. It was more creative and thought-provoking. **—Vice President**

This was a great experience and I have been encouraging my staff to attend programs that are suitable for their contributions to our firm. The takeaway of class interaction with the faculty and fellow executives reinforced the idea that other people were struggling with and solving problems similar to ours. Their different approaches have been invaluable. **—Chief Financial Officer**

11. Pennsylvania State University

Smeal College of Business Administration
310 Business Administration Building
University Park, Pennsylvania 16802

Corporate ranking: 10	*Consumer ranking*: 16
Number of programs: 22	*Number of programs in 1986*: 18
1990–1991 participants: 1034	*Years in executive education*: 36
Annual revenues: $4.0 million	*Change since 1986*: 50 percent

Contact: Albert A. Vicere, assistant dean for executive education, 814-865-3435

Executive Management Program

A lot of executive education programs are so intense that you feel like they're sapping your very life's blood. But Penn State will ask you to hand over a test tube full of the real thing. For nearly two decades, the famed football powerhouse has made physical fitness an integral part of management training, and one of the most popular aspects of the Executive Management Program is its access to the school's state-of-the-art executive health and fitness program. While their brains are undergoing EMP's four-week mental workout, an overwhelming 98 percent of participants choose to overhaul their bodies as well.

Soon after arriving on the bucolic State College campus, you receive a physical examination, complete with blood tests, EKG, and treadmill stress test. The results are run through the computers at Penn State's College of Health and Human Development, one of the country's premier centers of study in the field of exercise and sports medicine. Doctors and fitness consultants then evaluate your current condition and prescribe a diet and exercise regimen to improve your level of fitness. Individual counseling is available on the subjects of nutrition, stress reduction, weight control, and heart disease prevention; a recreation director will coordinate use of the school's vast sports facilities, including three indoor pools, tennis, squash, racquetball, handball, and basketball courts, a bowling alley, and two 18-hole golf courses. You couldn't ask for more if you signed up for a month at Canyon Ranch.

Of course, there's more to EMP than jogging and playing tennis. The program, which is offered once in summer, once in winter, and in a "time-phased" session one week a month between August and November, falls squarely on the side of the highly integrated, big-picture general management courses, with little time devoted to functional review. The course covers four major segments: strategic management, which includes competitive strategy and globalization; operational effectiveness, including financial planning and control; multidimensional thinking, or how business interacts with government, society, and international businesses; and network building, including leadership and organizational development. The subject matter is up to date, and the program is constantly being reevaluated to keep it current. "We've seen huge changes in the curriculum in the last 5 to 10 years," says Albert A. Vicere, assistant dean for executive education. "Globalization and international changes are now prominently featured. There's a much stronger focus on team-building and leadership. And we're spending more time on the external issues—government, the political process, ethics."

In fact, Vicere says he prefers to think of EMP not as a program, but as an "experience." Foreign students comprise at least a third of each class (except the time-phased session, which is almost entirely domestic in origin), and class sizes are among the smallest at any of the B-schools. With just 32 to 35 students, they are designed to encourage discussion and idea-sharing. An outdoor experience on the program's second day acts as both an icebreaker and a lesson in team-building, with groups challenged to complete a task such as building and racing a sailboat or crossing a stream using ropes and pulleys in a single afternoon. In the program's third week, participants return to the outdoors for yet another more strenuous team-building challenge. Throughout the month, more time is devoted to case study in small groups and computer-based business simulations by teams than to lectures. "We're trying to create a highly interactive situation where people teach each other," says Vicere.

Unfortunately, self-teaching has to pick up some of the slack left by the faculty, which is not EMP's strongest suit. Part of the problem is a lack of consistency. Each of the four annual sessions has a different academic director, and about half the program's core faculty is made up of visiting professors. Managers complain that teachers are rarely available to students outside assigned lectures; that professors could better coordinate their presentations; and that, compared to other schools, they don't appear to be on the leading edge of knowledge in their fields. "The visiting professors were excellent; the resident professors by and large were not up to the challenge," says Susan Lawrence, director of planning for General Motors, who attended EMP in 1991.

Still, Penn State's resident professors have forged strong ties to the outside world. The revolving band of directors includes Peter D. Bennett, a marketing professor, who started his career as a marketer at IBM and has consulted for Eastman Kodak, Borg-Warner, Sperry Rand, and Hershey Food; Edward T. Reutzel, a statistical maven, who has worked for USX and helped the Pennsylvania Public Utilities Commission launch a consumer services information system; and John J. Coyle, author of a best-selling textbook on logistics management.

Despite those varied backgrounds, managers also fault the school's professors for not making the best of the students' own experience and expertise. "The knowledge base of foreign nationals was completely underutilized," says Lawrence. "Foreign students were handled as if they were in the United States to learn about American business practices, versus all of us being executives from international firms interested in exploring emerging issues from various perspectives." Students had high praise for the simulation games run by Finance Professor Anthony J. Curley, who joined the Penn State faculty in 1970. "We broke up into four teams, each with a different business, using the same set of parameters," says Candy Obourn, an Eastman Kodak vice president, who attended in 1989. "Based on the market conditions we had to decide whether to raise or lower prices, invest in new factories, expand into new geographies. Each evening the team got together and decided what to do, and the next day the computer told us whether our stock went up more than our competitors'—or we lost our shirt." The faculty also has a strong base of knowledge in business logistics—the procurement of raw materials and distribution of products after they're manufactured—which helps attract a significant number of students from manufacturing companies (some 20 percent of each class).

The typical EMP participant is a midcareer, upper-middle or senior manager from a mid- to large-size, top 500 company, and corporate sponsors seem to be satisfied with what they're getting—92 percent use the program more than once. Penn State uses its ongoing relationships with companies to try to draw in more women and minority participants, who each make up about 10 percent of the typical class. The school also hopes to use its continuing corporate relationships with companies such as Conrail, General Motors, and AT&T to attract more customers for its growing business in company-specific programs, which Vicere believes will form the bulk of Penn State's exec-ed offerings in the coming years.

Facilities at Penn State run to the comfortable rather than the flashy. Students stay and eat at the Nittany Lion Inn, a university-run colonial hotel that was recently renovated; room and board is included in the $13,250 tuition. The inn is adjacent to the building that houses the exec-ed classes, so you don't have to be daunted by the prospect of shuttling across the school's sprawling, 5000-acre campus. Night life centers mainly around study groups or organized social activities, many of them sports-oriented, like a contest to see who can guess how long it will take to walk around the perimeter of one of the golf courses. That's about all the excitement you're going to find in State College, which is located halfway between Philadelphia and Pittsburgh in the middle of nowhere. But that's just another reason to take part in the fitness program: If you can't find anything else to do, you can always exercise.

Organizations sending most participants: AT&T; Petroleos de Venezuela; General Motors; Eastman Kodak; A.P. Moller

Other Programs of Note

Program for Executive Development: Designed to familiarize rising, early-career executives with a general management perspective, focusing on corporate strategy and encompassing the integration of functional areas, leadership, ethics, and international business. Includes a team-building white water rafting trip down the Youghiogeny River over the second weekend of the program. Led by Professor J. Randall Woolridge, a corporate finance expert who has been teaching at Penn State since 1980. Intended for high-achieving functional managers with 8 to 18 years' business experience and at least 5 years' experience beyond first-line supervision, who have been targeted for greater responsibility. Three weeks; held annually, in early summer; 42 students; $10,250, including tuition, room, board, and supplies; by application.

Program for Strategic Leadership: Focuses on improving corporate strategy development and implementation through more effective communication, leadership, team-building, and decision-making skills. Led by Associate Professor Scott Snell, a former IBMer with a background in human resources. Intended for upper-middle and senior executives at the corporate or division levels, mainly general managers or top functional managers with at least eight years' experience. Two weeks; held annually, in May; 40 students; $6400, including tuition, room, board, and supplies; by application.

Human Resources Management Program: Outlines ways human resources managers can more effectively tie in to overall corporate strategy, with an overview of the basics of financial analysis and general management. Led by Assistant Dean Albert

85

A. Vicere. Designed for upper-level executives with at least eight years' management experience who have human resources responsibilities. Two weeks; held annually, in early fall; 30 students; $6400, including tuition, room, board, and supplies; by application.

Managing the Global Enterprise: Explores management of multinational companies, including the current global business environment, world economics, international finance, leadership of diverse business cultures, and global strategies. Encompasses an investigation of global business by specific geographic area, including Africa, China, Europe, Japan, Korea, Pacific Rim, the former Soviet Union, and the United States; half of each class is from outside the United States. Led by Professor Stewart W. Bither, an active consultant who has been teaching strategy at Penn State since 1968. Designed for executives with at least eight years' experience who have international responsibilities. Two weeks; held annually, in spring; 40 students; $7500, including tuition, room, board, and supplies; by application.

Organizations sending most participants: AT&T; Petroleos de Venezuela; Eastman Kodak; Northern Telecom; Consolidated Edison

Smeal Consumers Sound Off

> *The integration of sports and social activities into the program was particularly well-managed, and the committed attitude of the faculty staff helped the group to gel rapidly.* **—Director**

> *Excellent balance of international business executives and faculty that allowed my group to explore not only various international business practices, but also the political and human factors that surrounded each topic.* **—Divisional Manager**

> *More instructor availability would have been helpful. You sometimes got the impression that their research and consulting were the major focus of their lives.* **—General Manager**

> *The program had some mediocre teachers, and I've noticed that the current program still carries them. Too bad.* **—Divisional Manager**

> *The health enhancement portion was excellent. It included a full physical, blood checks, stress checks, follow-up recommendations on diet and exercise, and counseling by a nutritionist. You lived, ate, and studied as a collaborative team. However, the atmosphere, tempo, and professionalism of the staff made the four weeks very short, fun, and not like work.* **—Production Superintendent**

> *Dramatically improved my overall knowledge and understanding of economic and political issues relating to the operations of a company competing in a global economy.* **—Coordination Manager**

This program is basically for U.S. executives, although they claimed it was for international businesspeople. Case studies with more cultural differences would be more interesting and promote more dialogue between the participants. **—Product Development Manager**

I loved this program because of its emphasis on teamwork, leadership, and interpersonal skills. At executive levels, it's the "soft" skills that are now making the difference. **—Marketing Manager**

I found the length of the course at Penn State, four weeks, to be one week too long. The first couple of weeks, I kept extensive notes on ideas I wanted to implement back on the job. By the last week, I'd almost forgotten who the first speaker was. It was a classic case of information overload. **—District Manager**

My educational experience at Penn State was exceptional. The quality of the course material as well as that of the presenters was excellent. The focus was very much in tune with current business issues. The mix of participants was right. It was a great program and I will recommend it to others. **—President**

This definitely was the most intellectually stimulating experience in my 23 years with AT&T. The program provided an opportunity to explore new managerial and business philosophies as well as to calibrate with other executives from around the world. I would recommend Penn State to any middle- to upper-management executive who could transport the knowledge gained to the everyday business environment. A side benefit is the personal enrichment offered by socializing with people of varied cultures. It was refreshing to learn that we all share the same management concerns and aspirations, no matter what part of the planet we may reside on. **—Manager**

Penn State's mission statement promises are an educational experience of a lifetime, and it certainly lived up to its promise. Top consultants offer you insight into the latest developments on the business front. Nowhere else is such up-to-date information so readily available. **—Technical Manager**

I feel strongly that all such programs rely too heavily on Harvard Business School case study methodology. You read three to four cases per night; the professor asks one or two questions about the case; long, rambling, unfocused discussion follows, and then the professor reviews what really happened at the end of the case discussion. If you are lucky, a new concept or two may be suggested. I've felt for some time that working on one case in depth for two to three days would be more valuable than the scattershot approach academia seems to prefer. **—Vice President**

12. Massachusetts Institute of Technology

Sloan School of Management
50 Memorial Drive
Cambridge, Massachusetts 02139

Corporate ranking: 11	*Consumer ranking*: 15
Number of programs: 18	*Number of programs in 1986*: 8
1990–1991 enrollment: 674	*Years in executive education*: 61
Annual revenues: $9.0 million	*Change since 1986*: 100 percent

Contact: Alan F. White, senior associate dean, 617-253-7166

Program for Senior Executives

When Robert M. Freund signed up for Sloan's Program for Senior Executives, he knew he'd better pay attention in class. He'd probably be teaching it one day soon. The tenured associate professor is the fourth Sloan faculty member to enroll in the program in order to become more familiar with the full range of management skills outside their own specialties. When Freund begins teaching a segment on operations research—the use of mathematical models to tackle management problems—during the program's 1993 sessions, "I'll have a broader view of how the different pieces of management fit together," he says. "While the costs to me and to MIT were quite high, the payoff in terms of my increased value as a teacher and as a management researcher has been enormous."

Sloan's willingness to educate its own staff—despite the loss of two months' teaching time while a professor turns student, not to mention the $31,900 in tuition that would have been paid by an outside executive—certainly says something about the school's level of commitment. Sloan has every reason to be confident: This is where executive education was invented 61 years ago, with the establishment of the famed Sloan Fellows Program, the original 12-month executive master's degree program. The Program for Senior Executives, or seniors program, as it's known around here, provides a good, strong taste of what the Fellows program offers, but in eight weeks (beginning in September 1993) instead of 12 months. Like the Stanford Executive Program, Sloan's seniors program is being shortened by a week, according to Alan F. White, Sloan's senior associate dean, to help ease the burden on students—particularly those from outside the United States—of being away from office and home for such a long stretch.

Foreign participants, who currently make up about 60 percent of each seniors class, are becoming more influential in the program, and the international perspective is reshaping the curriculum as well. As of the fall 1992 session (the program is held twice a year, beginning in March and September), managers will take a weeklong international field trip, designed along the lines of the three-day stay in Washington, D.C., that for years has been one of the program's most popular segments. With some help from the Brookings Institution, recent classes have enjoyed informal, question-and-answer-style discussions with such Washington notables as C. Boyden Gray, counsel to the president; Senators Paul Sarbanes and William Cohen; embassy representatives from Japan, Brazil, and Argentina; members of the Council of Economic Advisers; State and Treasury department officials; and Brookings think-tank wizards. During the first foreign excursion, to London (other European sites are being earmarked for upcoming sessions), students will also meet informally with international policymakers, government officials, business leaders, and media representatives. The program will continue to visit Washington, White says, because understanding the government decision-making process can shed light on an executive's own organization, and because the city is a "marvelous example of an international capital right in our own backyard."

While the global context of management seems to be taking center stage in the curriculum right now, there are two other important components of study. Foremost is the program's longtime emphasis on technology and its growing importance as a basis for competition in business. After all, this is MIT, and the technological, analytical bent is a key feature distinguishing the seniors program from the flagship executive programs at Harvard and Stanford, to which Sloan is most often compared. Another distinction is the seniors program's small class size, with each session limited to 50 students. Also, at Sloan you're going to run into a bigger share of executives from tech-heavy industries, like computers, engineering, electronics, and telecommunications.

The third significant area of study is organizational change, which encompasses human resources, leadership, team-building, and organizational behavior. One of the program's icebreakers during its first few days is a set of team problem-solving exercises, in which small groups tackle such dilemmas as crash-landing their plane in the remote Canada wilderness and then trying to determine whether it's better to stay with the wreckage until help arrives or strike out and search for civilization. "You can find out a lot about people in a short period of time based on how they react," says William Shover, a Martin Marietta manager who attended the program in 1989.

With the program cut back a week, and the foreign trip requiring an additional week's time away from Endicott House—MIT's conference center in Dedham, Massachusetts, about 20 miles outside Boston, where managers reside—something's obviously got to go. Most of the cuts will be in the functional areas, White says, leaving the business basics to be covered by the Fellows program. (After all, the seniors program does aim for a more experienced, higher-level executive, whose average age of 45 is some 10 years older than the typical Fellow and who stands two or three rungs farther up on the management ladder.) White is hoping to better integrate the curriculum by establishing a modified core faculty, with professors assigned to the program for at least a year at a time, perhaps longer. A lack of coordination among the program's various segments and a lack of faculty involvement in the learning process are two weaknesses managers mention in our surveys, so this change may address those shortcomings.

Sloan does have access to MIT's wealth of big-name professors, even if only on a limited basis. Student-generated special-interest sessions are encouraged, and past classes have picked the brains of economist Paul Samuelson, the Nobel laureate and MIT professor emeritus, and B-school Dean Lester C. Thurow, author of *The Zero-Sum Society*. Among the program's regular teaching staff, students adore "learning organization" guru Peter Senge, author of *The Fifth Discipline*, who amazes and amuses each class with his "beer game." Teams representing different segments of the beer industry, from brewers on down to retailers, make supply-and-demand decisions that affect one another, but without having access to the same pool of information about market conditions. Order slips fly up and down the imaginary line, as do the piles of pennies used to represent cases of beer. "You'd see these horrendous swings in inventory, and you could see how quickly the system gets out of control," says Shover, who says he's become something of a Senge disciple since observing him in action.

One reason managers may feel a bit distanced from the faculty is logistical. Although students spend one day a week on the Sloan campus in Cambridge, the lion's share of the program's days and nights are spent at Endicott House, a beautifully appointed, restored mansion on 20 acres of gardens and woodland. Participants have the option of sharing one of Endicott's large, luxurious rooms, or taking a smaller, more modest single in nearby Brooks Center. Either way, the facilities are first-rate, with outdoor walking and running trails, an exercise room, and excellent food. Much of the program's social life revolves around the dinner hour, with students hanging out in the lounges to watch the news or chat before the meal. Since Dedham is not far from Cambridge and Boston, you can take advantage of the area's many restaurants and clubs, although students tend to stick close to home base, attending an occasional evening lecture or musical performance at Endicott House when they're not studying.

The last week of the program is devoted largely to the extremely popular Spouses' Program, which participants rated highest of all the schools we surveyed. This is not just a tea party; wives and husbands are expected to do advance reading for sessions that summarize the material their spouses have been studying for the previous seven weeks. Then participants and spouses together attend classes involving organizational studies, covering topics such as life planning, career planning, career choices, and personal development. Ninety-five percent of spouses attend, an astonishing figure considering the fact that most have to take time out from their own careers, and many are traveling at their own expense from overseas.

This level of devotion can be found among Sloan alumni as well, who are a fiercely loyal bunch. A three-day Triennial Convocation draws dozens of past exec-ed participants. There is also a 16-member alumni board which is regularly consulted on changes being considered in the exec-ed curriculum—including the dramatic ones now taking place in the seniors' program.

Organizations sending most participants: AT&T; Boeing; General Motors; Eastman Kodak; Unilever

Other Programs of Note

The Alfred P. Sloan Fellows Program: The world's first executive education foray, this 12-month master's degree program broadens the typically specialized experience of mid-career executives to prepare them for more general management responsibilities. It's the real thing—the model for similar programs at Stanford and the London Business School. For further details, see Chapter 6, The Ten Most Innovative Programs.

The MIT Executive Program in Corporate Strategy: Explores the importance of strategy and strategic management to corporate success, while teaching methodology for development of companywide and functional strategies through four afternoon workshops. Led by Professor Arnoldo C. Hax. Intended for senior line managers and staff planners with corporate strategic responsibilities. One week; held annually, in May; 50 students per session; $4200, including tuition, room, board, and supplies; by application.

Current Issues in Managing Information Technology: No school scores higher than MIT for its courses in information technology. This course is a forum for MIT's Center for Information Systems Research to present and discuss significant issues in the management of information systems, with topics changing annually. Led by John F. Rockart, senior lecturer at Sloan and director of CISR. Intended for senior and high-level information-systems managers in mid- to large-size organizations, both public and private, as well as general managers with information-systems responsibilities. Four days; held annually, in June; 200 students per session; $2500, including tuition, room, board, and supplies; by application.

The MIT Management of Technology Program: A joint offering of the Schools of Engineering and Management, this 12-month master's degree program prepares mid-career executives with engineering or science backgrounds for senior management of technological and manufacturing companies. For further details, see Chapter 6, The Ten Most Innovative Programs.

Organizations sending most participants: AT&T; Boeing; General Motors; Eastman Kodak; Unilever

Sloan Consumers Sound Off

The education was very focused on North American business circumstances. I think MIT must decide if the education shall be an international executive education with international participants, or a North American executive education with international participants. **—President**

One of the most rewarding aspects of the program is the 50-50 mix of U.S. and non-U.S. students, set in a relatively small class and in a wonderful setting for learning and interaction with other participants.
—Compensation and Benefits Manager

The main disappointment of the program appears to come from its success. Of concern is the minimal involvement of the head of the Sloan School and a number of the school's more famous professors. It was notable that the professors rated as the most effective by the class came from schools other than Sloan. Another concern was the program administration. Both the head of the program and the faculty representative were incapable of relating to program members and of directing faculty members to provide additional requirements requested by the class. In short, success appears to have made MIT complacent. **—General Manager**

An excellent balance between case study and formal lecture. When compared to other programs, the smaller course size aided considerably in

both classroom interaction and interstudent communication. And the school's staff and visiting lecturers were better able to understand the mood of the class and to adjust accordingly during the period. —**Managing Director**

One drawback to the program was the immense amount of preparation that was required for each day's classes, with no obvious coordination between teachers as to scope or context. This situation drove one to focus on specific subjects of interest rather than obtaining a good overall flavor. —**Program Director**

The peer group was a bit of a problem. Our group was one-third North Americans, two-thirds from overseas. The Asians, in particular, were of little use in exchanging information and working case studies. Their presence was intended to globalize the student group and focus. I would have preferred a 1:1 mix. The situation as it was put a burden on the North Americans to deal with the case-study activity (which was mostly North America-based). —**General Director**

Stimulating and grueling, a long time away from home. I'm glad I went, and I'm glad it's finished. —**Technology Manager**

Just before I attended the program, I was promoted to the position of joint managing director (joint CEO in U.S. terminology). Having had no previous management training, I felt that the program was excellent in preparing me for my new role. I found the material to be very relevant; it was attended by high-caliber executives (although a somewhat high proportion had engineering backgrounds); was international in its participant mix as well as material taught; and the facilities were outstanding. —**Joint Managing Director**

The size of our class (47 executives) was just right—large enough for diversity, but not too large that it made one feel lost in the crowd. Instead, it created an attitude of friendship and support among all. —**Group Manager**

The program opened my eyes and mind to a larger world. We had 48 students in our class, of which 26 were international representing 18 countries. I believe that we in the United States become too narrowly focused as we climb the corporate ladder. As the world becomes one global economy, we need corporate leaders with much broader vision and greater breadth of experience. The Senior Executive Program at MIT creates this awareness, and for me it shifted my paradigm of how I look at world events and large structural issues within my organization. —**Regional Manager**

13. University of Tennessee

College of Business Administration
708 Stokely Management Center
Knoxville, Tennessee 37996

Corporate ranking: 14
Number of programs: 30
1990–1991 participants: 1600
Annual revenues: $6.0 million

Consumer ranking: 10
Number of programs in 1986: 20
Years in executive education: 20
Change since 1986: 34 percent

Contact: John E. Riblett, director, Management Development Center, 615-974-5001

Executive Development Program

In the early 1970s, the University of Tennessee launched a capital drive to create an endowment for its B-school, which had been around for some 30 years but was still languishing in the minor leagues of regional education. The drive was a success, raising more than $3 million, but with a string attached: The contributing companies insisted that interest from the fund be earmarked for the development of executive education. That stipulation has turned out to be one of the best things that ever happened to the school. Since it was founded in 1972, Tennessee's Management Development Center has gained a national reputation for excellence and has carved out a niche for itself with its forward-thinking emphasis on the quality movement.

The school's early linkage with the all-important issue of quality put it on the map. Even when quality guru W. Edwards Deming began attracting widespread attention in the 1980s, most other business schools looked the other way, thinking Deming and quality were little more than a management fad. They were slow to recognize the importance of the quality revolution sweeping Corporate America, and many schools still pay short shrift to the subject. Not so at Tennessee. The first quality sessions in 1981 at Ford Motor Co.—one of the first American companies to discover Deming—were taught by the master himself and a statistics professor from Tennessee. Today, managing quality permeates most of the school's 30 different programs, including eight courses known as the Institutes for Productivity Through Quality and more than a dozen custom programs for such major players as Procter & Gamble, Campbell Soup, and Eli Lilly.

Being a relative newcomer does make for some limitations, however, and Management Development Center Director John E. Riblett is the first to point out that Tennessee's Executive Development Program cannot and does not want to be all things to all executives. The program, offered once a year, has chosen to space its four weeks over four months' time, from January through April, even though the extended schedule keeps foreign participation down to a minuscule 5 percent (even West Coast residents rarely sign up). That doesn't mean the geographic mix is Dixie-saturated; in fact, the program draws more managers from the North Central and Midwestern states than it does from the Southeast. But the current curriculum only touches on globalization, and most participants are from mid-sized domestic firms rather than giant multinationals. Riblett says the faculty is becoming more comfortable with the international angle through team-teaching excursions like the ones recently held for Eli Lilly employees in Ireland and Warner-Lambert workers in Belgium.

What you will get for your $8900 is a pragmatic, down-to-earth, customer-oriented overview of management in the 1990s. Case study is downplayed in favor of lecture/discussion sessions; the small class size of 32 encourages plenty of student participation, making the course feel more like a graduate seminar than an undergraduate lecture. Be prepared to work hard, with readings assigned for the three-week breaks to prepare for fully packed weeks on campus, Sunday through Saturday. The first week focuses on managerial skills such as human resources issues, job design, leadership, team-building, and communication. Week 2 covers strategic management of the organization, with a cross-functional perspective on marketing, finance, accounting, and corporate strategy. The third week encompasses the external influences on companies, including financial markets, global economics, legal issues, and labor relations.

The last week, called the "Executive in Action," brings everything together in a competitive business game that wins kudos from alums. Each three-student team sets up its own "headquarters" in a room at the Knoxville Hilton, where participants are housed throughout the program. (Classes are held on a special floor of the Stokely Management Center, the College of Business Administration's building.) A computer simulation—which was redesigned in 1991 to include timely material on customer value and managing for continuous improvement—then leads the teams through three years' worth of business decisions, with a team of faculty members performing such roles as banker and government regulator. The winner, Riblett says, "is not just whoever has the best numbers at the end of the week—it's who is positioned best for the long run." Participants say the simulation is a key factor in making the program relevant to their real-world jobs: "It helped put material from weeks one to three into practice, but also created teamwork, interaction, and competition," notes Steve R. Semeyn, a manager for Howmet Corp., a Virginia-based maker of aircraft components.

The last week also encompasses the program's highly rated Spouses' Program, which is included in the tuition fee. This is a meaty, capsule look at the program's content, with husbands and wives put through a case study, an economics lecture, and classes on topics such as health and stress, dual-career families, and changing American values. Some 90 percent of spouses participate, and at least two-thirds of those have their own careers, says Riblett, so the week has to be substantive. "There are no trips to Dollywood," he jokes.

Social life throughout the program is necessarily limited by the "commuter" orientation and the physical plant. Since Tennessee doesn't have a residential center, dinners are set up at the Hilton, at area restaurants, or at the college, where a Louisiana corporate official who's scheduled to speak might bring in a mammoth crawfish-and-shrimp boil, as it happened not long ago. But the few extracurricular activities are enhanced by the active role taken by faculty members, who hang out with students before class, during breaks, and at meals. When Riblett was named director of the center in 1976, only 15 percent of the program's teaching staff was from the Tennessee faculty. That ratio is now reversed, with a well-established, permanent core faculty, and the visiting professors and consultants who remain involved with the program all have long-term, ongoing relationships with the school.

Among the faculty standouts are William V. Haney, a consultant who brings his extensive experience in working for firms such as Caterpillar, IBM, Pillsbury, and Metropolitan Life to his popular segments on interpersonal relations; Professor William B. Locander, one of the resident quality gurus; and Associate Professor James M. Reeve, whose expertise with cost-management systems and activity-based costing puts a new slant on the accounting and finance segments. There's no academic director, per se; instead, Riblett and a handful of key staffers make decisions about the program's direction. The faculty involvement goes well beyond graduation; it's not unusual for Riblett to head out to visit an executive who attended as long ago as 1977.

If you're hoping to parlay your exec-ed networking into a high-powered position at a Fortune 50 firm, Tennessee is probably not the place for you. Participants tend to be upper-mid-level, either functional managers or those who are just entering general management, in their early 40s, making upwards of $100,000 at companies with under $1 billion in sales. A good number of them are Deming disciples, too. Obviously, the school lacks the caché of a Northwestern or Wharton because its MBA program is not among the Top 20. "We don't draw the same level of participant that Harvard or Stanford does," Riblett readily admits. "You're not going to rub shoulders with the vice president of Sony here." But as the program's alums climb the corporate ladder, they're probably going to send their minions here as well—and that suits Riblett just fine.

Organizations sending most participants: Procter & Gamble; General Motors; Campbell Soup; Ford; Martin Marietta

Other Programs of Note

Cost Management Institute: Focuses on new cost management systems necessary for operation of globally competitive firms, including activity-based accounting, constraint management, and performance management. Led by Professor James M. Reeve. Designed for accounting and financial managers responsible for systems improvements. One week; held twice a year, in May and October; 20 students per session; $3500, including tuition, room, board, and supplies; by application.

Marketing and Customer Value Institute: Examines the strategic nature of quality management in connection with marketing and customer value, including the functional relationships between marketing, accounting, and manufacturing, and how they affect the quality of products. Led by Professor William B. Locander. Intended for managers with responsibility for marketing, sales, and promotion. Two nonconsecutive weeks; held annually, in January and February; 18 students per session; $4500, including tuition, room, board, and supplies; by application.

Executive Development Program for Distribution Managers: Designed to broaden the cross-functional perspective of managers responsible for corporate logistics. Led by Professors James Foggin and John Langley. Intended for distribution managers, transportation managers, or other executives in charge of corporate logistics. One week; held annually, in spring; 34 students; $2800, including tuition, room, board, and supplies; by application.

Senior Executive Institute for Productivity Through Quality: A one-week crash course for senior-level managers in using statistical methods to improve delivery of customer value; explores the relationship between statistics, quality, cost, schedule, and value in a competitive market. For further details, see Chapter 6, The Ten Most Innovative Programs.

Organizations sending most participants: Procter & Gamble; General Motors; Campbell Soup; Ford; Martin Marietta

Tennessee Consumers Sound Off

The focus on developing leadership skills within the philosophy of CQI, or continuous quality improvement, was extremely helpful to me. I felt that the teachers were truly at the leading edge of knowledge within their fields. —**Director**

The total quality philosophy that was the common thread to the program was the primary reason I attended Tennessee. In total, I found the experience to be a "shot in the arm" to help me personally—I have aggressively pursued both corporate and personal goals set during this experience and am reaping fine results. It's not just a "here are the facts" course, but a challenge to respond. —**Vice President**

The large difference in ages—from 27 to 60—made it difficult to have the curriculum meet the needs of all. I was under the impression that the program was primarily for seasoned management levels, not entry-level people. Several had no knowledge of how businesses operate. —**President**

The program had a very high intensity level. Fortunately, the course was only one week per month over four months. Four consecutive weeks would have been way too much to take and would severely limit participation due to job-related activities. —**Marketing Vice President**

The quality of instructors was excellent, so much so that I would have preferred less class discussion and more lecture. Way too many group projects, and too few individual projects. —**Manager of Procurement and Sales**

Local instructors came to most all break sessions, also before classes and after classes. I got 30 minutes' personal time with [William V.] Haney, a world-class behavioral scientist. —**Operations Projects Director**

After attending the program in 1981, the experience and knowledge I gained was used either on the job or for personal career decisions and action each and every day. In 1991, I elected to repeat the program to update my manufacturing experiences with the latest trends and improvements in manufacturing, marketing, and accounting concepts. 1991 was also a good decision. —**Plant Manager**

If all business schools taught with the same excellence as the University of Tennessee, American businesses would have no fear of the Japanese. The school provides that which it teaches, namely, "the best comparative net customer value." —**Operations Manager**

The overall program was very well done. It's a cohesive approach to tying the various aspects of the business environment together for today's manager.—Vice President

The one week per month approach allowed me to keep up and also to keep focused. Attempting to cover this amount of material for a continuous six to eight weeks or longer would have been discouraging. In total, I found the program to be a "shot in the arm" to help me personally. I have aggressively pursued both corporate and personal goals set during this experience and am reaping fine results.—Director

This is an excellent program for executives who have several years of working experience. The program covers a lot of the things you already know or have been doing, but they do an excellent job of explaining how and why. On a scale of 1 to 10, I would have to give the UT staff a 10. It is a very professional and well-organized program.—Sales Manager

The course gave me the opportunity to prove to myself that I was capable of working with and competing at the same level with some pretty impressive people. Aside from the education value, I developed more than a few long-term relationships with classmates. There are people in the course who know more about me than people I have worked with for 10 years. —Engineering Manager

Every member of our senior management team has attended UT's Executive Development Program. We all feel we have gained a lot and the common experience adds to our team effort. We continue to support the program with one to two participants every year.—Vice President

14. University of California at Los Angeles

John A. Anderson Graduate School of Management
405 Hilgard Avenue
Los Angeles, California 90024

Corporate ranking: 21
Number of programs: 12
1990–1991 enrollment: 1300
Annual revenues: $3.0 million

Consumer ranking: 6
Number of programs in 1986: 6
Years in executive education: 38
Change since 1986: 100 percent

Contact: Victor Tabbush, associate dean, 310-825-2001

The Executive Program

Like surfing, Hollywood, ritual murders, Jerry Brown, and so many other things quintessentially Californian, UCLA's Executive Program is a breed apart. For one thing, it has to be the only management course in the country to tout free parking as one of its attractions—and an important attraction it is, considering the fact that this is basically a commuter course for residents of the car-crazed, freeway-happy greater Los Angeles metropolitan area. While a handful of the 40 to 60 students in each session hail from outside the Golden State—a few have even come from as far away as Nigeria and Taiwan—it's the rare executive who wants to fly in once a week over nearly 10 months to attend the program's evening classes. It's also one of the only exec-ed courses around to bring in an attorney and an accountant to offer personal tax and estate planning as part of the curriculum. All that's missing is Johnny Carson cracking a Forest Lawn joke.

For many, the idiosyncracies only add to the charm of both the locale and the school. Participants gave this program an overall ranking of sixth in our survey, besting such heavy-hitters as Duke, Harvard, and Wharton. Teaching quality was rated on a par with consumer favorite Virginia. "Dean Victor Tabbush and his staff do an excellent job of preparing this program," notes one participant. "They were always ahead of the issues," says another. The program also scored well for encouraging innovative thinking, being relevant on the job, and treating students as professionals.

However, even though Anderson has been involved in executive education for almost 40 years, and its MBA program is well-regarded, its management training programs are surprisingly unfamiliar to companies outside the West Coast (in our national corporate poll, UCLA didn't even break into the Top 20). Besides the Executive Program and the two-week Advanced Executive Program, the school's offerings are mostly short, single-topic seminars no more than a week long. And while UCLA has forged an interesting partnership with Johnson & Johnson to train directors of Head Start programs around the country, its company-specific ventures so far are few in number and pretty much limited to Southern California firms like GM Hughes Electronics. "We don't draw nationally, and we just don't get recognition among companies back East," says Tabbush, UCLA's exec-ed director. "We're flying under the radar."

But if you're looking for a general-management course that won't disrupt your worklife and is within driving distance of Westwood, the trendy L.A. suburb that is home to the sprawling, palm-dotted UCLA campus, the Executive Program may be just your ticket. There are two sessions each year: One begins in February, breaks for the summer, then continues through December; the other begins in September and runs through the following May. Each session is divided into two semesters, and each semester begins with a three-day in-residence stint an hour up the coast at the Ojai Valley Inn and Country Club. For the next 12 weeks, classes are then held once a week on campus, on Tuesday or Thursday evenings from 4 to 9 p.m. Since the second semester of the session that begins in February overlaps with the first semester of the session that begins in September, you may choose to attend classes twice a week and complete the program in just three months (an option that only a few students traveling from long distances have ever taken).

Confused? UCLA makes you work pretty hard just to understand its class schedule, and that's an omen for the future. Participants rate the program's workload as heavier than any other school's except Duke, perhaps in part because they're continuing to work full time throughout the program and don't have the luxury of grabbing an hour or two during the day for reading or study group meetings. The three-day residential sessions are intense, one focusing on leadership and motivational issues, the other on formulating and implementing strategies. The weekly classes, which cover the gamut of general management topics from functional reviews of accounting, finance, marketing, and information technology to international environment and human resources, have to pack a lot into five hours, with a working dinner (included in the $9100 tuition fee) served in a lounge adjacent to Anderson's modern, tiered executive classroom.

There isn't much time for group project work. Between lectures and group discussions of the week's assignment, the evenings pass quickly. There's also little time for fraternizing with classmates. Most of the informal interaction comes during students' voluntary dinner-hour presentations of management problems they're encountering on the job, such as downsizing, personnel, or technical challenges. Then, the floor is opened for suggestions and recommendations. When 9 p.m. rolls around, students are quickly out the door and headed for their cars, since everyone faces the drive home and work the following morning. "We didn't really socialize after class," says Anthony O. Hester, product assurance manager for Bendix Oceanics Inc., who attended the program in 1990–1991. "There are a lot of bars and restaurants nearby, and I was hoping people might head out for a drink and continue talking about what was going on in class, but that didn't happen." Tabbush says he hopes to boost the bonding factor a bit when the program adds a third three-day in-residence session just before the black-tie graduation ceremonies. Starting in February 1993, this session will include spouses and encompass such personal issues as career paths, life choices, and tax and estate planning.

The professors also try hard to lend a little camaraderie to the classroom by encouraging students to share their experience and expertise. "If you're talking about reading financial pages, for some people who do that all the time that could be laborious—but not if they can convey their insights," says Hester. The staff is made up of a 50-50 mix of Anderson faculty and consultants and visiting professors; among those singled out for praise are Professor Jose de la Torre, whom Anderson recently lured from France's INSEAD and who is helping to strengthen the program's international focus; Professor William G. Ouchi, author of the best-seller *Theory Z* and a specialist in organization and strategic studies; and Professor Moshe F. Rubinstein of

UCLA's School of Engineering, whose dynamic presentations enliven his segments on problem solving and decision making.

Because of the program's local nature, the participant list reflects the Southern California business community. Most are top functional managers or newly appointed general managers in their early 40s from the aerospace and electronics industries, entertainment, retailing, the petroleum industry, and local government. Whether because of the industry mix, or because the nonresidential format is more compatible to their lifestyles, women make up an unusually large percentage of each class, typically about one-fifth. The alumni association, called the Executive Program Network, is more active than most, meeting quarterly for breakfast; since most of the alums are from the area, attendance is steadily high. And the network offers something that most Californians can't pass up—free parking.

Organizations sending most participants: GM Hughes Electronics; TRW Signal Corp.; Allied-Signal Corp.; Atlantic Richfield; Northrop

Other Programs of Note

Advanced Executive Program: Subtitled "Competing in a Global Environment," this program examines the interrelationship between business strategy, environment, and organization. Led by Professors William G. Ouchi and Jose de la Torre, two of the school's top-rated teachers. Intended for senior executives of large and medium-sized companies with significant cross-functional experience at the level of vice president or above. Two weeks; held annually in July; 35 students per session; $7500, including tuition, room, board, and supplies; by application.

Medical Marketing Program: Focuses exclusively on sales and marketing techniques in health-care industries, including developing marketing plans and strategy, market research, managing a sales force, sales forecasting, team-building, and pricing. Led by Associate Dean Victor Tabbush, who had headed up UCLA's exec-ed business since 1979. Intended for marketing and sales managers in the pharmaceutical, device, diagnostic, biotechnology, hospital, and health-care service industries. One week; held twice a year, in March and October; 60 students per session; $3185, including tuition, room, board, and supplies (discounts available for Medical Marketing Association members, early registration, or group registration); open enrollment.

Purchasing Executive Program: Explores ways to integrate the purchasing function into corporate strategic planning and communication. Led by Associate Dean Victor Tabbush. Intended for senior and functional executives with purchasing, materials, or procurement responsibilities. One week; held annually in April; $2795, including tuition, room, board, and supplies (discount available for National Association of Purchasing Management members and early registration); open enrollment.

Managing the Information Resource: Examines innovative and creative information technologies, how they can be implemented, and how they can impact on other corporate segments. Led by Lewis E. Leeburg, director of the Information Systems Research Program and an Anderson lecturer. Intended for senior executives with information technology responsibilities, top-level functional managers of computer-based technologies, and high-level managers responsible for managing information technology within a function. Five days; held twice a year at UCLA, once in Hong Kong, and once in Malaysia; 45 students; $3690, including tuition, room, board, and supplies (costs vary for non-U.S. locations; discount available for early registration); open enrollment.

Organizations sending most participants: Pacific Bell; Ciba-Geigy; Transamerica Life Insurance; TRW; Johnson & Johnson

Anderson Consumers Sound Off

The quality of lecturers was exceptional, the material well integrated and presented in the correct sequence. Each of the two semesters began with an off-campus session devoted to a single well-focused subject and provided significant group/faculty interaction as well as group preparation and presentations.—**Vice President**

While I generally found the experience excellent, I was a little disappointed in the level of detail in which certain subjects were covered. For example, you won't learn a heck of a whole lot about corporate financing strategy in one four-hour module. We were exposed to the concepts, not drilled in them.—**Project Manager**

Excellent across-the-board survey course at the executive management level. Level of detail was excellent, and where more detail was desired, all the tools required to obtain it were provided.—**Evaluation Director**

Virtually no mention of total quality management, continuous process improvement, etc. Very traditional discussions of management styles. Does not reflect revolutions in some industries on employee involvement.
—**Program Manager**

I don't think the program required as much discipline as it should—written reports, presentations, quizzes, etc. It was too easy to stint on the reading and rely on the lectures for an overview of the subject. While I realize that such programs are not designed to match the rigors of an MBA, less of the information sticks without accountability devices.—**Executive**

Keeping in mind this was a certificate program based on attendance as opposed to a degree program based on classroom performance, I still feel the program could have challenged us more through specific work assignments and practical exercises.—**Consultant**

Excellent faculty (with minor exceptions); emphasis on teamwork and communication, camaraderie; widely varying student backgrounds gave insights to new thinking, very mind-broadening.—**Operations Manager**

The UCLA program was excellent in all respects. I have recommended it to peers and subordinates. In my particular class, many of my fellow stu-

dents had advanced degrees in technical areas, and were now rounding out their educations in management. The caliber of the students was exceptional. —**Manager**

The program was not as relevant to my industry (computer software) as I had hoped. But I did make some excellent professional contacts. —**Vice President**

The case studies and group interpersonal decision making is unique and outstanding for future development. It was an outstanding program in which theory was brought to practical and day-to-day business experience. —**General Manager**

The UCLA course gave me explicit tools for dealing with management situations and responsibilities that I formerly used implicitly or not at all. —**Director**

I can now sit in pricing meetings and reference elastic and nonelastic markets as a rationale for my decisions, rather than gut feelings. I felt the marketing and management information system modules were not of the same caliber as the rest of the program—that may have been because those were two areas that I had the greatest experience in. —**Marketing Consultant**

The quality of the facilities, accommodations, and instructional staff made it worthwhile. The two retreats away from the classroom to kick off each semester were particularly good to build class rapport unencumbered by daily routine. The only negative comment deals with curriculum composition. Much of the program dealt with finance and marketing. Since I am in government service, these topics were not as important to me as other subjects such as leadership and management. —**Manager**

15. Carnegie Mellon University

Graduate School of Industrial Administration
Pittsburgh, Pennsylvania 15213

Corporate ranking: 22   *Consumer ranking*: 7
Number of programs: 4   *Number of programs in 1986*: 3
1990–1991 enrollment: 310   *Years in executive education*: 38
Annual revenues: $1.9 million   *Change since 1986*: 208 percent

Contact: Peter M. Vantine, associate dean and director of executive education, 412-268-2305

Program for Executives

You're the chief executive of a·chemical firm that was just found responsible for a massive toxic spill in a local waterway. The press is clamoring for information; it's time to make your statement. Palms damp, heart pounding, you enter a room crowded with reporters, and as the cameras roll, you face a barrage of piercing questions and tough accusations.

Playing out this scenario in the Program for Executives' media skills workshop may not be as nerve-wracking as a real-life press conference, but the professors and consultants who pose as reporters do their best to make you sweat. One executive, a Soviet manager whose job it was to export nuclear-power technology, had the unlucky timing to arrive at Carnegie Mellon just six months after the Chernobyl reactor accident. When his turn came to meet the "press," Peter M. Vantine, the school's director of executive education, said slyly, "You can guess what the questions were like." And if the workshop itself isn't humbling enough, you get a videotape of your performance to review once you get back home.

Learning to manage the media is just one of the surprising areas of study in store for managers who arrive in Pittsburgh still thinking of Carnegie Mellon as a school for gear heads and computer jocks. Sure, you'll find plenty of technically trained managers in the program, along with more than the average share of controllers, accountants, and auditors. After all, at CMU, business has always been a science. The GSIA was the nation's first B-school to have its own computer, and even the master's program awards not an MBA but an MSIA (master of science in industrial administration). Along those lines, the Program for Executives does tend to look at the often-fuzzy art of management through a sharply focused quantitative lens. "We believe you can apply other disciplines to the study of management," says Vantine. "You can think of it in economics terms or in psychological terms. You can apply linear programming, mathematical models, and even physics. It's not just case study and telling war stories."

But there's plenty more to the program than number-crunching and running regressions. The school's techy reputation tends to belie its considerable strengths as a keen innovator in management education. Besides the media skills workshop, there are the informal question-and-answer sessions with such distinguished speakers as former Bendix CEO William Agee, Mellon Bank CEO Frank V. Cahouet, H.J. Heinz CEO Anthony J.F. O'Reilly, and former U.S. Attorney General Richard Thornburgh.

There's the team business simulation competition, with groups of five or six students acting as rival electronics manufacturers, each drawing up its own corporate strategy and comparing performance through five years' worth of business cycles. There's the world economics game, in which student teams representing different countries fight it out in the import-export arena. And there's the faculty, many of whom have a solid grounding in the real world through consulting and work experience. Vantine, for one, used to run the international divisions of Pepsico and Frito-Lay, and program director W. Robert Dalton is a former chief economist with Gulf Oil.

If you're looking for individual attention, Carnegie Mellon is the place to find it. The school's foray into executive education has been intentionally limited to just four programs, and two of those are custom offerings for AT&T Bell Labs and Bristol-Myers Squibb. In the Program for Executives, which is offered twice a year, in May and September, the class size of 30 to 35 makes it easy for the faculty to get to know every single participant on a first-name basis, and for classmates to become well acquainted with one another.

The intimacy level may be affected somewhat when the program shrinks from six weeks to four beginning in the spring of 1992; like other general management courses that are downsizing, CMU officials say that in lean times, companies are simply not willing to keep employees off the job for more extended periods of time. Vantine says he thinks the program can cover virtually the same amount of material in the shorter time frame simply by working the students a bit harder and making a few scheduling adjustments. The media workshop, previously required, will become an elective. But alumni who believe the workload was already fairly heavy say something will have to give, either by cutting back on the amount of reading or cutting into the unscheduled time for R&R or chatting with classmates. "If they're going to try to cover the same number of books," laughs Ronald L. Widner, director of steel development for The Timken Co. in Ohio, who attended the program in 1989, "that would certainly be more pressured."

In keeping with the fact that participants tend either to be upper-level functional managers from technology-driven companies such as IBM, Digital Equipment, and Boeing, or to manage technical functions in "non-tech" firms such as Unilever, the curriculum does bring a technological twist to its otherwise traditional overview of general management skills. The corporate strategy segment, for example, covers such material as technology spillover and the effects of rapid learning on industries. Operations management includes a piece on the management of new technology. The segment on global environment offers information on international technology transfers. Many of the CMU professors have engineering backgrounds: "We look at the world as engineers," says Vantine.

But that perspective is broadened by the core faculty members drawn from outside Carnegie Mellon—nearly one-third of the staff—and by long-term, continuing involvement with such well-known management educators as Robert S. Kaplan of Harvard, who brings his expertise in management accounting; Jay E. Klompmaker of the University of North Carolina, a marketing specialist; and John R. Percival of the Wharton School, who specializes in finance. (Among the more popular CMU staffers are Robert Kelley, who teaches the importance of both leadership and "followership" in organizational behavior, and Jeffrey R. Williams, whose innovations in strategic planning have been tapped by such companies as AT&T Bell Labs, Westinghouse Electric, Ford Motor Co., and NASA.) And two growing areas of importance in the program are decidedly "un-technical": the management of change, particularly in the current economic climate, with the trend among large companies to use cross-functional work units; and globalization, which is perhaps affecting technology-based industries most of all. The new international emphasis is reflected in the program's increasing number of foreign participants, who now make up about 35 percent of each class; that figure will probably grow after the course is shortened. (The program also draws a surprisingly large number of women—15 to 20 percent of each class—which Vantine speculates may result from the fact that female techies are such a rare breed that they may feel they need to get a leg up on the competition by boosting their education.)

Whether it's because of the small class size, or the relatively homogeneous career paths and interests, participants tend to be a tightly knit group, spending their free nights and weekends at a Pirates game, taking a riverboat excursion, or sailing and rafting on one of the Steel City's newly cleaned-up waterways. Or maybe it's commuter camaraderie: Since there are no exec-ed accommodations on campus, students are housed at a hotel across town and bused 15 to 20 minutes each way to class at the GSIA. Those rides often turn into mini-study sessions, says Widner: "You could talk with people on the bus about what you studied the night before, so it wasn't totally lost time." Administrators try to minimize the inconvenience, offering lunch on campus at the Faculty Club and scheduling numerous social dinners, but you're on your own for breakfast, some dinners, and weekend meals, adding a good $500 outlay to the $14,000 tuition and room tab. The spouses' program, held during the last three days, will continue to be a part of the four-week format.

Besides the media workshop, there is another part of the program that offers the same opportunity for humiliation to techies and non-techies alike—the song-fest celebrating the end of the competitive business simulation. After spending the morning justifying their business performance to peers and professors, each team heads off to write a skit, complete with songs and costumes, to be put on that night at what Vantine calls "a suitably grungy, disreputable bar." He adds, "I hope we don't run out of places too soon."

Organizations sending most participants: AT&T; U.S. Navy; General Motors; Boeing; Digital Equipment

Other Programs of Note

Program in Engineering Design: A highly technical program to help managers of engineering design teams improve their organization's ability to produce high-quality, cost-effective designs rapidly and efficiently. Focuses on state-of-the-art research, tools, and methods, with some discussion of organizational skills. Led by Bernd Kiel, executive director of the Carnegie Bosch Institute. Intended for engineering design team managers in large multinational manufacturing companies. Nine weeks long with a two-week break after the fifth week; held annually during the summer, with 20–25 students per session; $25,500; by application.

Organizations sending most participants: AT&T; U.S. Navy; General Motors; Boeing; Digital Equipment

Carnegie Mellon Consumers Sound Off

Carnegie Mellon was very responsive to the needs of the group, constantly looking for feedback and input to help improve the program. It was evident they have improved the program over time.—**Business Resource Manager**

Bob Dalton and his staff were exceptional! They personally cared for each one of us as individuals.—**Senior Engineer**

Outstanding speakers who identified with our environment and sought out an exchange of ideas rather than straight lecture.—**Senior Manager**

Several members of our class observed that some of the faculty did a fine job of faking interest in class input, while others responded in a genuine fashion.—**Product and Process Engineering Manager**

Too little subject matter and discussion on doing business internationally. Zero discussion on Japan.—**Automotive Programs Director**

Too manufacturing-oriented with dated cases. The curriculum should have more general management/service-retail orientation.—**Vice President**

A key distinguishing factor of the program was the press relations module. They use videotaping to train you on how to react to press interviews. It is an important skill for executives.—**Systems Director**

Spouses and significant others should not be included. Learning stopped the week they arrived and the group interactions diminished.—**Personnel Secretary**

In my opinion, a significant portion of the learning experience was to learn how to manage time appropriately, fully utilize team members, and better prioritize tasks when all cannot be accomplished. Given the above, no amount of work would be considered excessive. If absolute completion of all tasks by each individual was a goal of this program, then the work was clearly excessive.—**Manager**

My two objectives in selecting a program were (1) a balance of coursework to complement my skills and (2) international participants. The CMU course was one of the best fits of all the ones I evaluated.—**Manager**

One of my greatest pleasures of the program was to meet Robert Kaplan, an outstanding authority on financial management. Since I had already read his magnum opus "Advanced Management Accounting" even before attending the program, it was an excellent opportunity to discuss some of the most interesting issues in accounting policies with him. I wish we had more time with him.—**Director**

All the lecturers were essentially American-based consultants. Their experiences had little value for non-U.S.-based company people. I also felt that the program allowed limited time for mixing with the international students.—**Director**

The program at CMU was excellent both in content and timing for me. I have an engineering background and most of my experience is in research and development. The small size of the group (about 30 managers) and the cross section of people represented an opportunity to broaden my understanding of other disciplines and other types of business that have similar issues to those I face each day. The course work in accounting was especially new, challenging, and helpful to me.—**Director**

I returned to my job as a more confident and better person for having attended the program at Carnegie Mellon. Having been a career Navy man, I gained a totally new perspective of the business world. Our class had very diverse backgrounds, and I am not sure if it was the diversity of my classmates or the diversity of the faculty, but we ended up with an exceptionally close group at the end of our short six weeks.—**Engineer**

16. Dartmouth College

Amos Tuck School of Business Administration
100 Tuck Hall
Dartmouth College
Hanover, New Hampshire 03755

Corporate ranking: 18	*Consumer ranking*: 12
Number of programs: 9	*Number of programs in 1986*: 3
1990–1991 enrollment: 264	*Years in executive education*: 21
Annual revenues: $1.4 million	*Change since 1986*: 53 percent

Contact: Professor Frederick E. Webster Jr., faculty director for executive education, 603-646-3134

Tuck Executive Program

If you loved going to summer camp, you'll feel right at home at Dartmouth's Tuck Executive Program. First off, there's the campus. You can either think of it as a peaceful, rustic hideaway, nestled in the pine-covered Hampshire Hills on the banks of the Connecticut River, or you can consider yourself stranded in the woods for a month. The lack of air-conditioning in the ascetically appointed B-school dorm rooms, where you'll be staying throughout July, can be either a charming reminder of long-ago summer nights, or a sweat-soaked impediment to a good night's sleep. The optional Outward Bound-style experience on the program's first weekend, when it invariably manages to rain, can turn into either an invigorating challenge or a torturous taste of Parris Island. As one sopping-wet participant remarked, with an almost-straight face, after spending the day working the ropes in a downpour, "We bond much quicker in the mud."

Recreation and the great outdoors do play an important role at Dartmouth. There are plenty of open-air hikes in the mountains and cookouts at the Dartmouth Outing Club, a ski-lodge-style facility on Occom Pond about a half-mile's nature walk from Tuck. Actually, there's not much else to do, seeing as how you're a good two to three hours from the nearest major metropolitan areas of Boston and Montreal, and the nightlife in sleepy little Hanover tends more to catching fireflies than barflies. The get-fit mentality begins on the first day of the program, when a physician talks to participants about stress, cardiovascular conditioning, smoking, and diet. "A lecture from your mother," quips Frederick E. Webster Jr., faculty director for executive education. Classes are wrapped up by 3:15 each afternoon so participants will be free to attend aerobics classes, go jogging, play tennis, or take a canoeing trip, and most of the 60 or so students take advantage of the opportunity. "There are always a few perched on their lawn chairs, reading the next day's assignments, but not very many," Webster says.

Does that mean you have to be a jock to enjoy this program? By no means. There's plenty of mental exercise involved here as well. TEP's emphasis is on strategic management, which is infused throughout the curriculum's five segments: strategy formulation and implementation; organization design and leadership; financial management, accounting, and control; marketing and operations management; and the international economic environment. "Cost accounting and finance were put forward as strategic concepts—I expected to be bored, but instead I was stimulated," says one participant. The strategic orientation culminates in a three-day computer simulation game, devised at Tuck, in which teams of six to eight students represent companies that are globally marketing an unspecified product. Each team must cope with such unforeseen events as suffering a major factory fire, losing a key salesperson, achieving a technical breakthrough, or plunging into a worldwide recession. There are no winners or losers here. Performance is rated against each team's own objectives (although "It's usually pretty clear who did best and worst," Webster says).

In fact, throughout the course, Tuck makes a special effort to tone down the competitive edge that many general management programs seem to engender. Small study groups are rotated weekly, and even the class seating assignments are scrambled every few days so participants can maximize exposure to their classmates; by the end of the program, you'll be on a first-name basis with pretty much everyone. "The group of individuals that I had the pleasure of interacting with was incredible," says Charles F. O'Donnell, manager of oil movements and pipeline support at Alyeska Pipeline Service Co. in Anchorage, Alaska, who attended TEP in 1991. "I've already had contact with 6 individuals out of 58 on business-related decisions in which we have exchanged ideas and opinions." The faculty gets very involved, as well, shying away from pure lectures in favor of spirited discussions, and spending a lot of time outside of class with the students, at meals and other social functions. Because Dartmouth is a small teaching college rather than a large research university, faculty members seem to have fewer time pressures here. And since the school is among the smaller players in the executive education game—its annual exec-ed revenues are lowest of our Top 20, and it offers no company-specific courses—managers get an inordinate amount of attention. (The school is negotiating with a handful of firms to offer tailored versions of its open-enrollment courses in hopes of boosting that revenue figure, but Webster says the staff limitations will continue to prevent any large-scale customizing.)

Thanks partly to its small size, Dartmouth's teaching quality ranks among the highest at the top business schools. Participants in our survey ranked it in the top one-quarter, on a par with Harvard. After all, Tuck is the oldest management school in the United States, dating back to 1900, and TEP's core faculty is composed almost entirely of tenured Tuck professors. Professors Brian Quinn and Richard D'Aveni's sessions on strategy, Professor Dennis Logue's classes on corporate finance, and the marketing sessions with Webster, who serves as the program's director, are singled out as stellar. You can also expect good things from a TEP newcomer, Professor Vijay Govindarajan (just call him "V.G.," like everyone else does), who directs Tuck's highly rated Minority Business Executive Program.

The program does come in for criticism in a couple of key areas. Many managers believe the international content is weak; although typically a third of each class is from outside the United States, foreign students complain that the case studies involve American companies almost exclusively and that they feel like invisible observers instead of actively tapped resources. Others say they'd like the program to be more directly applicable to their real-life jobs. (Tuck ranked in the lowest third of the schools we surveyed on that question.)

In response to the relevance question, the program is introducing several new features that aim to boost its linkage to students' full-time jobs, according to Webster. During the computer simulation, professors plan to take more hands-on control of the leadership and team-building lessons that are a natural outgrowth of such an exercise. In addition, the second week will begin including a segment on innovation, product development, and market development, with participants using their own companies as examples in lieu of prewritten cases. And in the third week, the program is developing a two-day group exercise in which executives are asked to detail management issues they expect to face when they return to their offices, then grouped according to common problems so they can work together to come up with ways to address those issues. "We have to be responsive to what our customers want," says Webster, especially when the month's price tag totals $15,500.

Those customers, both the companies and their employees, are becoming an increasingly diverse group. While a good 50 percent of participants continue to be 40-something top functional managers from the 500 largest U.S. companies, more and more are drawn from smaller firms or from entrepreneurial offshoots of the big corporations. The school is also working to attract more women, which currently make up about 10 percent of each class. The new participant profile is causing some rethinking of segments like the Couples Program, which takes place during the last three days. In one recent session, says Webster, a vice president of sales at a major food manufacturer introduced her husband, an Eastern Orthodox priest who said he found the marketing sessions quite applicable to his job of building a congregation.

Organizations sending most participants: General Motors; Price Waterhouse; General Reinsurance; General Mills Restaurants; Hercules Inc.

Other Programs of Note

Minority Business Executive Program: A week-long crash course in management for minority entrepreneurs. For further details, see Chapter 6, The Ten Most Innovative Programs.

Tuck Marketing Strategy Program: Reviews and updates strategic marketing management concepts in consumer, industrial, and service industries, as well as addressing topics of current interest in the field. Led by Professor Frederick E. Webster Jr. Intended for marketing specialists, including executives in product planning and development, sales force management, market research and information systems, pricing, distribution, advertising and sales promotion, and marketing planning, as well as general managers with marketing responsibilities. One week; held annually, in August; 50 students per session; $3950, including tuition, room, board, and supplies; by application.

Effective Management of Production Program: Examines developments in customer service, workforce management, control of costs, new product transfers, and optimal use of production capacity. Led by Professor Kenneth R. Baker. Designed for managers involved with manufacturing, operations, materials management, production control, and related functions. One week; held annually, in August; 40–50 students per session; $3950, including tuition, room, board, and supplies; by application.

Strategic Cost Management Program: Designed to enhance the strategic perspective of financial managers and controllers, the program demonstrates how managerial accounting and control systems can be linked with the design and implementation of business strategy. Led by Professor John Shank. Intended for executives with 10 years' experience in managerial accounting and control, including corporate senior financial officers, controllers, audit partners, and management consultants. One week; held annually, in September; 30–35 students per session; $3950, including tuition, room, board, and supplies; by application.

MBA: Update 2000:   Designed to keep your MBA investment current. Updates the education you received years ago in such critical areas as strategic alliances, empowerment, workforce diversity, the quality movement, industrial ecology, strategic analysis, and the revolution in management accounting. Intended for managers and executives who received their MBAs sometime before the mid-1980s. Program is offered at the Basin Harbor Inn, directly on Lake Champlain, just 40 minutes from the Burlington Airport. Two five-day modules, one in September and the other in June; $7500, including tuition, room, board, and supplies; by application.

Organizations sending most participants: AT&T; Digital Equipment; IBM; Norton; Texaco

Tuck Consumers Sound Off

*This is an excellent program. The underlying strategy focus provided by Brian Quinn puts the ongoing turmoil and restructuring of American business in a context that helps to understand the opportunities and challenges.—****Executive Vice President***

*The program met or exceeded my expectations in all areas. Of particular value were courses on strategy and activity-based costing. The teaching staff was seasoned, professional, and absolutely first class.—****General Manager***

*We had two professors who were really weak—their classes were a waste of my time. The majority were outstanding, but those two brought the overall rating down for me.—****Vice President for Sales***

*The case method was used too extensively. Two to three cases a day was too much to cover properly.—****President***

The setting was superb. The fact that the dorm rooms were spartan and not air-conditioned led to even more group interaction as people moved outside to study and socialize. I actually didn't watch TV for a month.
*—****Customer Service Manager***

*The facilities were uncomfortable. Too much lecture and sitting in one place. Not enough time for peer interaction.—****Supply Director***

The Tuck organization functions like a well-worked machine. The teaching faculty is world class. The workload is taxing, but in the end keeps

you focused and prevents you from contacting your office everyday. I wholeheartedly recommend it to seasoned upper-level executives!—**Group Vice President**

My appreciation for the Tuck program increased significantly six to eight weeks after returning to work. The cohesive nature of the various classes enforced new and creative ways of approaching business problems. It's a "must program" for executives who have reached the pinnacle of their "technical" careers and must learn to assimilate technical opinions to broad business issues.—**Partner**

Courses on executive health and exercise rounded out a well-balanced program.—**Facilities Management Director**

As the sole nonprofit representative among nearly 60 executives, I found the entire Tuck experience beneficial. The program helped me expand my management skills, and this should serve me well in the future. The notion that executive programs are for business executives is a myth. Perhaps the most valuable skill that I developed during the program is "strategic thinking." All too often, nonprofit managers are simply concerned with the "survival" of the institution. Given this short-term outlook, it's no wonder so many nonprofits are in trouble.—**Director of Development**

17. Cornell University

Johnson Graduate School of Management
319 Malott Hall
Ithaca, New York 14850

Corporate ranking: 13
Number of programs: 11
1990–1991 enrollment: 350
Annual revenues: $1.4 million

Consumer ranking: 18
Number of programs in 1986: 5
Years in executive education: 40
Change since 1986: 100 percent

Contact: Joseph Thomas, acting director of executive education, 607-255-4854

Executive Development Program

Each summer, a lucky Johnson MBA student has the good fortune to get paid a pittance to be used and abused by a group of high-powered managers. Whoever is chosen as an intern to the school's Executive Development Program spends a month providing computer tutoring, doing library research, acting as an all-around gofer, and making some invaluable contacts and learning a few lessons about Corporate America to boot. Michael Adkins, who interned in 1991, found the whole experience exhausting. "I never really understood what service meant. Now I do," he told Johnson's exec-ed director. But the payoff made it all worthwhile: He landed three job offers as a direct result of the internship and accepted a position at The Timken Co., the Ohio-based steel products firm.

At Cornell, customer service is more than just lip-service. The university whose famed School of Hotel Administration has turned out some of the nation's finest purveyors of food, drink, and lodging prides itself on giving the folks what they want, and executive education is no exception. Besides the traditional management training courses offered by Johnson, an array of more narrowly defined executive programs can be found throughout Cornell's vast network of schools and departments. The hotel school offers a number of programs for executives in the hospitality industry, including a three-week Advanced Management Program for senior managers. Companies give high ratings to the human-resources and labor-relations programs for executives sponsored by the School of Industrial Relations. Even the Department of Agricultural Economics weighs in with management programs for food executives.

Johnson's Executive Development Program is a good example of the service mentality. As of the summer of 1992, the program is being reduced from five weeks to four, following what the school calls its regular "reality checks" to find out what major clients want. By eliminating a mid-session break and adding class time to an opening day that was previously set aside just for registration, Cornell figures there won't be much lost from the schedule. Another change is that during the last two weeks, EDP's 50 or so participants will now be allowed to specialize in one of three elective areas—human resources, manufacturing strategy and operations, or finance—supplementing the basic curriculum in their chosen subject with additional readings, lectures, and discussion. That's a major difference between Cornell's general management program and those served up at other schools. Students also get their choice of extracurricular activities around 5 p.m. each day, between the end of

113

classes and the start of dinner, when they can join an aerobics group, take a golf or tennis lesson, or sign up for special-interest seminars on subjects like computers, public speaking, or estate planning. All this on top of the typical regimen of classes throughout the day and group case-study sessions in the evening. Maybe that's why participants rank Cornell's workload among the Top 20's heaviest, just below Duke and UCLA.

As far as the curriculum goes, the program's announced theme is "Continued Organizational and Individual Development," and, indeed, interpersonal skills are given more attention than strictly functional ones. Among the topics covered are boosting individual and organizational productivity, decision making, the social and economic environment, finance, marketing, and strategy. The faculty, which receives high marks for its accessibility to students, nicely balances the research orientation of an Ivy League university with a strong interest in classroom teaching and a substantial amount of consulting work to stay in touch with what's going on inside companies today. Program director L. Joseph Thomas, a professor of manufacturing who teaches EDP's productivity segments, has consulted for Hershey, Alcoa, GTE, and AT&T; John A. Elliott, associate professor of accounting, has worked for Arthur Andersen and Westinghouse; and Professor Richard H. Thaler, who is publishing a book of collected writings on the psychology of economics, has consulted for Concord Capital Management. EDP also hauls in name-brand guest speakers such as Ken Blanchard, author of *The One-Minute Manager.*

Case study plays a significant role in the course, with assigned discussion groups regularly rotated for maximum diversity, but less orthodox teaching tools are used as well. The Cornell Management Game runs throughout most of the course. It's a computer-based simulation designed by Professor Jerome E. Hass, a finance and strategy specialist who served as special assistant to Energy Secretary James Schlesinger in the late 1970s and who has consulted for such firms as Standard Oil of Ohio, Exxon, and the Long Island Lighting Co. Teams of 8 to 10 students compete against one another, and against computer-generated wild-card companies in the same market, where they are forced to deal with workforce, marketing, and production problems as well as performance. At the end of the game, Hass hands out awards dubbed "The Good, the Bad, and the Ugly." You'll also be witness to a workshop put on by the Cornell Interactive Theatrical Ensemble, professional actors who role-play issues involving workplace diversity, such as age discrimination and sexual harassment, then answer participants' questions in character to further the discussion.

Johnson is quite concerned about its own diversity, making special efforts to push companies to send minority and female employees to EDP. The program also brought in one of the rare woman professors to teach in executive education, Maureen O'Hara, a finance expert who has consulted for Goldman Sachs and the Federal Savings & Loan Association. Last year, the program drew 20 percent women, so the efforts are paying off. At 40, participants are slightly younger than the typical general-management clientele, and the school strives for a broad corporate representation, including executives from small companies.

The program also attracts a sizable number of students from outside the United States, who now number about half of each class. One recent class featured 48 students from 19 countries representing 41 companies. Following the upheaval in Eastern Europe, Dean Alan Merten met with President Bush to explore ways B-schools could assist the new generation of fledgling capitalists; as a result, three students from that part of the world attended EDP during the summer of 1991. "I've continued to correspond with a student from Croatia about what's going on over there," says James F. Haven, assistant to the president of Texaco USA in Houston, who was a member of the 1991 class. Despite the special efforts, however, students still complain that the course's international content is underemphasized and that the foreign participants' unique experiences are underutilized. Another frequent complaint is that EDP has little immediate applicability to participants' jobs. The new elective areas of concentration may help students find more relevance to their work; the program is also using feedback questionnaires, to be filled out by subordinates before the session begins, to help students gauge their personal strengths and weaknesses in dealing with other people.

You sure won't hear any complaints about the facilities. In fact, this is Cornell's chance to showcase its expertise in the hospitality game. The campus' isolated setting, in the Finger Lakes region of upstate New York, is conducive to a retreat-like atmosphere. Weekends will find students headed out for sailing on Cayuga Lake, a tour of New York's wine country, a night-golf tournament, or even a jaunt up to Niagara Falls, a favorite among the foreign participants. As far as nightlife goes, Ithaca offers a surprisingly wide range of restaurants and bars, many of them staffed by hotel-school grads. Participants are housed in the sleek J. Willard Marriott Executive Education Center and Statler Hotel, built in 1989 and state-of-the-art as far as conference centers go. Since the hotel school uses the Statler as one of its teaching facilities, participants are treated to gourmet meals, fine lodging, and precision service. The program's administrative and support staffs also win praise for making things run like clockwork. At $12,950, it's practically a bargain. And as any of the program's MBA interns will tell you, you can't put a price on service.

Organizations sending most participants: Boeing; Chevron; AT&T; Digital Equipment; Conoco

Other Programs of Note

Managing the Next Generation of Manufacturing Technology: This program introduces new technologies that will revolutionize manufacturing operations in the coming decade, then explores how management will have to adapt to these innovations, including the ways management accounting, financial analysis, and production control must change as cost structures, speed and flexibility of operation, and marketing patterns evolve. Senior executives from large industrial firms such as Emerson Electric, Xerox, and Corning are scheduled to discuss their own success and failures in dealing with automation. Led by Professors John A. Muckstadt and L. Joseph Thomas. Intended for senior managers in engineering, manufacturing, or general industrial management functions. One week; held annually, in November; 40 students per session; $2950, including tuition, room, board, and supplies; open enrollment.

Manufacturing Executive Program: Explores ways to boost manufacturing performance through enhanced motivation and utilization of employees, and reduce customer response times and improve manufacturing efficiency through new technology. Intended for senior manufacturing executives, including plant managers, vice presidents or directors of manufacturing, and their direct subordinates. Two weeks;

held annually, in March; 20 students per session; $7500, including tuition, room, board, and supplies; open enrollment.

Purchasing Executives Institute: Examines business issues that affect purchasing, including accounting, the world economy, legal issues, relationships with suppliers, and multifunctional teamwork. Led by Professor Ronald W. Hilton. Intended for vice presidents and directors of materials or purchasing. One week; held annually, in September; 25–40 students per session; $2495, including tuition, room, board, and supplies (discount for National Association of Purchasing Managers members); open enrollment.

The Effective Executive Program: Focuses on improving strategic planning, decision-making, problem-solving, and innovation and technology management skills. Intended for upper-level managers, with company team involvement encouraged. One week; held twice a year, in May and September; 25 students per session; $1995, including tuition, some meals, and supplies (room and other meals extra); open enrollment.

Organizations sending most participants: NYNEX; Federal Reserve; SmithKline Beecham; 3M; Tenneco

Johnson Consumers Sound Off

*The program was wonderfully rigorous, enlightening, and satisfying. I would not hesitate doing it again.—**Publisher***

*The course was best when it stuck to its core faculty with the subjects they know best, and worst when imported "motivational" speakers were used. Outside speakers recruited from the ranks of the "captains of industry" with current upper-level management experience would be more valuable.—**Chief Engineer***

*A nice mix of social events and education. The program was well-run, informative, and overall a pleasure in which to participate.—**Marketing Director***

*Interaction with other participants was a very large part of the learning experience. Often the "expert" for a topic was a participant.—**Exploration Manager***

*Target market needs to be better defined. The range of skills and experience was so broad that the course tended to be aimed at the lowest common denominator.—**General Manager***

*One of the program's major selling points was the international aspect. However, this focus was not apparent in either the lectures or reading material. I felt this was a gross misrepresentation on Cornell's part. —**Comptroller***

I was pleasantly surprised that Cornell did not attempt to "overwork" its executive students with excessive case study work. This was my going-in expectation based on "horror" stories of peers who attended similar programs at other schools. Cornell appeared to have an excellent balance of lectures and reading. The assignments also maximized opportunities to network among the students.—General Manager, Research & Technology

Absolutely top-notch program. Many of the sessions will be with me for much of the rest of my professional career. I highly recommend it. —Director

My general feeling about the program is that it may be well adapted to executives who have been involved in exclusively technical and commercial fields with little to do with management and finance. Being specialized in these fields and rather well acquainted with accounting and industrial strategy, I didn't find the program all that useful. Overall, the social experience was more important to me than the knowledge gained through the program.—Vice President, Finance

Careful attention needs to be paid to managing the expectations of program participants. Sponsoring employers need to know the programs to which they are recommending their executives in order to ensure a positive experience.—Director

It was an outstanding program. There was a very good balance of professors and guest lecturers. The material was well-organized, and we had super accommodations with gourmet meals complemented by plenty of opportunities for exercise. The attention paid to the makeup of the class added a great deal to the educational experience. There were 48 students from 19 countries, representing 41 companies, in my class. The international flavor really added to class discussions.—Assistant to President

18. Babson College

School of Executive Education
Babson Park, Massachusetts 02157

Corporate ranking: 19   *Consumer ranking*: 14
Number of programs: 20   *Number of programs in 1986*: 14
1990–1991 enrollment: 893   *Years in executive education*: 19
Annual revenues: $2.7 million   *Change since 1986*: 170 percent

Contact: Morton Galper, dean, 617-239-4355

The Consortium for Executive Development

You know the old joke about the guy who doesn't want to belong to any club that would have the likes of him for a member? Don't tell it to the companies that belong to Babson's Consortium for Executive Development. They probably won't laugh. As you might have gathered from the name, the consortium is not your typical general management program, and it is a lot like a private club: Only employees of its member firms participate in the four-week course held each summer.

This is a hybrid of an open-enrollment program and a customized company-specific program, and the members reap the advantages of each. The participants are exposed to other corporate cultures and business lines; at the same time, their companies retain a good deal of control over the program's format and content. Those advantages are a strong drawing card. While the consortium's lineup has shifted to some extent over the 12 years it has been in existence, four of the nine current corporate partners—New England Telephone, AT&T, Norton, Digital Equipment, Textron, Eli Lilly, North American Philips, DowElanco, and Perkin-Elmer—have been part of the program since its inception.

It's only fitting that Babson originated the consortium idea because the Massachusetts school is a bit of an odd duck itself. Undergraduates can earn only business degrees; no other majors are offered. Babson has the only accredited MBA program in the United States not affiliated with a large university and one of the nation's 20 largest part-time master's programs, which attracts many employees from Boston's high-tech Route 128 perimeter nearby. Founded by financier Roger W. Babson in 1919, the college didn't get into management training until 1973, the same year Morton Galper, the current dean of the School of Executive Education, joined the faculty. Galper recalls that even the first exec-ed program offered by Babson was a bit outside the norm, an evening course targeting women who were re-entering the workforce at entry-level management positions rather than the usual group of male upper-middle managers.

The consortium, founded in 1980 as Babson's first residential program, was seen as a way to offer general management education without making the overwhelming commitment of resources required of what then were typically eight- to twelve-week programs. "We felt we could get more accomplished in a shorter period of time this way," Galper says. "We didn't have to be all things to all people." One reason the concept has remained relatively limited in use among executive educators (Indiana University's Partnership for Management Development and the University of North

Carolina's Consortium Program for Global Executives are two of the few in operation) is that a lot of schools don't like to yield authority over what goes on in their programs. (It's the same reason some schools have stayed away from company-commissioned courses.)

In Babson's case, in return for their verbal commitment to send four to six managers a year to the school at a cost of $11,000 per person, an advisory council made up of representatives of the consortium members gets to meet twice a year with school officials to discuss curriculum, faculty, and participant selection. In 1991, for example, the council decided to shorten the program from a split-session, five-week format to four consecutive weeks. If a company must leave the consortium, as Polaroid did a few years back when the firm was fighting a hostile takeover attempt, the members have veto power over the replacement choice. "The basic philosophy is that we want companies that are compatible but noncompetitive, or at least essentially noncompetitive, because as these companies grow, they sometimes start to rub up against one another at the edges," says Galper.

The school hasn't the least objection to sharing the helm. "Babson has operated on the philosophy, from the inception of executive education, that we are serving customers, whether they're undergraduates, graduate students, or executives," Galper says. "We're not of the opinion that we have all the wisdom and they should grasp the pearls we throw out." As a matter of fact, the faculty is strongly grounded in Corporate America. Before arriving at Babson in 1989, President William F. Glavin was vice chairman of Xerox Corp.; Galper spent 15 years in management at high-tech firms such as Raytheon before entering academia. "Several other of our faculty have spent 5 to 10 years in industry before they had another calling and made the transition," Galper says. "That gives us a more balanced perspective."

Participants by and large are happy with the concept as well. You're not going to get off easy just because your company has a say in how the program runs. You'll be expected to attend classes from 8 a.m. until 4:30 p.m. weekdays and Saturday mornings, work with your assigned study groups in the evenings, and manage to read numerous case studies, just like in any other general management course. In fact, the small class size of 20 to 30 makes it painfully obvious if you don't pull your weight; you could wind up essentially flunking the course and ticking off your classmates, as one student did in 1989. "She seemed to feel class attendance was optional," recalls Michael W. Hucks, regional sales and service manager for Perkin-Elmer, who attended that session. "There was a lot of resentment, and when they handed out certificates at the end of the program, she didn't get one."

The curriculum begins with an overview of the basic functions, including human resources, marketing, accounting, finance, and operations, then moves to a more strategic focus. Much of the last two weeks is devoted to a computer simulation game devised by Associate Professor Robert Eng, in which teams of students representing manufacturers and suppliers in the same industry must come to terms with such issues as product definition, pricing, volume, and marketing. The teams negotiate face to face rather than just dealing through the computer, so students get a good dose of leadership, team-building, and interpersonal relations practice as well. Besides Eng, who has brought his expertise on both computers and Chinese business to consulting gigs for General Foods, AT&T, and St. Regis, the core faculty includes Professor Allan R. Cohen, author of *Influence Without Authority* and a consultant on organizational change for firms such as Digital Equipment, Chase Manhattan, and General

Electric's WORKOUT project; Division of Management chairman, Robert F. Reiser, who spent 20 years at Xerox before joining Babson; and Galper. Professor Stephen A. Allen, the consortium's founding director, recently turned over the leadership to Professor William C. Lawler, an expert in financial planning and strategic cost analysis; Allen remains on staff, handling segments on global competition and competitive strategy.

The consortium does have its limitations. The foreign representation in the program is quite small, consisting of one or two workers from a multinational member's overseas segments, so exposure to cultural diversity is minimal. There is no spouse program, which some participants felt was a major lapse. But the facilities are first-rate, with the four-year-old Center for Executive Education providing large, comfortable bedrooms, delicious meals, and state-of-the-art classrooms with amphitheatrical seating and personal computers. Babson's picturesque campus, with red-brick buildings on 450 wooded acres, is large enough to act as a buffer to the busy suburbs surrounding it. Participants are particularly impressed by the new recreation center, with its full-service health club, indoor ice skating rink, and the Bottom Line, a quasi-bar where study groups tend to hang out on weeknights. The suburban location is ideal for weekend tours of historic Boston or jaunts up the coast to Maine.

Galper believes that the consortium was at the forefront of the current exec-ed trend toward more company-specific programs, which is one of Babson's strongest suits, for customers such as Digital Equipment, New England Telephone, IBM, and Hewlett Packard. Its newest custom client is the giant Japan-based consumer electronics company Sony. While some schools are scrambling to get into the custom game, Babson is already there. "Organizations are looking much more to organizational development instead of individual development," says Galper. "Attitudinally, a lot of schools have a lot of re-education to do. Our faculty already feels that executive education is a valuable learning experience for us as well as for the participants—every time we dialog with executives, we learn about what's going on inside companies and what we might want to research. It's an important feedback loop." Companies certainly can't argue with that attitude—but only if they're members of the club.

Organizations sending most participants: New England Telephone; Digital Equipment; AT&T; Eli Lilly

Other Programs of Note

Strategic Planning and Management in Retailing: Emphasizes the implementation of strategy in the rapidly changing retailing industry through competitive assessment, financial and productivity analysis, assortment planning, consumer research, merchandise management, personnel management, and the creation of an effective corporate culture. Led by Babson Professor Douglas J. Tigert and College of William and Mary Professor Lawrence J. Ring. The marketing duo's consulting clients include IBM, Reynolds Metals, Coors Brewing, and Dominick's. Intended for senior managers in retail operations, including senior merchandise managers, general merchandise managers, and senior and regional operations managers, as well as general managers, research directors, financial managers, and information and human resources managers. One week; held three times a year, in May at William and Mary in Williamsburg, Virginia, in June at Babson, and in October in The Netherlands at

Nijenrode University; 40 students per session; $3900, including tuition, room, board, and supplies (Netherlands session is $3400, not including room); by application.

Developing Managerial Effectiveness: Gives line and staff managers an overview of functional, managerial, and strategic skills needed to successfully lead their areas of responsibility. Led by Babson Associate Professor Jeffery Ellis, a strategy expert and consultant to John Hancock, Bank of Boston, IBM, and Xerox. Intended for middle managers with at least five years' experience who must organize projects and motivate teams. Two weeks; held twice a year, in a split-session version in the spring and consecutively in the fall; 30 students per session; $5100, including tuition, room, board, and supplies; by application.

Technology Managers Program: Designed to broaden the business skills of technology managers, from product costing to strategic implementation to leadership. Led by Babson Professor Ivor Morgan, who has also taught at Boston and Brandeis Universities and at IMD in Switzerland. Intended for mid-level technology managers at manufacturing, high-tech, and technology-driven companies. Two weeks; held annually in split sessions, with the first week in March and the second in May; 25 students per session; $5700, including tuition, room, board, and supplies; by application.

Leadership and Influence: Subtitled "For those who lead what they cannot always control," this program focuses on improving interpersonal relations with subordinates, peers, and superiors, including ways to cut through interdepartmental barriers and motivate colleagues; experience-based, with pre-program confidential questionnaires, video case studies, and role-play simulations providing the basis for discussion. Led by Babson Professor Allan Cohen, an organizational behavior guru whose consulting clients include General Electric, Chase Manhattan, Digital Equipment, and Textron. Intended for cross-functional managers at all levels. One week; held annually, in May; 30 students per session; $3250, including tuition, room, board, and supplies; by application.

Organizations sending most participants: C&A; King Soopers; Norton; Hannaford Brothers; GenRad

Babson Consumers Sound Off

This program broadened my knowledge of the interrelationship between core business functions and the need to develop teamwork and a driving strategy known and understood by all to be successful. Too little time was spent discussing how to change the culture of an organization to accept change and thrive on flexibility.—MIS Manager

As someone with a "hard science" background, the weakest portion of the curriculum was the human component—motivation, interaction, group dynamics, etc.—Regional Sales Manager

One area that needs more attention is discussion and practical focus on how to implement new skills.—R&D Director

One thing I found very enlightening was the balance between analysis and judgment: One should always run the numbers, but one must never lose sight of the strategic objective. —**Director of Tactical Design Engineering**

This is a very valuable program, particularly for a functional manager with no previous business education. I found the sessions on financial measurements, net present values, and cost of capital particularly useful. —**Manager**

This course allowed me to step back from my normal day-to-day activities and think about the broader issues that face businesses today, how those issues developed, and how other companies have dealt with them. This broader perspective has given me a great insight into the rationale for what my top management team is trying to do and has enabled me to do my job better. —**Engineering Director**

My experience in the program gave me a greater sense of the priorities that drive other divisions within my own company and of the measurement tools they're applying to track their success. —**Sales Manager**

19. Southern Methodist University

Edwin L. Cox School of Business
Executive Education
Dallas, Texas 75275-0333

Corporate ranking: 23
Number of programs: 71
1990–1991 enrollment: 3603
Annual revenues: $2.4 million

Consumer ranking: 8
Number of programs in 1986: 46
Years in executive education: 13
Change since 1986: 79 percent

Contact: Robert R. Gardner, director of executive education, 214-692-3191

Management of Managers

Deep in the heart of Texas, with its love for all things big, SMU has carved out a niche in executive education by thinking small. As a relatively small school, whose excellent reputation is still mainly regional, Cox has played it smart by not even trying to compete with the big names in the general-management training game. The school began offering its first in-residence programs just 13 years ago and still does not teach the kind of full-fledged, 4- to 12-week senior management overview found at most top schools; its 2-week Management of Managers program is strictly an exercise in leadership and personal relations skills.

Instead, Cox presents a huge menu of more than 50 different short, open-enrollment courses—a larger number than powerhouses like Wharton and Michigan—many of which are aimed at drawing local execs on a commuter basis. The list ranges from such universally applicable titles as "How to Understand, Deal with, and Prevent Sexual Harassment in the Workplace" to such arcane offerings as "Industrial Bar Coding" and "Internal Auditing to the ISO 9000-Q90 Quality Standards." It's the kind of stuff that would turn up the noses of many of the directors at the elite schools, but they're critically important topics for many practicing managers. "We've made a strategic decision to keep our longest programs under two weeks, but we offer many one-, two-, and three-day programs," says Professor Robert R. Gardner, who has been the exec-ed director since 1984. "We have to figure out ways we can impact areas that larger schools do not."

One of those areas of impact is Cox's specialty: the energy industry. The school, which is named for a Dallas oil and gas entrepreneur, has a corporate customer list that reads like a Who's Who of the drill and derrick brigade: Arco, Amoco, Unocal, Enron, LTV, Brooklyn Union Gas, and Petroleos de Venezuela. Cox's two-week general-management seminar for senior energy executives and one-week financial planning course for oil and gas company managers have become almost rites of passage among their target audiences. And while Cox has, out of necessity, kept its company-specific work to a minimum, Gardner says the school is beginning to "broaden its portfolio" by taking its energy-industry expertise international. This year, a one-week mid-management course will be run on site at a firm in Abu Dhabi, and Gardner says he hopes to steadily add other foreign locales in the coming years.

While Cox's specialization and limited scope have kept it a bit of a secret among corporations around the country—SMU ranked twenty-third in our survey of companies—participants gladly attest to the high quality of the school's programs, rating its Management of Managers program eighth in our consumer poll. But if you're looking for a mini-MBA update, this is not the place for you—no marketing, no finance, no accounting. All that functional material was eliminated from the program a few years back, when Professor John Slocum came up with the current format modeled on similar courses he'd been involved with at Penn State and Michigan. What you will get, twice a year, in spring and fall, is what Cox bills "A Leadership Renewal Program"—a sort of executives' encounter session in which participants learn how to enhance their leadership skills and management styles using reward systems, information management, negotiation tactics, and decision-making skills.

The introspection begins even before you arrive on campus, when your superiors, peers, and subordinates at work fill out surveys detailing their opinions of your managerial skills—sometimes an embarrassing though helpful exercise for participants. It continues throughout the course, which spends much of its time in group role-playing exercises and confessional-type discussions of the assigned casework. (Even the computer-based competition, in which teams simulate different companies operating in the same industry, is based not so much on financial performance, but on how each company's actions affect the others and how team members work together.) And it follows you out the door: At the end of the course, each participant devises a personal action plan for changes to be made back on the job; a few months later, Cox holds a free, one-day reunion in which the class is invited back to Dallas to report on their successes and failures in carrying out their plans. This kind of follow-up is one reason participants rated the $5650 program highest of our Top 20 in terms of teaching material that was directly useful on the job.

This is not a program for the timid: The entire class of 30 or so is expected to bare their souls to relate their own personal experiences and operating styles to the theories being presented by the faculty. "This isn't a canned course," says Peter Langlois, corporate communications manager for Iowa Public Service Co., who attended in 1989. "The professors have a knack for getting a classroom full of people stirred up and involved, giving everybody the opportunity to benefit from one another's experience. The classes can be quite lively." (A little too lively for some, who can find the rough-and-tumble, free-for-all atmosphere and heated exchanges of some sessions quite unnerving.)

Because of its size, Cox is not shy about looking outside its own faculty for instructors, so you can expect to find equal parts SMU staffers, visiting professors, and consultants at the lectern. Besides Slocum, Professor Michael E. McGill, the academic director, and Professor Robin L. Pinkley, an expert in conflict and negotiation, make up the Cox contingent; Arthur L. Anderson, chairman of the sociology department at Fairfield University, handles the segments on changing values; and Barry Leskin of the University of Southern California teaches reward systems. The computer simulation is run by consultant Maynard H. Southard; A. Dale Thompson, who runs a Dallas-based outplacement company, and Mike King, a specialist in line-staff relations from a Houston-based consulting firm, round out the current lineup.

In keeping with the program's personal development orientation, an optional "wellness" segment is offered, which draws a good two-thirds of each class. A thorough medical screening on the first day includes blood tests, weigh-in, body-fat tabulations, and strength and flexibility evaluations. A computer analysis then comes up with individual diet and exercise prescriptions for the participants, who are encouraged to use the university's field house and gymnasium after class. Students can also work out at the full-service health club at the nearby Radisson Hotel, where participants are housed during the program. While there's not much time for recreation in a two-week course—classes are held Saturday mornings, and there's not enough room in the schedule for a spouse program—there's usually an afternoon or two set aside for golfing, and a group sightseeing tour of Dallas or Fort Worth might round out the in-residence weekend.

Although there are no facilities on campus for exec-ed housing, participants do get to take advantage of Cox's recent expansion and refurbishment, which tripled the size of the school over the past three years. New amphitheater-style classrooms are hooked into the B-school's Business Information Center, an electronic hub that networks all the classrooms, offices, and labs and provides computerized access to business statistics and research data. Breakout rooms, reception areas, and catered dining rooms, where participants share most of their meals, are also located in the complex.

Because Cox attracts a heavy concentration of executives from multinational, energy-industry firms even in a general-interest, open-enrollment program such as this one, the classes include a much larger number of managers from outside the United States than might typically be expected at a small regional school. Some 30 to 40 percent of each session's participants are foreign, many from large, state-owned companies. "We had students from the Middle East, Africa, and Europe," says Langlois. "The photo of our class looks like a group of delegates to the United Nations." In this type of course, however, the diverse population can be both an advantage and a drawback: Participants get to share a global viewpoint, but some foreign students can be a bit baffled by the indigenously American corporate culture issues that are the program's focus.

Even some American executives scoff at the "touchy-feely" nature of this program. Langlois says he was a bit skeptical going into the course, but he came out a true believer in the need for leadership training: "A lot of what they teach here should seem very obvious, but it's not." And his experience back on the job has only convinced him more—since attending the 1989 program, his company, Iowa Public Service Co., has become involved in a merger with another utility. "Every day I'm trying to resolve differences and get on with new ways of doing things," he adds. "The course prepared me to deal with all this change and upheaval."

Organizations sending most participants: LTV; Arco; Ericsson; Brooklyn Union Gas; Army & Air Force Exchange Service

Other Programs of Note

Seminar for Senior Executives in the Oil and Gas Industry: Examines strategic, financial, and operational management issues within the context of the oil and gas industry; includes 50 percent foreign participants. Led by exec-ed director Robert R. Gardner. Intended for general managers or senior functional managers in the oil and gas industry. Two weeks; held twice a year, at SMU in November or in Vail/Beaver Creek, Colorado, in June; 30–35 students per session; $6850, including tuition, room, board, and supplies; by application.

125

Financial Planning and Control Seminar for Oil and Gas Company Managers: Concentrates on financial management techniques specific to the oil and gas industry, including capital investment and project evaluation, financial accounting, financial planning and forecasting, performance measurements, operating budgets, financial analysis, and the financial implications of globalization. Led by SMU Professor John W. Peavy III, a Wharton MBA who worked for Goldman Sachs & Co. for six years. Intended for mid- to senior-level managers in the oil and gas industry. One week; held twice a year, in March and September; 30–35 students per session; $3850, including tuition, room, board, and supplies; by application.

Financial Techniques for Improved Operating Effectiveness: An intensive finance and accounting seminar for nonfinancial managers, providing a working knowledge of financial decision making, financial statements, financial forecasting and analysis, capital budgeting analysis, operational budgeting systems, and performance measurement systems. Led by SMU Professor John W. Peavy III. Intended for middle- and senior-level executives in nonfinancial functions or general management. One week; held twice a year, in April and September; 20 students per session; $2950, including tuition, room, board, and supplies; by application.

Leading the High-Performance Sales Organization: Explores techniques for building successful sales organizations, including building and motivating the sales force, influencing the customer, closing the sale, establishing strategic sales planning, and conducting a sales management audit. Led by exec-ed director Robert R. Gardner, who consults with several large multinational companies and has authored more than a dozen case studies. Intended for sales executives with at least 10 years' experience and responsibility for managing both salespeople and operations. One week; held twice a year, in March and October; 20 students per session; $3250, including tuition, room, board, and supplies; by application.

SMU Mid-Management Program: A commuter course providing a broad survey of subjects typically covered in an MBA program, including marketing, financial and management accounting, quality management, financial management, human resources management, management information systems, organizational behavior, operations management, international management, and strategy. Led by exec-ed director Robert R. Gardner. Intended for middle managers with 5 to 10 years' experience and technical professionals moving into management. Twelve weeks, with one three-hour evening session per week; held three times a year, in spring, summer, and fall; 50 students per session; $1500, including tuition and supplies (discount for group enrollment); by application.

Organizations sending most participants: Arco; Amoco; Petroleos de Venezuela; Enron; Unocal

Cox Consumers Sound Off

A very good program—it has changed the way I view my peers and subordinates. The program definitely changes your outlook on business and managing styles.—Vice President

SMU did a particularly nice job of handling course logistics. The support staff was extremely accommodating and responsive to students' needs, providing group entertainment and assisting with course work when necessary. SMU wrote the book on Southern hospitality.—**Corporate Communications Manager**

The business case method of teaching needs constant updating to remain relevant. This is a challenge that was not always met.—**Assistant Manager of System Services**

The duration of the seminar was just right. Course materials were readily available and the opportunity was there for anyone to read further on topics of special interest.—**Personnel Manager**

The computer-based business simulation during the last two days was very effective in terms of transferring lecture/theory into practical application under near-real conditions. I plan to recommend that similar simulations be used in my company, tailored to our specific type of business.—**General Manager of Operations**

My personal relations with my staff have improved in large part due to the skills I learned at SMU. I can now even manage my boss a little better.—**Technical Manager**

Management of Information Systems laid an egg—too basic. Also, could have used better control of disruptive class elements in some sessions.—**Senior Project Director**

20. Indiana University

School of Business
Bloomington, Indiana 47405

Corporate ranking: 15
Number of programs: 18
1990–1991 enrollment: 510
Annual revenues: $1.5 million

Consumer ranking: 19
Number of programs in 1986: 14
Years in executive education: 40
Change since 1986: 200 percent

Contact: Cam Danielson, director of executive education, 812-855-0229

Indiana Partnership for Management Development

A corporate love story: In the late 1980s, two of the founding members of Babson College's Consortium for Executive Development found themselves with an unusual problem. The program was too popular. While each of the consortium's nine member firms was limited to enrolling six executives a year in the program, N.A. Philips and Eli Lilly were being deluged with 20 or 25 nominations of qualified managers who wanted to attend. So, with Babson's blessing, the companies decided to search for another school that could develop a program with a similar format, a general-management program open only to a select "club" of regularly affiliated companies. Around the same time, Indiana University had been talking with AT&T, another Babson consortium member, about custom-designing a mid-management course focused on globalization. The two ideas met, married, and in 1988, the Indiana Partnership for Management Development was born.

The concept has been so successful that Indiana is moving its entire executive-education philosophy away from the open-enrollment programs the school has offered for 40 years and toward sharing responsibility for course content and design with regular customer companies. "We're just beginning to wake up to the real power of this structure," says Cam Danielson, Indiana's director of executive education. "It's not so much that our content is significantly different from anyone else's general-management programs, but we can place the concepts in a context people can relate to"—their own companies. While open-enrollment programs provide the opportunity for benchmarking performance through contacts with other companies and industries, says Danielson, custom-designed programs allow study materials to be tailored to individual needs. The business school now believes that these partnerships offer the best of both worlds.

In addition to the Indiana Partnership, which includes nine U.S.-based firms, the school is developing an International Partnership for Executive Development in conjunction with INSEAD, the European business school, in which a mix of American multinationals and foreign companies would send executives to a two-week general-management program. One week would be spent in France, the other in Bloomington, with a target start date of October 1993. Indiana is also considering the reconfiguration of its two middle-management open-enrollment courses, The Professional Manager and Managing Business Strategies, into a single program that would be supported in part by a guaranteed number of participants from a "strategic alliance" of a dozen firms. While the allied companies would have input into the curriculum and schedule, other student slots would be reserved, open-enrollment-style, for executives from nonallied companies. Modified versions of the two programs may be offered as early as fall of 1993, but the final curriculum and format will depend largely on the desires of whatever companies join the alliance.

Having that kind of control, while still being able to expose their employees to other corporate cultures, is what attracted firms like AT&T, N.A. Philips, and Eli Lilly to the Indiana Partnership. A steering committee made up of representatives from each of the partner companies, which also include Amoco, Bristol-Myers Squibb, Dow Chemical, DowElanco, Whirlpool, and Xerox, meets two or three times a year with Danielson, Program Director and Finance Professor John Boquist, and other key faculty to discuss changes they'd like to see in the course content, staffing, or schedule. They help shape the makeup of each class by reviewing applications, and if a company has to drop out of the partnership—none has so far—they'll be able to choose a replacement. In return, each firm is committed to sending four to six managers a year, at $9500 per person, to the four-week, split-session program (two weeks in May and two more in August).

Much of the program is centered around team-building, with a variety of exercises involving participants in a variety of combinations. During the first few days, each company's employees get to know one another. With organizations this large, most managers arrive in Bloomington never having met colleagues that may work in farflung locations. They immediately prepare presentations for the rest of the class on the opportunities and challenges their corporation faces. (The same issues are revisited at the end of the program, and participants are often surprised at how their perspectives have changed.) A second set of teams, with four to five people from different companies, is also formed the first week for case-study work.

A third lineup of 8- to 10-member teams takes on the popular Indiana Leadership Challenge Course, an outdoor facility located a few miles off campus on Lake Monroe, where students must work together to perform tasks such as crossing an imaginary river on wooden planks. "I went into this with a cynical attitude, figuring it would just be more 'touchy-feely' stuff, but I was surprised," says Martha A. Laing, executive assistant at AT&T Microelectronics, who attended the program in 1991. "You really get a lot of messages about the value of team-building and ways to do it." It took Laing's group more than 20 tries to cross the river, and when everyone had finally made it to the other side, an over-eager, over-tired team member "fell in" while trying to retrieve the last pieces of equipment, forcing everyone to start at the beginning again. "It was awfully hard to be nice and positive about that one," Laing recalls.

Finally, a fourth set of teams during the second half of the program tackles INTOPIA, a computer simulation of the microchip business that requires each group to formulate a strategy for their "company." Because of the nature of the partnership firms, the program attracts a small number of foreign participants, with a mere 10 percent of each class consisting of foreign nationals working in the United States or in divisions abroad. To help fill in that gap, much of the simulation game centers around international trade and overseas operations. With a vast range of 300 variables available to affect team performance, participants say this is one of the most realistic games around: "There was even a form you had to fill out for everything," jokes Laing.

One drawback to all this team-building is that it tends to obscure the one-on-one give-and-take with professors that executives in other programs often find of great value. To add a more personal touch, the partnership has begun including individual leadership assessments, with subordinates, peers, and superiors evaluating participants' interpersonal skills. Participants also carp about uneven teaching quality and say they'd like to get more cutting-edge information, but they applaud the program's efforts to bolster the staff with outside stars such as Dartmouth Professor Ronald M. Green, a business ethics specialist, and USC's William H. Davidson, who specializes in global economics and has taught at B-schools in France, China, and Japan. Excellent teaching in-house can be found in Program Director Boquist's segments on finance; Professor Michelle Fratianni's insight into the European monetary system (a former staff economist for the Council of Economic Advisers, he has lent his expertise in currency and banking reforms to the governments of Italy and the emerging Baltic states); and Associate Dean George W. Hettenhouse, who helped develop the state of Indiana's strategic economic plan.

You won't hear any complaints about the scenery. Bloomington, a quaint Midwestern town nestled in the rolling hills of Indiana farm country, is dominated by the university's picturesque campus. Partnership students stay at the Indiana Memorial Union, which bills itself as the world's largest student union and houses a full-service hotel. Participants also like the unique meal system the program has set up: Rather than shuffle the class of 50 off to a cafeteria for dinner, the school has contracted with some 20 Bloomington restaurants to provide dining services. Students need only show their badges and sign the check, and the usual evening ritual has classmates gathering in the hotel's hospitality suite to divide up and head off to sample a surprisingly broad range of ethnic cuisines. "Some people might want Thai, some might want burgers—there's even a Tibetan restaurant in town," says Laing.

Participants here tend to be on the young side, in their late 30s; the school has encouraged the companies to send women, who make up about 25 percent of each class. The partners have also made a conscious decision to send mostly managers with technical degrees and functional backgrounds, rather than general managers and those with MBAs. Danielson says he's also seen a trend toward companies' sending teams of managers who work together. Xerox, for example, has been using the program as a training ground for its reorganized, crossfunctional work units. That's fine with Danielson: "We let the group set its own standards." And that's apparently fine with the companies and their employees: Several firms report that they're getting 30 to 40 nominations a year for the course. Perhaps they'll have to begin looking for a third school to take up the slack.

Organizations sending most participants: Dow Chemical; Bristol-Myers Squibb; Amoco

Other Programs of Note

The Professional Manager: Designed to enhance leadership skills in professionals who are increasing their management responsibilities, examining the development of managerial skills, leadership and team-building, organizational behavior, and managing in a global environment. Led by Professor Philip M. Podsakoff, an organizational behavior expert who has conducted research and training at several major corporations. Intended for middle and upper-middle managers with 10 years' experience who have responsibility for developing high-performance work teams. Three weeks; held annually, in spring; 35 students per session; $7800, including tuition, room, board, and supplies; by application.

Managing Business Strategies: Expands the strategic business skills of operational managers through a general management overview including strategic planning, financial management, marketing, manufacturing, the legal and global environments, and the economy. Led by Professor George W. Hettenhouse, who has won awards for his teaching prowess. Intended for new general managers or functional managers with general management responsibilities, with 10 years' experience. Three weeks; held annually, in spring; 35 students per session; $7800, including tuition, room, board, and supplies; by application.

Indiana Business Seminars: A series of nine one- to three-day seminars at the functional and technical level, which can be taken individually or as a group; topics include finance and accounting for nonfinancial managers; financial statement analysis; the multiple dimensions of leadership; total employee involvement programs; total quality management; and creating the high-yield organization. Intended for mid- to upper-level executives of small businesses (under $100 million). Held annually, between March and May; fees, including tuition, breakfast and lunch, and supplies, range from $225 to $885; open enrollment.

Organizations sending most participants: General Motors; Arvin Industries; Kimball International; AT&T; Eli Lilly; IBM

Indiana Consumers Sound Off

The great advantage to the Indiana Partnership is that the course material can be tailored specifically to the companies involved. For example, financial ratios were given for each company as they were covered in class, marketing strategies for each company, etc. **—Facilities and Engineering Director**

A real high point was the fact that many of the financial analyses were done on the member companies so the material could be applied on the job. **—Manager of Product Design**

It has taken four to five years to fine-tune the program to meet each company sponsor's needs. The university has been committed to continuous improvement and reacts to feedback provided during and after the program. The quality of the faculty was excellent and the overall experience very positive. **—Information Systems Manager**

The major weakness of the program was the discrepancy between best and worst teachers. The best were excellent, the worst few quite bad. **—Group Marketing Manager**

Indiana University's use of talented faculty from a number of schools (Ron Green from Dartmouth on ethics, Bill Davidson from USC on global

economics) really was a plus. It supplemented the excellent work by their own professors (such as John Boquist and Michelle Fratianni).—**Executive Assistant**

Overall, I would rate the program a B. Too much time was spent on the simulation model, time that could have been better used in some other way. The Pacific Rim sections were poorly done—in fact, they missed the mark. The program covered the European Community, but nothing on Eastern Europe or the Soviet Union. Finance, marketing, operations, human resources management, and cultural diversity courses were excellent.—**Manager**

The long-term value could be greatly enhanced with a one- to two-year follow-up program that challenges the executive to utilize the skills on the job.—**R&D Director**

I believe the program has merit for business specialists who may be ready to move into general manager positions. I saw the program enlighten and frighten a majority of participants to the breadth and complexity of business issues facing international companies.—**Senior Counselor**

The experience made me realize how much harder I need to work to keep up with this rapidly changing world.—**Manager**

One clear benefit of the program was to remind us that we must focus on meeting our customers' needs in order to succeed. Companies tend to focus on internal needs far too often. Success in the 1990s will depend on meeting customer needs and increasing customer satisfaction. That's an important lesson reinforced by this program.—**Director**

Overall, the program is an important and good stimulus to shift one's perspective from task-specific management to a more general management view. Personally, I would have welcomed more opportunities to "fail" on issues and topics presented because errors committed in a risk-free environment are usually the best prevention against future mistakes in the actual workplace.—**Marketing Manager**

I found the classwork relevant and the instructors fascinating. The mix of functions in the program allowed for realistic discussions of actual business problems from many different viewpoints. Long term, this program will provide a stronger foundation for future growth.—**Manager**

CHAPTER 5

THE RUNNERS-UP

All the fanfare about ratings tends to obscure the fact that there are some 150 schools offering executive education out there. The array of offerings is vast, ranging from one-day, single-topic seminars on subjects as specific as "Using Bar Codes in Warehousing and Distribution," to longer, grand-scheme programs that aim to groom the next generation of top CEOs. There are many variables to consider in choosing a course: subject matter, cost, location, scheduling, time required away from the job. What's right for one person may not be right for another—and what's right for someone this year may not fit his or her needs five years down the road.

With that in mind, BUSINESS WEEK has chosen 10 schools we consider to be the next best in overall quality of executive education, based on our surveys of corporate users of programs and the business school directors of these programs at the leading schools. Some, like the University of Texas at Austin, the University of California at Berkeley, and the University of Southern California, are big names, well-known and well-respected for their MBA programs. Others, like the University of Hawaii and the International Institute for Management Development, may be less familiar but offer outstanding training as well.

BUSINESS WEEK lists this group without an actual ranking.

Emory University

Emory Business School
1602 Mizell Drive
Atlanta, Georgia 30322

Number of programs: 13
1990–1991 enrollment: 555
Annual revenues: $1.0 million

Number of programs in 1986: 3
Years in executive education: 36
Change since 1986: 130 percent

Contact: Gregg Jesse, acting dean for executive education, 404-848-0543

Across the country, universities have been steadily downsizing their flagship general management courses to meet the economic realities of the 1990s. The list of short-ened programs is a long one, from Stanford and MIT to Cornell and Carnegie Mellon. But Emory has gone them all one better: In 1992, it scrapped its Executive Program altogether. The school thought long and hard about cancelling a program with such a proud tradition, dating back to what was originally called the Advanced Manage-ment Program, a 10-week Sea Island retreat for senior executives initiated in 1956. "We ran it in 1991 with only 20 people—believe me, it was a gorgeous program, the participants loved it," says Harry B. Bernhard, former head of exec-ed. "But in 1992, we would have had only 15 enrolled."

It wasn't just a matter of money, says Bernhard. "One of the major values is the other people in the class, and the critical mass just wasn't there. We could have bro-ken even, but I chose not to do that. I didn't think it was right." Instead, Bernhard, and several other of the B-school faculty members Emory has recently lured from such top schools as Harvard, Wharton, Northwestern, and MIT, believe they have seen the handwriting on the wall: Long, expensive, university-based training for top-level managers, with its skew toward individual development, is simply not the way of the future. "The people coming to these programs are not 'senior management' as they were considered after World War II," says Professor Jeffrey A. Sonnenfeld. "Back then, they didn't have MBAs; now most do. They already know the fundamentals of busi-ness, and they can't spare the time off the job."

What companies want now is an immediate payoff, Bernhard says: "They want people back in the office on Monday, starting to apply what they learned." Bernhard's in an excellent position to gauge the corporate pulse. He spent the first 30 years of his career at IBM, where from 1981 to 1985 he directed the firm's management de-velopment programs. Armed with that experience, as well as the lessons he learned during stints as a Harvard fellow and associate dean of exec-ed at the University of Southern California, Bernhard began to consider alternatives to Emory's current line-up soon after landing there in 1990.

Does that mean Emory is giving up on executive education? Not on your life. The B-school, which is on the verge of attaining breakthrough national prominence, has quadrupled its offerings and more than doubled revenues from management pro-grams since 1986. In 1991, exec-ed moved out of the rapidly overcrowding B-school headquarters on Emory's suburban campus and into 12,500 square feet in a high-rise building in Atlanta's thriving Buckhead business district, north of downtown. The site, which is linked electronically to the main campus, boasts two state-of-the-art amphi-theatrical classrooms seating 60 apiece, break-out rooms, faculty offices, and houses the executive MBA program, which is kicking off an evening degree program in the summer of 1992. The location offers conveniences that weren't available on campus, including housing and meals for exec-ed participants, provided by the adjacent J.W. Marriott Hotel; the lively night life of Buckhead; and a nearby MARTA subway station, which can have you at the airport in under half an hour.

All these resources are being directed toward a new vision of executive education, one that will aim squarely at the company-specific market. Emory already offers nine custom courses for such clients as Lockheed, Goldkist, United Parcel Service, Pitney-Bowes, Champion International, and the American Cancer Society. The school is also looking to revamp the Executive Program consortium-style, following the lead of Babson and Indiana, and is seeking a half-dozen regional companies to join Southern Cos. in an agreement to regularly send executives to a general-management course of the companies' own design. As far as open-enrollment courses go, Emory is seeking out novel approaches or topics that have been underexplored by other schools, such as its new investor relations course. The weeklong program looks at law, public relations, marketing, and security analysis as they affect investor relations. Taught by both academics and professionals, classes wind up visiting a brokerage house to see their lessons in action.

Another interesting exec-ed development at Emory is the niche Sonnenfeld has carved out with his Center for Leadership and Career Studies, which runs a school-cum-encounter group exclusively for corporate chieftains called the CEO Leadership Workshop. Twice a year, Sonnenfeld, who arrived at Emory in 1989 after winning acclaim at Harvard for his book on CEO departure styles, invites several dozen chief executives for a two-day meeting of the minds on the challenges that are unique to being a company's ultimate authority. Less than three years old, this is already a high-wattage program, with plenty of star quality. In spring of 1992, a panel including Katharine Graham of the *Washington Post*, Edward B. Rust Jr. of State Farm Insurance, and Harvey A. Weinberg of Hartmarx exchanged views on leading transformation as an insider, while T. Marshall Hahn Jr. of Georgia-Pacific, C.B. Rogers Jr. of Equifax, and Warren L. Batts of Premark discussed how to leverage external experience.

Indeed, while the number of applications for Emory's Executive Program was barely breaking into double digits, as many as 90 CEOs have been showing up for workshops that Sonnenfeld expected to draw 50 participants—attesting to the lack of arenas in which top guns can connect with others who can truly identify with their problems. "The technological jolts, the marketplace shifts, the erosion of regulatory barriers, the demographic changes—the model of their predecessors just doesn't measure up for these people," Sonnenfeld says. "We can't read our old, yellowed notes on outdated cases to them, and a kindly backslap from a mentor won't do it. The best source of data is sitting side by side with other chief executives who are letting their hair down."

What is most amazing is the level of candor achieved during these workshops, which spend much of the first day in a huge roundtable discussion among the entire group of invitees, with Sonnenfeld moderating á la Phil Donahue. One notable session featured former President Jimmy Carter talking about what it was like to deal with defeat in high office and how he has managed to shape a new, well-respected role as a sort of social missionary. "There in the room were the recently dismissed chief executive of Continental Airlines, the departed CEO of People Express, and the former head of Sears," Sonnenfeld recalls. Those who had experienced failure gave a stern warning to any counterparts who were riding a wave of success: Beware the adulation, lest you begin to believe it yourself.

135

On the second day, participants break up into smaller, industry-specific groups such as travel and transportation, retail, financial services, communications and information, and professional services (attorneys, accountants, consultants, and advertising and executive placement executives). Before the workshop, each group votes for a "Legend in Leadership" for the session; those choices, such as Bernard Marcus, chairman of The Home Depot, for retailing, or Kemmons Wilson, founder of Holiday Inn, for travel and transportation, are on hand to join in the discussions. But even in that arena, with proprietary interests looming overhead as fierce competitors sit shoulder to shoulder, bonds are forged—"even among the retailers," Sonnenfeld jokes.

There's only one problem with these workshops: They're free. Attendance is by invitation only, and the CEOs are not charged to participate; so far, the workshops have been quietly and generously funded by United Parcel Service. What Emory has to do now is figure out how to offer its new exec-ed vision—and get paid for it.

Organizations sending most participants: Southern Bell; U.S. Postal Service; AT&T; Eastman Chemical-Kodak; Southern Cos.

Other Programs of Note

Management Development Program: Explores general management skills, including international perspectives, and leadership techniques. Each participant develops an individual strategic plan for his or her current job; a progress check is made by the faculty director after six months. Led by Charles Frame. Intended for mid-level, functional executives with five years' experience who want to broaden their managerial skills. Two weeks; held twice annually, in spring and fall, with each session split by a three-week break; 30–40 students per session; $4200, including tuition, some meals, and supplies; by application.

Financial Management for the Nonfinancial Manager: A crash course in financial management for general managers and executives in nonfinancial functions. Led by Timothy O'Keefe. Designed for functional or general managers with limited training in accounting and finance. Four and a half days; held twice annually, in spring and fall; 20–25 students per session; $2300, including tuition, most meals, and supplies; open enrollment.

Marketing Strategies and Analysis for Competitive Advantage: An intensive, interactive exploration of marketing strategies and competitive analysis, built around the Markstrat computer simulation game. Led by Edgar W. Leonard. Intended for mid-level marketing specialists or general managers with new marketing responsibilities. One week; held twice annually, in summer and winter; 20–25 students per session; $2300, including tuition, supplies, and most meals; open enrollment.

Investor Relations: Issues, Strategies, and Techniques: An overview of investor relations. Led by Greg Waymire. Intended for investor relations specialists, including new arrivals, as well as general managers who want to broaden their skills in this area. One week; held twice a year, in February and October; 40–45 students per session; $2490, including tuition, supplies, and most meals; open enrollment.

Organizations sending most participants: Southern Bell; Marco Equipment Co.; New York Times; Northern Telecom; SunTrust Banks

University of California, Berkeley

Haas School of Business
350 Barrows Hall
Berkeley, California 94720

Number of programs: 16	*Number of programs in 1986*: 5
1990–1991 enrollment: 735	*Years in executive education*: 33
Annual revenues: $2.5 million	*Change since 1986*: 400 percent

Contact: James L. Kelly, director of executive education, 510-642-4735

The Executive Program

In September of 1989, Jim Kelly was busy running his own corporate communications consulting firm when he got a desperate phone call from one of his board members, who also happened to be dean of the Haas School of Business: The director of Haas' Executive Program had been killed in a horseback-riding accident. With 60 executives scheduled to arrive on campus in October for the annual four-week course, the school was in a terrible bind. Would Kelly be willing to help out his alma mater by pinch-hitting as program director? "I became so hooked on it, I just stayed," recalls Kelly, who by the following autumn had left his business to take on the entire executive education department as director.

Berkeley has always been a school full of passion, and it still has an intoxicating effect on a lot of people, Kelly included. Although the "Summer of Love" generation has largely disappeared, along with tie-dyed T-shirts, Volkswagen minibuses, and peace-sign medallions, the 1960s mythology lives on here in the form of health-food restaurants, protest marches, petition drives, and liberal politics. As you might expect, the exec-ed philosophy marches to the beat of a different drummer as well. The Executive Program, for example, included a segment on trade with Asia, a hot topic for the 1990s, as far back as the first session in 1959, and from its inception aimed to offer something apart from the typical management overview. "It was originally decided that there was room for only one MBA-style program on the West Coast," says Kelly. Stanford, Berkeley's friendly rival across the Bay, already owned that franchise. So Haas modeled its flagship course after MIT's rather than Harvard's, emphasizing globalization and innovation instead of functional skills.

Those themes continue to dominate the program's curriculum and format. There is a strong international flavor to all of the program's main segments of study. The first week, which examines the effects of change on global, national, and industry markets, kicks off a series of presentations by managers analyzing either their own industries or, for the 50 percent of each class from outside the United States and Canada, their home country or region. (Foreign participants are split about evenly between Europeans and Asians, and a typical session includes presentations on Japan, the former Soviet Union, the European Community, Central Europe, the Middle East, and Mexico.) The study of corporate strategy formulation includes a comparison of Japanese and American strategies; the segment on leadership and organizational behavior takes a look at different corporate cultures around the world. Assigned study groups that gather each morning to review world news and discuss how it might have an impact on business are rotated several times during the program to maximize diversity. "In a class with 21 different countries represented, discussing economic, political, and business events from the perspectives of the attendees provided a truly global perspective for all of us," a 1989 participant recalls.

The stress on diversity carries over into the program's extensive teaching staff, which reaches out to include experts from other Berkeley departments such as engineering; Slavic, Near Eastern, Asian, and Latin American studies; and demographics. Unfortunately, the breadth of scope has also led to a fuzzy focus, with participants complaining that the program's content is disorganized, that the faculty is poorly coordinated, and that teaching quality ranges from excellent to downright awful. Our survey shows that some students also find the faculty to be generally inaccessible, aloof, and uninvolved outside of class. Nevertheless, a number of top-quality instructors can be found here. Among those singled out by alums are Sara Beckman, a specialist in manufacturing strategy and former program manager for Hewlett-Packard; former Haas Dean Earl F. Cheit, who teaches economics; Russ Winer, a marketing specialist; former Haas Dean Ray Miles, and Charles O'Reilly, who teach the segments on organizational behavior; and Bob Cole, a quality expert who sits on the judging panel for the Baldrige Award. Cole, drawing on his 10 years' experience at Volvo in Sweden and 10 years at Toyota in Japan, leads a popular on-site visit to the Nummi joint venture auto manufacturing plant in Fremont, where students hear union and management representatives speak, tour the facility, then contrast the different automakers' strategies in three major markets. Haas also strives to bring in a meaty lineup of outside speakers, who in the past have included a panel of Mexican executives and the Canadian consul general giving their views on the North American free trade agreement, a *San Francisco Chronicle* editor discussing press relations, and the retired chairmen of Bank of America and Chevron.

Haas' connections with the corporate arena are strong. Kelly, prior to starting his consulting business, had been CEO of a TRW subsidiary; B-school Dean William A. Hasler, who just came on board in 1991, was vice chairman in charge of international operations for KPMG Peat Marwick. In large part as an outgrowth of their own experience in business, the two have committed to a dramatic expansion of the school's executive programs in the coming years. While exec-ed has already gone through rapid growth in the last five years, Haas' outmoded, overcrowded facilities have become a major stumbling block to further increases. The B-school shares its 30-year-old quarters in Barrows Hall with three other Berkeley departments, and the Lipman Room, where the Executive Program holds its classes, is described by participants as "not up to standards" and "woefully inadequate."

However, a new, 200,000-square-foot Haas mini-campus, with four state-of-the-art exec-ed classrooms, a business library, computer labs, and faculty offices, is scheduled to open in 1994. There still won't be any exec-ed housing, with students continuing to stay at the Hotel Durant, a five-minute walk from campus. Except for the twice-weekly dinners at the Faculty Club, managers have to scrounge up their own evening meals most of the time. (Since the price tag has reached $12,500, these inconveniences are provoking more grumbling than ever.) But once you get in the Berkeley groove, you might even look forward to heading out for sprouts and tofu.

Organizations sending most participants: AT&T; Boeing; Digital Equipment; IBM; General Motors

Other Programs of Note

Managing in the Global Economy: Examines the causes and implications for managers of such recent developments as the liberalization of Western economies and the opening of the former Soviet Union and Eastern Europe to the West. Led by exec-ed director James L. Kelly. For mid- and upper-level functional managers and newly appointed general managers. Two weeks; held annually, in spring; 40–50 students per session; $6950, including tuition, room, most meals, and supplies; by application.

Strategic Management of Innovation Program: Held in Tokyo with Nomura School of Advanced Management, this program explores the organizational and strategic conditions necessary for creating corporate innovation. Led by David J. Teece of Berkeley and Ikujiro Nonaka of Nomura, with an internationally drawn faculty. Intended for senior managers with strategic responsibilities. Two weeks; held annually, in late winter; 70 students per session; $8000, including tuition, room, most meals, and supplies; by application.

Management Development—A Comprehensive Approach: Outlines management skills and concepts needed to cope with the downsized, focused business units being created in the 1990s; among the topics discussed are management strategy, innovation and organizational change, organizational politics, conflict management, global economics, and ethics. Led by Ray Miles for mid- and upper-level operating and staff managers and human resources executives. One week; held annually, in July; 40–50 students per session; $3600, including tuition, room, board, and supplies; by application.

Competitive Marketing Strategies for High-Tech Products: Shows managers how to recognize, analyze, and solve marketing problems in businesses with rapidly changing technologies. Led by Russell S. Winer and Rashi Glazer for mid-level marketing managers as well as functional and general managers in technology-based businesses. One week; held twice annually, in March and October; 30–40 students per session; $3600, including tuition, room, board, and supplies; by application.

Organizations sending most participants: Hewlett-Packard; Pacific Telesis; Pacific Gas & Electric; Bank America; Chevron

University of Hawaii

College of Business Administration
Center for Executive Development
2404 Maile Way
CBA B-101
Honolulu, Hawaii 96822

Number of programs: 32   *Number of programs in 1986*: 22
1990–1991 enrollment: 1325   *Years in executive education*: 38
Annual revenues: $2.5 million *Change since 1986*: 108 percent

Contact: Meyer A. Washofsky, assistant dean for management development, 808-956-8135

Advanced Management Program

If your company does business in the Pacific Rim—or would like to—you can't beat the University of Hawaii's Advanced Management Program for its Asian perspective. More than 75 percent of each class of 60 comes from Japan, Korea, Taiwan, Singapore, China, Malaysia, the Philippines, Hong Kong, and Australia, with less than a quarter of the participants from the United States. Of the program's big U.S. users— Boeing, AT&T, Hewlett-Packard, Digital Equipment—most of those send employees who do business with or in Asia as well.

Started in 1954 by Harvard as an offshoot of its AMP, the Hawaii program does give a Pacific twist to its otherwise straightforward general management overview, drawing many of its case studies, computer simulations, and classroom examples from Asian firms. In fact, the university has capitalized on its unique location and culture to develop a wider range of Pacific-oriented executive programs than any other U.S. school. As far as degree programs go, the 10-month Japan Management Program and the 15-month Japan-focused Executive MBA offer an unparalleled immersion in Japanese language, culture, and business practices, culminating in a three-month internship at a major corporation in Tokyo. The International Managers Seminars bring in Asian corporate teams for company- or industry-specific lectures that are presented with simultaneous translation into the team's native language. And research on the region is kept current by the university's Pacific Asia Management Institute.

AMP does draw a few all-American executives each summer—curiously, the state of Kentucky recently enrolled an employee—for its other attractions, not the least of which is the magnificent Hawaiian climate and scenery. Although the heat is definitely on in Honolulu during June and July (the AMP brochure pointedly notes that the classrooms, dining room, and bedrooms are air-conditioned), who wouldn't want to spend five weeks studying in a tropical paradise? Once executives get here, they're not exactly champing at the bit to get back to the office, which may be one reason the program has no plans to shrink to four weeks, as so many others around the country have done, anytime soon. "It's the sabbatical effect—what is the minimum length of time you need to be away for that magic to work?" Meyer A. Washofsky, Hawaii's assistant dean for management development, points out.

While the curriculum's Harvard roots are readily apparent, Hawaii has put its own stamp on the program, which it has run independently since the mid-1970s.

Washofsky, a former Air Force pilot who's spent his entire academic career at Hawaii, says that in the 10 years he has directed the program, he's seen a de-emphasis on case study in favor of more interactive forms of teaching, particularly those involving video and computers. You still get a solid grounding in basic management concepts. There's even an optional three-day finance segment before the program starts, for anyone who feels shaky in that area, and up to 60 percent of the participants sign up, particularly Asians who want to become more familiar with American terminology. The course then flows "from micro to macro," Washofsky says, examining group dynamics, marketing, and information technology before moving on to corporate culture, global economics, planning and strategy, and multinational operations.

The Pacific influence permeates every topic. For example, one of two major negotiation exercises, in which teams use a computer simulation as the springboard for face-to-face business dealings, is based on the Tylenol contamination scare, but is set at a fictitious Taiwanese company. "It's amazing to watch the different ethnic groups deal with this," says Washofsky. When the simulated press begins clamoring for information, "the Taiwanese just look at one another and say, 'But we don't talk to the press!'"

While most participants enthusiastically embrace the opportunity to learn firsthand how managers from other countries operate, it can take a while to get everyone on the same wavelength. While most all the students consider themselves senior or upper-middle managers from large companies, "large" is a relative term, notes Washofsky: A firm with 20,000 employees would be near the top of the list in Taiwan, while in the United States, you'd need 120,000 workers to qualify. The final week's Spouse Program points up some of the marked differences in corporate culture between West and East. Nearly 100 percent of the husbands and wives of Western participants attend, but very few Asian spouses do so. The gulf is still a large one. The program enrolled its first Japanese businesswoman last year; at the same time, a woman manager from Australia arrived with her infant and nanny in tow.

The program's faculty lineup is ever-shifting, so it's sometimes hard to predict exactly who will be up in front of the classroom. In fact, there are two staffs appearing in alternating years. That is, the group teaching during the summer of 1992 will be back in 1994, with a few changing faces; a different group, the one that taught in 1991, is slated for 1993. Hawaii's own staff is small—only two or three professors are free to teach at each AMP session—but the school has gathered a notable group of supplementary visiting instructors. Among those who have been involved with the program in recent years are Wayne Cascio, a management controls specialist from the University of Colorado; Dennis Logue, a finance professor from Dartmouth's Amos Tuck School who has consulted for Citibank, Atlantic Richfield, Price Waterhouse, and the U.S. Department of Labor; MIT's Ed Schein, whose *Organizational Psychology* textbook has been widely used for more than 20 years; and Donald Sexton, a marketing specialist from Columbia who brings a vast consulting experience with such firms as Pfizer, General Electric, AT&T, DuPont, General Foods, IBM, Johnson & Johnson, and Kodak. The 1993 staff will include faculty from INSEAD, New York University, the University of Washington, Columbia, Dartmouth, Colorado, and MIT.

For 26 years, AMP has been held in its entirety at the Ilikai Hotel, which is outfitted with breakout rooms and computer labs. The $11,700 tuition fee, which includes meals, supplies, and accommodations, will net you only a double room; you have to pony up an extra $2350 for a single, which 75 percent of students do. Extracurricular activities tend to be low-key, with local companies sponsoring dinners and

141

picnics, and local participants, who make up 10 to 15 percent of each class, inviting classmates to their homes. Most of the non-Hawaiians take advantage of the long weekend break after the third week to go island-hopping. But you won't be lacking for entertainment. All you have to do is walk outside and bask in the sunshine, beaches, and dramatic topography that surround you.

Organizations sending most participants: Boeing Aerospace; Digital Equipment; Hewlett-Packard; Ssangyong Group; Westpac Banking

Other Programs of Note

Hawaii Management Program: A general management overview, with emphasis on increasing functional competence in accounting and finance, marketing, human resources management, planning and strategy, information systems management, organizational structure, and leadership skills. Led by Steve Dawson. Intended for middle managers. Four months; held annually, on Tuesday evenings and Wednesdays of alternate weeks between August and December; 35 students per session; $2500, including tuition, some meals, supplies, and parking; open enrollment.

Self-Managing Work Teams: Outlines how to organize small teams of employees from within a function or department who meet regularly to discuss proposals for improvements to corporate quality, productivity, and service. Led by consultant Frank Anbari. Intended for upper and middle managers with responsibilities for quality improvement. Two days; held annually, in February; 15–25 students per session; $795, including tuition and supplies (group discount available); open enrollment.

Deming Procedures for the Public Sector: Examines ways to apply W. Edward Deming's quality improvement principles to public-sector services and administrative operations. Led by consultant Hal Bergan. Intended for government officials and managers in public-sector organizations, including hospitals, courts, the military, police and fire departments, post offices, and schools. Two days; held annually, in May; 15–25 students per session; $795, including tuition and supplies (group discount available); open enrollment.

Innovative Compensation Packages: Explores new approaches to compensation, including gainsharing, and how to choose the most effective structure to motivate your employees. Intended for human resources, personnel, quality assurance, and compensation executives, as well as plant managers and managers of operations, manufacturing, or industrial relations. Two days; held annually, in November; 15–25 students per session; $795, including tuition and supplies (group discount available); open enrollment.

Organizations sending most participants: Bank of Hawaii; Hawaiian Dredging & Construction; Outrigger Hotels; Hawaiian Electric Co.; U.S. Navy

University of Illinois at Urbana-Champaign

College of Commerce and Business Administration
Executive Development Center
205 David Kinley Hall
1407 West Gregory Drive
Urbana, Illinois 61801

Number of programs: 29   *Number of programs in 1986*: 18
1990–1991 enrollment: 1390   *Years in executive education*: 25
Annual revenues: $2.1 million   *Change since 1986*: 40 percent

Contact: Fredric L. Barbour II, director, 217-333-3885

Executive Development Program

You might not expect a school with more than 36,000 students to be well-versed in delivering the personal touch, but the University of Illinois' Executive Development Program will surprise you. Its loyal core of six faculty members has been together for seven years, and every May and June they put their lives on hold for four weeks so they can share lunches, dinners, coffee breaks, receptions, guest lectures, and even softball games with the program's 30 to 35 participants. If they got any closer, they'd be sharing the students' showers and beds.

The framework of the program, which dates back to 1957, is a straightforward overview, with the requisite case studies, lectures, and small-group discussions, of general management skills for newly appointed senior and fast-rising upper-middle managers: strategic management, financial management, management control and information systems, marketing, human resources management, and the external environment. But this is not just a "Business Through the Ages" retrospective. The second half of the course is shaped around the examination of cutting-edge topics, with corporate executives and consultants sharing their first-hand knowledge and experience with the class. A day-long look at the quality movement might be capped by a roundtable talk with the director of General Motors' corporate quality program; a bank chairman might be invited to shed light on growth and reorganization in the banking industry. "We spend the first few days giving everyone a common vocabulary, then we quickly move on to tomorrow's issues," says Mary Porter, assistant director of the B-school's Executive Development Center. "Historical perspective is simply no longer relevant to today's executives."

Hot topics in recent sessions have included corporate governance, the Japanese perspective, and large-scale startups, but the subjects change annually based on world events and the personality of each particular class. This is where the faculty's close involvement really pays off: They may even fiddle with the lineup midway through a session if it becomes apparent that the group has some special needs or concerns, as in 1991, when an impromptu segment on downsizing was added. The core teaching staff are all full professors at Illinois: James A. Gentry, the program's faculty chairman, specializes in finance; other segments are handled by Fred M. Gottheil, external environment, whose expertise on the oil industry in the Middle East was tapped by the

143

Carter administration; Peter Holzer, management control and accounting, whose vast international teaching experience has ranged from France and Austria to China, Thailand, and Tunisia; Howard Thomas, strategic management and policy, author of the widely used book *Decision Theory and the Manager*; David Whetten, human resources management, who has consulted with private corporations and Illinois state agencies in his specialty of managing rapid growth and retrenchment in large social systems; and Frederick W. Winter, marketing, who has consulted for General Electric, McDonnell Douglas, GTE, FMC, and Bell Helmets, among other firms.

Despite the emphasis on currency in the curriculum, you won't find a lot of trendy teaching techniques here—no computer simulation games, "no tree-climbing or tugs of war," laughs center director Fredric L. Barbour II. But there has been a growing stress on globalization. Three of the core faculty members are foreign-born and -educated, and about a third of each class is from outside the United States, automatically bringing an international perspective to discussions. (There's an optional four-week English language review given before the program for any non-American who feels the need to brush up on those skills.) EDP's foreign following has been boosted by several other distinguished programs for overseas students, including the one-year MBA-style Program for International Managers and its one-semester version, the Specialized Program for International Managers, and the one-year PEATA-Illinois Business Program, exclusively for Japanese middle managers.

Illinois has had less luck lately with longer-term domestically focused programs. A planned general management course for smaller-company executives never got off the ground. Barbour hopes to revive it in a consortium-style format. Nor did a novel idea to train Western European managers to compete in the U.S. market by matching them up with American counterparts who want to form strategic alliances overseas. With the flood of business opportunities now available in Eastern Europe and the former Soviet Union, Barbour says he'd like to turn the tables and play matchmaker for U.S. managers who'd like to plunge into the overseas market, aligning them with European counterparts. (The rest of the exec-ed lineup here consists of one- to three-day single-topic seminars, mostly held off campus in Chicago, Toronto, and New York.)

In EDP, interaction among participants is encouraged through assigned case-study discussion groups, which meet each morning to review the day's material and are rotated every few days for maximum diversity, and "living groups," Illinois' version of the Harvard can group. All managers are housed in single rooms on two floors in the University Inn, an independently run hotel on the edge of campus, and a conference room for evening bull sessions is set aside for each living group of six to eight students, which stays together throughout the month.

Each bedroom is equipped with a kitchenette, which participants find to be a real plus late at night, on weekends, and during the three-day break midway through the program. Lunches are set aside for organized socializing: a buffet at the football stadium training facility, with a behind-the-scenes look at the home of the Fightin' Illini; a tour and reception at the university's World Heritage Museum, with its extensive collection of ancient art, or the stunning Krannert Center for the Performing Arts; or an initiation into the art of the tea ceremony at Japan House, one of the university's ethnic research centers. Also included in EDP's $10,600 tuition, which is a bargain rate compared with other programs of similar scope, are a spouse program during the last three days of the course and free run of the university's extensive athletic facilities—after all, this is the Big 10.

It's a good idea to take advantage of all the extracurricular offerings on campus, because Urbana and neighboring Champaign don't offer much excitement, and it's a good two-hour drive north through farm country to Chicago. Should you find yourself with time on your hands, however, there's one sure bet for company—call up one of your professors. They're just waiting to hear from you.

Organizations sending most participants: Nestle; Ciba-Geigy; Hoechst; ABB; IBM

Other Programs of Note

Program for International Managers: Familiarizes international managers with American and international business practices, both through classroom study; field trips to industrial, commercial, and financial institutions around the country; and seminars with American corporate executives. Participants can design their own programs of study, including an optional intensive eight-week English language course if desired. Led by Kendreth Rowland. Designed for international middle managers. One year; held annually, beginning in June; 15–25 students per session; $18,200, including tuition, summer room and board, supplies, and activities; by application.

Specialized Program for International Managers: A one-semester version of the Program for International Managers. Four months; held twice a year, in spring and fall; 15–25 students per session; $5900, including tuition and supplies; by application.

PEATA-Illinois Business Program: A joint effort with the Pacific Economy and Technology Association of Tokyo, this program is designed to familiarize Japanese managers with American management concepts and culture, provide contact with American executives, and ensure adequate English skills for functioning in the international business community. Classroom study is supplemented by field trips to U.S. industrial, commercial, and financial institutions, and seminars with American corporate executives. Intended for Japanese middle managers. One year; held annually, beginning in June; 20 students per session; $18,200, including tuition, room, board, and supplies; by application.

Organizations sending most participants: Nestle; Ciba-Geigy; Hoechst; ABB; IBM

International Institute for Management Development

23 Chemin de Bellerive
P.O. Box 915
CH-1001 Lausanne, Switzerland

Number of programs: 40   *Number of programs in 1986*: 0
1991–1992 enrollment: 2500   *Years in executive education*: 2
Annual revenue: $18 million   *Change since 1986*: not applicable

Contact: Paul Adams, director of marketing, 41-21-618-01-11

Program for Executive Development

Ask any European executive to name the top management schools, and it's a sure bet that IMD will be on the list. Ask an American executive what IMD is, however, and you'll be told the initials stand for anything from a new designer drug to a secret government agency instead of a purveyor of executive education.

Although still relatively little known in the United States, the International Institute for Management Development is beginning to gain a following on this side of the Atlantic, especially among American firms that do a significant amount of their business in Europe. IMD was created in 1990 by the merger of two long-standing exec-ed institutes—IMI, a Geneva school founded in 1946 by Alcan Aluminum, and IMEDE, which was set up in 1957 by Nestlé with the support of the Harvard Business School. (IMEDE's newly expanded campus, on the shores of picturesque Lake Geneva in the French-flavored city of Lausanne, is where IMD now resides.)

This history of corporate involvement in the school continues today through IMD's unique partnership program with 128 companies from more than two dozen countries around the world. In contrast with many American B-schools, which guard their independence jealously, these sponsors, which include such powerhouse firms as ABB, AT&T, Digital Equipment Corp., Nestlé, Ciba-Geigy, Citicorp, Dentsu, Credit Suisse, Baxter Health Care, Philips, and IBM Europe, play a critical role in IMD's operation. "Senior executives from these companies devote a lot of time to helping us define programs and telling us about their needs," says Paul Adams, IMD's director of marketing. For example, a recent decision to double the enrollment of the school's full-time, 12-month MBA program, was prompted by sponsors.

In fact, the partnership plays a role in almost every aspect of IMD. The school's research projects are designed to address sponsoring companies' needs, are funded by industry, and are conducted in conjunction with sponsors' line managers. Senior executives from both sponsoring firms and others have formed a network that holds seminars of special interest to chief financial officers, personnel directors, and marketing chiefs, as well as an annual roundtable for CEOs, under the guidance of IMD faculty members. Partnership firms commission some 20 company-specific programs a year. They also sponsor company employees in IMD's open-enrollment programs who provide much of the feedback that is used to re-evaluate program content and design.

Another distinction you'll find at IMD is its international makeup. While many U.S. schools are rushing to include foreign content and encourage foreign participation in their programs, IMD, partly by virtue of its location, comes by globalization

146

naturally. The 2500 managers who attend IMD's programs each year are drawn from some 90 countries; a U.S. participant in the flagship Program for Executive Development shouldn't be surprised to find that he or she is the only American among 50 or 60 students from more than 20 countries, ranging from Venezuela and Germany to Kenya and Malaysia. The school's 41 professors are of 16 different nationalities (12 are from the United States and Canada). However, the international aspect goes deeper than that, notes Adams: "This isn't just a matter of employing faculty members from several countries; it's a commitment to integrate business practices and systems other than the Anglo-Saxon model. (The only drawback, particularly for Americans, may be the language barrier: While classes are conducted in English, only about one in five managers count English as their native tongue.)

The Program for Executive Development is no exception to the school's international thrust. Fully half the program—which targets high-potential mid-level, mid-career managers of large corporations, senior executives of smaller companies that aim to expand, or entrepreneurs who want to launch new businesses—is devoted to "global thinking for a global market." But PED's ambitious curriculum includes much more, which is one reason the course is 10 weeks long, broken into two 5-week modules. (Managers may opt to take the halves consecutively, as about one-third do, or with a 6- or 12-month break in between; each module is offered twice a year, beginning in January or August.) Atttending this program requires a commitment of time—and money, with tuition topping $21,000 by 1993, not including lodging, many meals, and travel expenses—on the part of both the participant and his or her employer.

The first five-week module is an overview of the basic management functions and how they work together—what IMD calls "system thinking for the general manager." Among the topics examined are managing others (communication, motivation, and team-building) and yourself (how to handle learning, change, and stress); marketing; accounting and finance; operations management; and product development. A week-long computer simulation dubbed IRIS—Integrating Reality into Strategy—caps the first half of the course, pulling together the various functions to show how they interact and how strategy design must reflect this interaction. Other topics touched on in the first module include world competition, the opportunities arising in Central and Eastern Europe, and environmental management. Case studies and other source materials are first read individually, then discussed in assigned study groups, and then dissected in class by the professor.

During the second five weeks, global issues are at the forefront. First, managers are taught skills for dealing with what IMD calls "the turnaround business world": industry analysis, understanding geopolitics and current developments in the economic environment, and customer relations. Then participants learn how to assess their own companies' capabilities for coping with the new demands on corporate culture, structure, and systems; this includes an examination of current thinking in manufacturing, finance, and technology management. Finally, the program delves into how management practices differ in different environments, how managing the multinational corporation requires special techniques, and what strategies are most likely to succeed. One- and two-day workshops on special issues, such as service quality or entrepreneurship, are held on an elective basis; participants also make a field visit to a corporation and meet with visiting executives on campus to hear their real-world insights.

A program of this scope requires a large teaching staff, and the core faculty numbers more than a dozen. A new program director, Ahmet Aykac, a Turkish expert on economics and quantitative methods, takes over in August of 1992. A look at the backgrounds of Aykac's staff shows just how international the faculty is: Derek F. Abell, a Brit, specializes in general management and corporate strategy; Ralf Boscheck, a German formerly with Monitor Co., teaches business policy; Yury Boshyk, a Canadian, is an expert in international politics and business; Terry L. Campbell, an American with experience as a manager in retailing and manufacturing, specializes in control and finance.

Classes are held on IMD's campus, which recently underwent a major renovation and expansion to add conference and group study rooms, a library, a restaurant, and a cafeteria. Each study group is assigned a meeting room equipped with a computer. Unfortunately, the construction did not include any on-campus residences, so participants continue to stay at nearby hotels. Although you're on your own as far as lodging and most meals go, the program hosts a number of social events to help participants get to know one another. By the time you get back home, you'll have a truly international experience under your belt, and you'll be able to share one of exec-ed's best-kept secrets—at least in the United States.

Organizations sending most participants: Nestlé; Ciba-Geigy; Hoechst; ABB; IBM

Other Programs of Note

Managing Corporate Resources: Aims to improve skills in allocating resources and using them efficiently, covering such topics as analyzing the competition, matching operations to strategy, mobilizing business units, and motivating staff. Led by James C. Ellert. Intended for newly appointed general managers with 20 years' experience. Four weeks; held twice annually, in spring and late summer; 55 students per session; $14,000, including tuition, lunch, and supplies; by application.

Seminar for Senior Executives: Emphasizes the making and implementing of strategic decisions, including defining the organization's vision, leading the staff to action, prospecting the changing business environment, sharpening the firm's competitive edge, and leveraging technology. Led by Kurt Schar. Intended for experienced general managers. Two and a half weeks; held twice annually, in late spring and fall; 45 students per session; $14,000, including tuition, lunch, and supplies; by application.

International Program for Senior Executives: Explores the changing role of the corporation in society from a simple creator of wealth to a steward of natural resources. Led by Ahmet Aykac. Intended for very senior executives with corporate strategic responsibilities. One week; held three times a year, in June, August, and October; 25 students per session; $6000, including tuition, lunch, and supplies; by application.

Mobilizing People: Examines ways to motivate individuals, teams, and organizations. Participants analyze their own leadership styles through feedback questionnaires from colleagues; strengthen team-building skills through outdoor exercises; then put these insights into an organizational context through case study and group discussion. Led by Christopher Parker. Intended for general managers and functional managers with line or staff responsibilities. Two weeks; held twice annually, in spring and fall; 40 students per session; $8300, including tuition, lunch, and supplies; by application.

Organizations sending most participants: Nestlé; Ciba-Geigy; Hoechst; ABB; IBM

London Business School

Centre for Management Development
Regent's Park
Sussex Place
London NW1 4SA, England

Number of programs: 44   *Number of programs in 1986*: 11
1990–1991 enrollment: 3000   *Years in executive education*: 26
Annual revenues: $11.1 million *Change since 1986*: 327 percent

Contact: Jerome Foster, dean for executive education, or Jean-Michel Beeching, marketing director, executive education, 44-071-262-5050

Senior Executive Programme

Jerome Foster, London Business School's dean for executive education, is a model of British efficiency. Tracked down by a reporter while doing business in Hong Kong, Foster can dig up a personal computer, compile a long list of detailed information about his school's programs while halfway around the world from his office, and fax back a response in under 12 hours. You get the feeling that he'd be more than willing to fax you a spot of tea while you're waiting, if only he could.

That's exactly the kind of efficiency you'll find imbued throughout LBS's Senior Executive Programme. The course has been around since 1966, when the independent school for graduate business studies was founded, and although it has gradually been compressed from eight weeks to four during its lifetime, it remains strongly wedded to its original goal of providing a solid grounding in general management skills to senior managers whose experience has been limited to a single function. As with the school's 20 other open-enrollment courses and custom programs for some two dozen firms, the byword here is substance, not flash.

But that doesn't mean you'll find yourself stuck in a 1960s corporate time warp, either. While U.S. schools are scrambling to globalize their programs, LBS, by virtue of its location and participants, has always provided a truly international perspective on business. Only 3 percent of each class of 35 to 40 is American; about one-third is British, one-third from continental Europe, and one-third from the rest of the world, including Asia, Africa, South and North America. The school has made a major investment in designing international cases and other course materials. And Foster himself brings a uniquely global background to his role as director, having previously headed executive programs at France's INSEAD, Carnegie Mellon, and Oxford's Templeton College before landing at LBS in 1990. "What we take for granted in terms of global perspective, U.S. schools would regard as huge progress in that dimension," Foster notes.

The curriculum is crisply divided into four major themes: strategy formulation and implementation, particularly global strategy and the effect of technology; the changing international business environment, including the role of government and society and the success of Japan; financial management, including defining profitability, measuring risk, and determining shareholder value; and managing change through leadership, with its focus on organizational behavior. Teaching techniques

149

cover the range of lecture-discussions, case studies, computer simulation games, and videotaped role-playing exercises; small study groups of six or seven are rotated weekly to allow classmates to get to know one another.

The program is coherent and well-integrated, thanks in part to a core faculty that has remained pretty much intact for several years now. Some tinkering with the mix may occur after Tony Eccles, a strategic management specialist who spent 10 years as a production manager at Unilever, takes over as program director in autumn of 1992. (The course is offered twice a year, in September and February.) In particular, the program may begin to embrace a couple of the more innovative aspects of LBS's Accelerated Development Program, including a subordinates' survey as well as counseling sessions and project work on individual managerial problems brought in from the workplace. "We're moving away from prepackaged theory and toward what I call 'just-in-time learning,' where a manager facing a problem can reach out for help to find a solution," says Foster. SEP has already begun six-month follow-up interviews to learn what managers have been able to apply from the program directly to their jobs and what gaps still exist in their performance abilities.

Eccles is joined on the core faculty by a well-traveled group of professors with substantial experience in business. Walter Reid, a previous director of SEP, is a chartered accountant who handles the finance segments; Paul Marsh, who had a career in corporate finance before joining LBS, specializes in stock market behavior and capital investment decisions; and John M. Stopford, a director of the Swiss Intermatrix Group and board adviser to Vickers PLC, teaches segments in international business. John W. Hunt, an organizational behavior specialist, is taking over the OB spot vacated by former program director Stuart R. Timperley. In addition, several other LBS professors teach classes in the program but are not part of the core faculty, and one or two external speakers appear during each session.

LBS is located on London's northern end at the edge of Regent's Park, the beautifully landscaped acreage that is home to the London Zoo. Classes are held in the school's state-of-the-art exec-ed classroom and discussion rooms, built in 1987, and managers stay in single rooms in the comfortable on-campus executive residence. While there's not a wealth of spare time available during the course, what with evening study sessions and a relatively heavy load of reading, the glory of London is just a short walk or tube ride away—everything from the lofty Royal Academy of Music to the less highbrow fun of Madame Tussaud's wax museum.

Meals are included in the program fee of about $6400 (it may vary with the exchange rate); while most lunches and some dinners are taken at LBS's campus restaurant, the class will often head off for an evening meal at some establishment with notable history or cuisine. Other extracurricular events include a reception at the home of Principal George S. Bain (LBS's dean), a distinguished speaker night in which participants may be joined by a superior or colleague from the office, early morning jogs through Regent's Park, and an optional wellness program. And one more thing: At 3:30 each afternoon, the class breaks for—what else?—tea.

Organizations sending most participants: ABB; British Telecom; British Petroleum; ICI; Shell

Other Programs of Note

Accelerated Development Programme: A mini-MBA-style overview, covering finance and accounting, marketing, operations, organizational analysis, personal computing, as well as leadership and team-building skills, strategic management skills, and international business. Special features include a weekend of outdoor team exercises, an optional health and fitness program, and an individual subordinate survey on interpersonal skills with a six-month follow-up to gauge progress. Led by Assistant Professor Gareth Jones. Intended for high-potential young managers with at least five years' experience and outstanding achievement records in their specialties. Four weeks; held three times a year, beginning in March, June, and November; 30–42 students per session; $6400, including tuition, room, board, and supplies; by application.

Competing Globally: The View from Japan: Held entirely in Japan, this program begins with a two-day mountain retreat for brainstorming on the topic of Japanese business success and its implication for competing globally. The group then tours companies in Tokyo, Osaka, Kyushu, Kyoto, Nagoya, and other cities, where participants meet with managers at all levels, engineers, and government officials. The class then breaks up into smaller, special-interest groups for industry- or function-specific visits; the course ends with a one-day debriefing. Led by Associate Professor Peter Williamson. Intended for senior managers of international companies that compete with or are considering competition with Japanese firms, companies that want to improve communications with Japanese subsidiaries, executives about to be posted in Japan, and corporate executives with responsibility for Japanese business. Two weeks; held annually, in fall; 15–20 students per session; $5550, including tuition, room, most meals, transportation within Japan, and supplies; by application.

Interpersonal Skills for Senior Managers: Explores practical solutions to management leadership problems involving the employment process (recruitment, motivation, goal-setting, dismissal); the control process (designing and maintaining structures, fact-finding, decision making; and interaction (teamwork, organizational behavior, staff assessment, managing diversity). Exercises before and after the program help participants develop personal action plans, and much of the course time is spent discussing how the participants' real-life situations apply to what is being learned. Led by Professor John Hunt. Intended for top management, including chairpersons, unit directors, general managers, or top functional managers. One week; held three times annually, in January, April, and December; 18 students per session; $1900, including tuition, room, board, and supplies; by application.

Organizations sending most participants: N.M. Rothschild; Cathay Pacific; British Telecom; Credit Suisse; Brent Chemicals

University of Pittsburgh

Joseph M. Katz Graduate School of Business
301 Mervis Hall
Pittsburgh, Pennsylvania 15260

Number of programs: 40
1990–1991 enrollment: 1226
Annual revenues: $1.8 million

Number of programs in 1986: 61
Years in executive education: 43
Change since 1986: 50 percent

Contact: Richard Headley, director, Center for Executive Education, 412-648-1610

Management Program for Executives

A Brazilian executive would like to attend a solid general-management program, but he thinks his English is a bit shaky—especially if he'll have to speak in front of American classmates. A Saudi banker is eager to expand his business skills but is intimidated by the vast cultural differences between his country and the United States, where he'll have to spend an entire month. These might be good enough reasons to stay away from American B-schools, but the University of Pittsburgh's Joseph M. Katz Graduate School of Business has answers to just such dilemmas.

Before every session of its four-week Management Program for Executives, which is held each spring and fall, Katz offers an intensive one- to four-week cram course in English and American customs to any foreign manager who wants to refine his or her language skills or become more familiar with U.S. culture before plunging into exec-ed. Each class has a couple of students who have taken advantage of the special training, just one of the ways Katz encourages foreign participation in the program by making students from abroad feel more at home. The school also arranges, through the Pittsburgh Council for International Visitors, for foreign students to visit with local families from their native countries and to meet local executives in positions and industries similar to their own. The effort is paying off: More than 50 percent of each MPE class is now from outside the United States. The roll reads like a little United Nations, taking in students from such farflung locations as the Bahamas, Guam, Tanzania, Australia, Peru, Sweden, and Pakistan.

Globalizing its flagship program is one of the steps Katz has taken in its recent quest to become as customer-responsive as it teaches its students to be. Although Katz was a pioneer in exec-ed—MPE, which dates back to 1949, was one of the country's first general management programs, following closely on the heels of Harvard and MIT—the school's audience has remained largely regional. Besides MPE, Katz's two well-regarded executive MBA programs and a one-week course for executives from expanding companies, the exec-ed portfolio has focused on one- to three-day single-topic workshops and seminars. But Katz is working hard to raise its profile. In March 1992, the school co-sponsored, with AT&T, the twentieth annual University Consortium for Executive Education, which gathered representatives from dozens of schools and companies to discuss how total quality concepts might be applied to exec-ed. A Corporate Advisory Council, made up of more than a dozen human resources and management development officials from firms like Xerox, PPG Industries, Frito-Lay, and Rubbermaid, as well as MPE alums, meets twice a year to offer advice on the program's direction.

152

The school is making a concerted effort to keep costs down, billing its offerings as "investments in executive development that make economic sense." MPE was reduced from five weeks to four after companies complained that they were having difficulty letting people go for so long under the current economy. Indeed, the program's $12,000 price tag is lower than the $13,000 to $15,000 tab for four-week programs charged by most private universities, including cross-town competitor Carnegie Mellon. Katz has also begun asking MPE's 30 to 35 participants per session to evaluate program content and faculty both upon completion of the course and six months down the road, when the value of some material may become more apparent. "The administrator of the program solicited an extensive feedback survey, and they evidently will act on it," one participant from 1991 notes. "I got a letter after the course concluded detailing several fundamental changes planned as a result."

As far as the curriculum goes, those changes include even more emphasis on globalization, a more sophisticated look at marketing, and the addition of a segment on managing technological change, says Richard A. Headley, who became director of the Center for Executive Education in 1990. Complaints about a lack of coordination among professors and uneven teaching quality have prompted a streamlining of the faculty into a smaller, more cohesive core, led by Dr. Edward Sussna, Headley's predecessor as director of the exec-ed center. Count among the teaching highlights Jack Baker's human resources and leadership segments, Anil Makhija's finance sessions, and Andrew Blair's insights on international business. (Blair heads the university's Center for International Business Education, which helped set up the first MBA program to be offered in newly capitalist Czechoslovakia.) An all-star slate of guest speakers, who in the past have included the CEO of Bell Atlantic, the president of BP America, the chairman of PPG Industries, the head of the United Steel Workers, and the retired chairman of United Parcel Service, will continue to round out the lineup.

While students will continue to get an overview of the usual general management basics, the stress here is on international business, corporate strategy, and leadership skills. "We want to build leaders who can operate globally and think strategically," says Headley. "We try to focus on both individual competencies and organizational competencies." Project work figures heavily into this scheme. Study teams, for example, not only bone up on the next day's cases, but also analyze their own development and performance as the weeks pass, with oral and written reports delivered to the class at the end-of-session celebration that culminates with a two-day Partners Program. The final week's management simulation brings all the disciplines together as competing teams formulate business strategy and make marketing, R&D, finance, production, and personnel decisions. On the personal side, managers fill out diagnostic questionnaires to assess their leadership skills, as well as how their lifestyle is affecting their health; one-on-one counseling with a psychologist is available for those who desire it.

Classes are held at the conference center in Mervis Hall, the B-school's sleek, glass-and-steel headquarters. Since Katz is within a stone's throw of city center, it's a short bus trip over to class from the Hyatt Regency, where participants are housed. The camaraderie level is low-key. Evenings center around team discussions in the study rooms set aside at the hotel, or solitary reading. During down time, you can tour the spiffed-up Steel City, take a riverboat ride, or take in a Pirates or Steelers game—if you can get tickets.

Organizations sending most participants: Conoco; Boeing; AT&T; Digital Equipment; Holderbank

Other Programs of Note

Executive Program for Expanding Companies: Known as EXPEX, this program is designed to broaden the leadership skills of top executives in small companies, with special emphasis on people management, strategy, finance, marketing, and total quality management. Led by Associate Dean Roger S. Ahlbrandt for key decision makers in firms with 20 to 500 employees; management teams are encouraged to attend together. One week; held annually, in January; 20 students per session; $2400, including tuition, supplies, some meals, and parking (discounts available for group enrollment); by application.

Benchmarking: A how-to course that brings one of the latest management buzzwords to life. Covers how to plan, implement, and gather data for benchmarking and use the data to trigger marketing and strategic plans. Led by the New York-based Quality Alert Institute for general managers as well as marketing, sales, and advertising managers. Two days; held twice a year, in spring and fall; 30 students per session; $825, including tuition and supplies; open enrollment.

How to Improve Your Negotiating Skills: How to sharpen your skills at negotiating and avoid common pitfalls. Led by management consultant Paul Clipp for executives, managers, and supervisors. Two days; held annually, in spring and fall; 30 students per session; $795, including tuition and supplies; open enrollment.

Target Marketing: Examines how to make the transition from mass marketing to niche marketing, with a step-by-step blueprint for planning, researching, and achieving market segmentation. Led by consultants Marvin Nesbit and Art Weinstein for marketing and sales managers as well as general managers with marketing responsibilities. Three days; held annually, in February; 30 students per session; $995, including tuition and supplies; open enrollment.

Organizations sending most participants: Conoco; Boeing; AT&T; Digital Equipment; Holderbank

University of Southern California

School of Business Administration
Hoffman Hall 800
Los Angeles, California 90089-1421

Number of programs: 38
1990–1991 enrollment: 1567
Annual revenues: $2.8 million

Number of programs in 1985: 25
Years in executive education: 39
Change since 1985: 65 percent

Contact: Karen Arden, executive director of executive education, 213-740-8990

The USC Executive Program

Trying to find your way through the maze of executive programs offered by the University of Southern California's School of Business Administration is like trying to navigate the Los Angeles freeways: It's best done with a map. Besides the courses offered by the Office of Executive Education, most of the school's eight independent research centers, which are all run by B-school faculty members, hold at least a symposium or two each year. USC has even put together a "map" to help prospective students figure out where to find the appropriate program—a 30-page booklet outlining the differences between the Center for Effective Organizations and the Leadership Institute, the SEC and Financial Reporting Institute and the Center for Crisis Management. Likewise, the sprawling B-school faculty of some 170 is listed in a separate 127-page guide that cross-references each instructor by specialty and department.

The sheer magnitude of available resources is a major asset of the USC Executive Program. Like so many other general management courses for senior executives, this one was downsized in 1992 from four weeks to three; previously run twice annually, either consecutively or as a split session, it is now being offered just once a year, in late spring. In its new, smaller format, the program has become less of an MBA-style overview and more focused on what are currently two key areas of interest for senior management: strategy and globalization (about 25 percent of each class is from outside the United States and Canada). But the program's true showcase is its organizational behavior component, true to USC's reputation among B-schools as a "touchy-feely" kind of place, with one of the strongest OB departments in the country.

The class size is small, held to around 25 to encourage plenty of give and take during discussions. Managers also are assigned to even smaller teams, which remain intact throughout the three weeks and are designed with geographic and cross-functional diversity in mind, for in-depth case projects. At the same time, each individual works on his or her own personal development plan, a set of goals for improving interpersonal skills that kicks off before the program begins with a personality assessment filled out by peers, subordinates, and superiors.

During the small-group work, managers set aside time to discuss the various behaviors observed during negotiations; faculty members sit in to comment on decision-making styles; and videotapes are made of some interactions for study later. By the program's end, each manager should have a set of objectives to take back to the office. To further boost the plans' effectiveness, beginning in 1993, three faculty advisers for self-assessment will be assigned to help participants identify the mana-

155

gerial skills they need to round out from the individual, corporate, and organizational points of view. "We want them to see the whole person in the whole corporation—how do I fit into the changing organization and the changing world around me," says Karen Arden, USC's executive director for exec-ed.

The faculty is first-rate. Led by Professor Tim Campbell, an expert on financial institutions and markets who took over the program's directorship in 1991, the core staff, all from USC, includes Philip Birnbaum-More, who specializes in technology in the global marketplace; Arvind Bhambri, an expert in implementing strategic change with an extensive consulting background; Morgan McCall, director of USC's Leadership Institute and a developer of the widely used "Looking Glass" simulation game; and David Stewart, a marketing and advertising specialist whose books on consumer psychology and focus groups are widely used in those fields.

You'll also rub shoulders with the school's OB legends, Warren Bennis, author of *Why Leaders Can't Lead* and chairman of USC's Leadership Institute, and Ed Lawler, an expert on "empowerment." Lawler is director of USC's Center for Effective Organizations, a research body which sponsors a human resources management seminar series each year for the center's 60 member companies (some open enrollment is available, too). You can also find some fine non-OB-oriented exec-ed offerings at USC. The Certificate in Management Effectiveness is one of the only executive programs in the country designed for women only, intended mainly to bring first-time managers with liberal arts backgrounds up to speed in the basics of business in a safe, nonthreatening, nonintimidating environment. The school is also launching a new program on strategic renewal and change, in which cross-functional corporate teams of three to five employees work on a project or problem their company needs to solve.

As far as the Executive Program is concerned, anyone familiar with the neighborhood surrounding USC—the campus was at the heart of the section of L.A. ravaged by the Rodney King riots in spring of 1992—won't mind spending the three weeks in Pasadena, where the program is held, classes and all, at the Ritz-Carlton Huntington Hotel (the room rate of $120 a day is not included in the program's $7800 tuition fee). The social atmosphere here is low-key and relaxed, West Coast-style: weekend tours of the Norton-Simon and Getty museums, receptions and dinners at faculty homes in the Pasadena area. There's no spouse program, but you won't need much help in finding ways to entertain yourself during late spring in Southern California, with its sunshine and beaches—as long as you have your map.

Organizations sending most participants: Pacific Telesis; AT&T; U.S. Navy Supply Corp.; Southwest Bell; Mitsubishi

Other Programs of Note

Certificate in Management Effectiveness: For women only, this mini-MBA overview boasts a strong finance component, with about half the curriculum devoted to quantitative subjects, such as finance, accounting and business math, and computer training. Other topics include business law, marketing, interpersonal and presentation skills, strategic planning, and current business trends. Led by a faculty committee with a majority of female instructors. Intended for first-time managers with liberal arts backgrounds; experienced managers whose expanding responsibilities require a broader base of business skills; entrepreneurs and professionals, such as physicians and attorneys, who need a grounding in sound business practice. Seven months; held every other Saturday from September to April and January to July, including two intensive retreat weekends; 50 students per session; $4500, including tuition, supplies, and room and board for retreat weekends; by application.

Advanced Management Program: A general-management overview, focusing on strategic thinking and decision-making skills; the organizational impact of financial analysis, market competition, government policies, and legal issues; organizational behavior and leadership; and social, political, and economic conditions that affect business. Led by Tim Campbell. Intended for senior corporate managers with functional backgrounds, nonprofit-sector organization directors, and entrepreneurial chief executives with 10 years' business experience. Five weekend (Friday and Saturday) modules spaced over four months; held twice annually, in spring and fall; 30 students per session; $4500, including tuition (discounted airfare and hotel rates available); by application.

Asia/Pacific Business Outlook Conference: Co-sponsored by USC's Center for International Business Education and Research and the U.S. Department of Commerce. Participants may choose from among 150 different workshops, seminars, and lectures led by senior commercial officers of the Commerce Department's U.S. & Foreign Commercial Service in Asia, the Pacific Rim, Mexico, and Canada, as well as executives from firms with well-established connections in those regions and USC faculty members. Led by John Windler. Intended for executives of firms interested in doing business in Asia and the Pacific Rim. Three days; held annually, in March; 400 students per session; $850 for three days, $325 for one day, including tuition, some meals, and supplies (discounted airfare and hotel rates available); open enrollment.

The Service-Driven Organization: An in-depth presentation on how to build a service-driven company, examining such necessary components as customer relationships, organizational structure, standards and measurements, reward systems, and guarantees, as well as their impact on corporate strategy, human resources management, operations, and marketing. On the final day, executives from such outstanding service providers as Federal Express, Scandinavian Airlines, Four Seasons Hotels, and California Federal Savings Bank will be on hand to share their experiences. In keeping with the program's theme, a guarantee promises a tuition refund to anyone not satisfied by the content or presentation. Led by Richard B. Chase. Intended for senior executives with the responsibility and authority to affect their organizations' quality of service. Four days; held twice annually, in April and October; 30–35 students per session; $2950, including tuition, some meals, and supplies (discount available for group enrollment); open enrollment.

Organizations sending most participants: AT&T; Hughes; TRW

University of Texas at Austin

Graduate School of Business
P.O. Box 7337
Austin, Texas 78713

Number of programs: 24
1990–1991 enrollment: 2045
Annual revenues: $2.6 million

Number of programs in 1986: 12
Years in executive education: 40
Change since 1986: 160 percent

Contact: Chantal Delys, assistant dean and director of executive education, 512-471-5893

The Management Institute for Engineers, Computer Professionals, and Scientists

When Chantal Delys took charge of UT-Austin's executive education department six years ago, there was almost nothing left to take charge of. The oil and gas industry recession, coupled with changing corporate expectations for executive programs, had almost forced the office to shut down. The department's 40-year-old flagship general management course, the Mid-Management Program, was showing its age; once five weeks long, it had been compressed into two weeks and was just barely limping along from session to session.

With her new domain languishing, Delys decided it was time for a radical change to the way the school was approaching exec-ed. "The long, four- to six-week programs are dinosaurs, a breed of the past," she declares. "The most precious resource for companies now is their managers' time—people who can leave for four or six weeks aren't necessary. Now the demand is for short, focused programs—and companies are telling us to show them results." So the old flagship was recast as a custom course, and in 1989, a new flagship was launched to take advantage of the burgeoning high-tech corridor springing up between Austin and San Antonio.

The Management Institute for Engineers, Computer Professionals, and Scientists is designed to prepare technical professionals for general management by presenting an overview of the business disciplines with which they may be least familiar: finance, human relations, marketing, and corporate strategy. But it also aims to keep them up-to-date on technological innovations in their own fields. And it does all this with minimum disruption of the participants' jobs and personal lives, meeting on Thursday, Friday, and Saturday once a month from September through May.

Each of the eight two-and-a-half-day modules focuses on a different theme, kicking off with "Managing the Technical Organization," which examines strategy formulation and implementation and interpersonal skills, and closing out with "Managing in a Global Economy." In between, the modules cover project management and team-building; business law, ethics, and the management of change; accounting and finance; marketing and customer service; quality management and risk assessment; and computer technology. Each Thursday evening, the 30 managers break up into small groups for case discussion, role-playing exercises, computer simulation games, and project work related to that module's topic. And one hour per month is set aside for a lecture by a technology expert, many of them drawn from UT-Austin's top-rated

College of Engineering, on his or her leading-edge research in such fields as genetic engineering, high-performance computing, and environmental protection.

With the Management Institute entering only its fourth year in September 1992, the curriculum and format are still being fine-tuned. Managers from the early sessions complained of muddled organization, poor coordination among faculty members, and a lack of course work that might be immediately applicable on the job. But Delys and her staff are praised for their quick responsiveness to participants' criticisms. "I participated in the first program, and as might be expected, there were a few areas where the curriculum and teaching methods needed adjustment," says one oil-company executive who attended in 1989–1990. "But the faculty and staff reacted very positively where change was needed. UT was very interested in class reactions."

One reason the program's faculty is hard to coordinate is because Delys has gathered a large staff from wide-ranging areas of the enormous state university's vast educational labyrinth: the B-school, the engineering school, the computer sciences department, and even the communications school. To help keep things on track, Delys has set up a core panel of four B-school professors to guide the direction of the program: Ajay Kohll, a marketing specialist; Courtland Huber, whose accounting classes have eight times earned him the school's Outstanding Graduate Professor award; Mike Jackson, director of UT-Austin's Continuing Engineering Studies; and Joanne Click, director of the department of computer sciences' professional education programs. And while you may not find much diversity among your classmates, who are all technical professionals almost exclusively from Texas-based firms, the faculty is quite cosmopolitan: Of some 15 professors who were involved in the program's most recent session, three were Indian, two Japanese, one Mexican, and two French (including Delys).

Classes are held at the university's Joe C. Thompson Conference Center, all the way across the 300-acre campus from the B-school; there is no housing on campus, but students can stay at a nearby Guest Quarters Suite Hotel for a reduced rate. Since this is basically a commuter course, the arrangements are satisfactory to most, particularly at the course's bargain price of $6200, including tuition, supplies, lunches, and dinners. There's not much time for socializing, what with the Thursday night workshops and Saturday classes, but Austin offers a lively nightlife for those rare occasions when participants steal away for a beer or late-night Tex-Mex snack.

Following the Management Institute's success, Delys has been concentrating her efforts on more specialized exec-ed offerings. The Mid-Management Program, for example, has been retooled as a two-level custom course in general management for employees of Halliburton, the oil services giant, with sessions held once a month on campus as well as in Singapore, The Netherlands, and Venezuela. The school is hoping to launch in September 1992 what will be called the Quality Management Consortia, a two-year program to help a dozen small, local companies implement quality improvement plans. Managers will meet once a month to learn how to organize and lead such a project. Then a team of two graduate students, one from business and one from engineering, will be assigned to each firm to assist in the arduous tasks of surveying and gathering the necessary data. For companies with 50 to 800 workers, the extra workforce may be what makes or breaks a quality movement's success, says Delys. After rebuilding her department almost from scratch, she knows firsthand.

Organizations sending most participants: IBM; Texas Instruments; Motorola; The Continuum Co.; Lockheed

Other Programs of Note

Customer Service: The Real Competitive Advantage: Explores ways to build a service culture by pinpointing customer needs and desires, assessing the effectiveness of your customer service operation, developing strategies for improving and integrating customer service into the whole company, and increasing profitability. Led by John Daly and Raymond Smilor. Intended for managers who deal with internal or external customers, including general managers and those in R&D, product design, manufacturing, marketing, sales, and finance. Three days; held annually, in May; 24–30 students per session; $1150, including tuition, supplies, and lunches (discount for early or group registration); open enrollment.

Managing Strategy in a Changing Environment: Examines current approaches for developing and implementing successful strategies, covering such topics as strategy formulation and evaluation, industry and competitor analysis, implementation, diversification, and management of change. Led by James W. Fredrickson and David B. Jemison. Intended for new general managers or those slated to enter general management within two years. Three days; held annually, in April; 24–30 students per session; $1150, including tuition, supplies, and lunches (discount for early or group registration); by application.

Quality Excellence Forum: Presents winning strategies and breakthrough approaches to quality improvement used by Baldrige Award-winning companies. Led by executives from several Baldrige-winning U.S. firms, as well as Japanese and European companies with high quality standards. Intended for senior managers with responsibility for implementing quality improvement. Two days; held annually, in March; 100 students per session; $795, including tuition, supplies, and lunches (discount for early registration); open enrollment.

Quality Self-Assessment Workshop: Designed as a follow-up to the Quality Excellence Forum, this program helps you diagnose your company's overall quality management effort, measure its progress using the Baldrige Award criteria, and devise an action plan to boost the firm's strategy to achieve total quality. Management team participation is encouraged. Led by consultant Jim Ziaja, a senior Baldrige examiner, and Raymond Smilor. Intended for upper-level executives involved in total quality management. Two days; held three times a year, in April, June, and September; 24 students per session; $795, including tuition, supplies, and lunches (discount for early registration); open enrollment.

Organizations sending most participants: 3M; GTE; IBM; Abbott Lab; Fisher Controls

University of Wisconsin-Madison

School of Business
Management Institute
432 N. Lake Street
Madison, Wisconsin 53706

Number of programs: 175	*Number of programs in 1986*: 120
1990–1991 enrollment: 9000	*Years in executive education*: 48
Annual revenues: $4 million	*Change since 1986*: 90 percent

Contact: Dr. Edward J. Marien, department chairman, 608-262-2155; Buck Joseph, director of executive development, 608-262-7878

The Executive Program

Befitting its location in what may be America's most socialist city, the University of Wisconsin-Madison's Management Institute is one of the most egalitarian schools for executives around. Forget the elitist attitudes you'll encounter at some schools that cater only to the management crème de la crème: The institute's vast list of courses—some 175 different programs, many of them taught several times a year—offers something for just about every managerial level and interest, from first-line, entry-level positions to senior executives. With 400 or so sessions to choose from annually, there's hardly a day on the calendar when there's not a class being held.

The freedom of choice hasn't been lost on the institute's target audience. In 1990–1991, a whopping 9000 managers passed through the doors of Wisconsin Center, the stone-and-brick building at the edge of UW-M's Lake Mendota that houses most of the executive programs. The institute has nearly doubled in size since 1986, and it will be none too soon when additional offices and classrooms open in Grainger Hall, the spanking new five-story home for both the institute and the School of Business, scheduled for completion in 1993.

Established in 1944 as part of a federal government plan to educate first-line business managers in the wake of the World War II personnel drain, the Management Institute has traditionally concentrated its efforts on short, single-topic seminars for lower- and middle-level executives. "This is still our bread and butter, the two- and three-day hard-hitting programs dealing with leadership development, team-building, and functional offerings," says institute chairman, Ed Marien. "People come in focused, and go away with good action items to bring back to the job." Topics range from the highly technical to the general, covering everything from "Using Bar Codes in Warehousing and Distribution" to "How to Work More Effectively with People."

The school encourages executives at all levels to make a broader educational commitment through its certificate series, in which participants who complete a number of required courses during a one- to two-year time span may "graduate" with certification of competence. The Office Administration Certificate Series, for example, targets office managers, executive secretaries, and administrative assistants; the Basic Management Certificate Series is aimed at first-level supervisors; other series are designed for mid-level general managers, procurement professionals, and functional managers of product service, maintenance, marketing, quality, sales, and transportation. There also has been an upsurge in demand for in-house programs for firms like CUNA Mutual Insurance,

Menasha Corp., and various state government agencies (the Capitol is just a stone's throw away from the downtown campus). Custom programs—ranging from company-specific versions of open-enrollment courses, such as the Executive Teambuilding program which has been tailored for insurance, manufacturing, and financial service companies, to long-term, collaborative research and training partnerships—now make up about 15 percent of the institute's business, according to Marien.

Unfortunately, while the institute has been busy in recent years trying to satisfy everybody from the bottom on up, executives at the senior level seem to have gotten short shrift. After 10 years in operation, the four-week Executive Program in particular has been languishing, with participants finding fault with everything from teaching quality to outmoded classroom facilities. (In our consumer survey, Wisconsin ranked twenty-third of 25 schools overall.) But all that is about to change: The program's 1992 sessions were suspended so it could undergo a complete overhaul.

Designed under the guidance of alumni and human resources directors at client companies, the revamped course will consist of four one-week sessions over the course of a year (in February, May, September, and December) to give students the opportunity to "digest what they're learning and apply what they're doing in the classroom on the job," says Buck Joseph, the institute's director of executive development and the Executive Program faculty leader. Intended for senior-level functional managers with at least 10 years' experience, the program will focus heavily on total quality management, leadership and team-building, and globalization (although Joseph expects the staggered schedule to keep foreign participation near zero).

A noteworthy innovation will be the centering of each week's material around a "living case study," in which executives of a firm under scrutiny will appear in the flesh to explain their actions. For example, during the first week, which examines total quality strategy and customer-driven organizations, the CEO, marketing director, and quality director of Harley-Davidson will be on hand to tell how they resurrected the ailing motorcycle manufacturer. The following week, which focuses on marketing and accounting, will see marketing, R&D, and finance executives from Oscar Mayer describe how they successfully brought out a new product line.

Another component Joseph plans to stress is the program's popular outdoor experience, which used to comprise a day and a half but will now encompass four days' time over the life of the course. The team-oriented exercises, which sound more forbidding than they really are, will include rockclimbing on the 400-foot cliffs at Devil's Lake, 35 miles outside Madison, and orienteering on water using a huge, 32-person canoe modeled on those once used by Great Lakes Indian tribes. "It's wild," laughs Joseph. "You have to see it to believe it." Other segments new to the program will feature workshops on enhanced communications and presentations skills, a session on managing diversity, and a business simulation on quality.

Nine B-school professors with extensive consulting experience have been tapped to form the program's core faculty. Joseph, a management specialist, has lent his expertise to such firms as Ralston-Purina, Abbott Laboratories, Allen Bradley, and Oscar Mayer. The quality and productivity segments are taught by Mark Finster, who has improved management systems for more than 40 different organizations, and Urban Wemmerlov; accounting by Mark Covaleski, who specialized in management control systems for high-tech and service-sector firms, particularly in the health care field, and Larry Rittenberg. Marketing is handled by J. Paul Peter, who has been a consultant to the Federal Trade Commission, and Jack Nevin, whose consulting has extended to such firms as Ford Motor, General Motors, and Frito-Lay. Rounding out the staff is Don Nichols, an economics professor who served as deputy assistant secretary of labor under the Carter Administration, and Randall Dunham, the author of a half dozen books on organizational behavior.

The new Grainger Hall will feature state-of-the-art amphitheaters to replace Wisconsin Center's overcrowded, outdated lecture halls, and participants will continue to stay at either the Friedrick Center, a campus conference facility with bedrooms and cafeteria, or the similarly designed Lowell Hall. The $12,000 tuition fee includes lodging and most meals. There won't be much time for socializing under the new schedule, which is designed to pack everything into day and evening classes between Monday and Friday. But should you have a few spare minutes, it's just a short walk from campus to State Street, the main drag in downtown Madison. You'll find everything there from the State Historical Museum and the Civic Center, to shops and restaurants, to leftover 1960s-era head shops, remnants of the university's days as a radical hotbed. In fact, Madison is a lot like the Management Institute: You'll find something for everyone.

Organizations sending most participants: Kimberly-Clark; Consolidated Paper; Wausau Paper; Telephone Data Systems; CUNA Mutual Insurance

Other Programs of Note

Leadership Audit and High-Performance Leadership: A highly individual leadership assessment, with surveys of peers, subordinates, and superiors on the job and a computerized report detailing your interpersonal style, along with an overview of effective leadership skills and development of individual action plans to boost performance levels after returning to work. Led by John Keenan. Intended for any manager who wants to improve leadership effectiveness. Five days; held twice annually, in April and October; 30 students per session; $1520, including tuition, supplies, and lunches; open enrollment.

Business-to-Business Marketing Strategy: Examines business-to-business marketing communications strategy. Participants are encouraged to bring their companies' promotional plans, ads, and sales material for evaluation. Led by Linda Gorchels, the Management Institute's director of executive marketing programs. Intended for product managers, sales managers, marketing directors, corporate communication specialists, and advertising managers. Three days; held twice annually, in June and December; 35 students per session; $795, including tuition, supplies, and lunches; open enrollment.

Professional Sales Skills Workshop Series: A week of one-day clinics emphasizing intermediate and advanced sales skills. You may enroll in one or any combination of the sessions. Led by Jerry Fritz, the Management Institute's director of sales and customer service management programs. Intended for experienced sales personnel. One week; held annually, in September; 30 students per session; $175 per day-long program, or $800 for all five days, including tuition and supplies; open enrollment.

Organizations sending most participants: Kimberly-Clark; Consolidated Paper; Telephone Data Systems; University of Wisconsin-Madison; Hutchinson's Technology

CHAPTER 6

THE TEN MOST INNOVATIVE PROGRAMS

Here are the management programs of the future, singled out by companies and deans in BUSINESS WEEK surveys as among the most innovative and creative approaches to executive education. Top scores went to a diverse array of programs, from the Wharton School's $33,000 International Forum, which takes 30 of the world's corporate elite around the globe for a series of seminars on global strategic issues, to Dartmouth's $2150 one-week crash course in management for minority entrepreneurs.

Many of the programs on the list are relative newcomers to the exec-ed market, products of the last few years of trends and research into managerial needs. The University of Tennessee's Senior Executive Institute for Productivity Through Quality, for example, is an outgrowth of the corporate total quality movement that took hold in the 1980s; Michigan's Global Leadership Program results from the ever-intensifying international scope of business.

But not all of these innovators are new kids on the block. MIT's Sloan Fellows Program, the granddaddy of all executive training, has been around for over 60 years, but its 12-month master's degree program for mid-career managers still offers one of the freshest formats and perspectives around. Harvard's Program for Management Development dates back to 1960, but its recent emphasis on computerization and use of "electronic cases" may be prototypical of the way general management courses will be taught in the next century.

What sets all of these programs apart is their willingness to experiment, to offer something you won't find anywhere else—at least not for long. In exec-ed, as elsewhere, imitation is the sincerest form of flattery, and successful ideas do spread fast. One of the latest likely to catch on is Dartmouth's novel "MBA: Update 2000" for MBAs who graduated before the mid-1980s who want to keep their MBA investment up-to-date. The program spans two $4000 five-day modules; one starts in mid-September of 1992 and the other in mid-June of 1993. It's a sure bet to make our next list of the most innovative programs. BUSINESS WEEK presents the following list without actual rankings.

Managing Cultural Diversity
Columbia University

Columbia Business School
310 Uris Hall
New York, New York 10027

Columbia Professor Anna Duran first realized she was getting the message of her Managing Cultural Diversity program across when she took some of her students out for lunch one afternoon. "I inadvertently said something that could have been taken negatively by a black person, and the group corrected me," Duran recalls with a laugh. The students then pointed out another way to say the same thing without a hint of prejudice. "I said, 'I've done my work!'"

The one-week program, the first of its kind in the United States, is designed to teach companies how to incorporate and effectively manage employees from diverse cultures—Hispanics, African-Americans, and Asian-Americans. The 16 to 24 participants in each session are asked to assess their own personal prejudices, to examine how the concepts of work and achievement among minority groups may differ from those of white male Americans, and to learn techniques to make both managers and multicultural employees more comfortable in the workplace. Each participant also formulates an action plan to take back to his or her office and disseminate throughout the workplace, so others can benefit from the new-found knowledge. "Our goal is to offer material for use in the company without our being there all the time," says Duran.

The $4750 program has proved so popular that in the three years since it was first offered at Columbia's Arden House executive retreat, it has expanded to two open-enrollment sessions a year (in spring and fall) and several custom versions for specific companies. Duran is even redesigning one large corporation's in-house general management course to include a segment on the topic. Unfortunately, Duran can't blow the program's horn too loudly. Participants and their firms simply don't want to be identified with such a sensitive subject, as if signing employees up for diversity management training is tantamount to an admission of prejudice. To protect clients' confidentiality, Columbia refuses to give out any names of companies that have been involved in the course. "People are very sensitive to litigation, to being seen as sexist or racist," notes Duran. That also accounts for the growing interest in company-specific versions of the curriculum: "If you have an in-house program, other companies can't see your dirty laundry," she says.

Duran, a trained psychoanalyst, had been on staff at Columbia's Teachers College for 10 years when Mary Anne Devanna, the B-school's exec-ed director, called her for some ideas on how executive programs might address Workforce 2000, the buzzword for the diverse makeup of the workforce of the turn of the century. After Duran came up with a successful pilot version of Managing Cultural Diversity for a major chemical company, the program "just zoomed off" in open enrollment, she says. The timid beware: Don't enroll unless you're willing to confront and share your innermost thoughts and feelings, some of which may not be very pretty. The course begins with lectures, but quickly moves into hands-on interaction with the concepts in small-group workshops, which then report back to the larger group for further discussion.

One workshop focuses on what Duran calls "microaggressions"—the subtle, sometimes unconscious ways people offend or condescend to those from different backgrounds. Participants work up skits to demonstrate microaggressions they've observed in their own workplaces, then faculty and classmates talk about ways to repair relationships that may have been damaged by such an act or comment. In another segment of the course, each participant's world view is assessed through a psychological test; the results are then interpreted to show how team development and functioning on the job might be affected by his or her perspective of other ethnicities.

Duran says she can gauge the program's success through the action plans that have been embraced by managers' companies. One company-specific customer came up with a three-pronged approach to handling cultural diversity companywide. First, a series of meetings were arranged over six months' time to present Workforce 2000 data to senior management; then committees were assigned across all functions and seniority levels to spread the word among the rest of the staff. Finally, the firm decided to incorporate the topic of cultural diversity into all its management training programs. "Another company had trouble keeping employees, and now they are keeping them," says Duran. "Some managers say they now see why they were losing people." A third firm developed a sort of reverse-mentorship program, pairing up lower-level black, female, and Latino workers with upper-level, mainly white male managers. "The person of color mentors the superior about diversity issues"—and is rewarded for internal leadership within the company, Duran says.

The teaching staff, while well trained in diversity management issues, also knows whereof it speaks from personal experience: Duran, who is Latina, has assembled a multiethnic panel of consultants to assist her. They include Anderson J. Franklin, an African-American; Derald Wing Sue, an Asian-American; Patricia Arrondo, also Latina; and the team of William Klepper, a white male, and Martha Stodt, a white female, who specialize in identifying gender gaps.

While most of the program's participants are white males (not surprising, since they are drawn from the ranks of senior and upper-middle management in the largest 500 corporations), minority managers do enroll on occasion—and find that they, too, have room to broaden their minds. "People of color, who know about this area, come away saying they have learned something they haven't in other programs," Duran says. And that is just the message she likes to hear.

Contact: Anna Duran, faculty director, 212-854-3274

The MIT Management of Technology Program
Massachusetts Institute of Technology

Sloan School of Management
50 Memorial Drive
Cambridge, Massachusetts 02139

Many managers have trouble taking even four weeks off the job for executive education; a year-long sabbatical would be unthinkable. But the MIT Management of Technology Program is so special that participants are willing to pack up their offices, uproot their families, and head off for a year of back-breaking study in Cambridge, Massachusetts—in most cases, with their companies' blessing and financial support to the tune of more than $35,000.

The MOT program is a lot like a Sloan Fellows program for techies: a 12-month master's degree program for mid-career managers with science and engineering backgrounds. Each June, some 40 executives, many in their mid-30s, return to the classroom to undergo the rigors of required, graded courses and even writing a thesis in order to earn the prestigious Master of Science in the Management of Technology degree, a joint offering of MIT's highly-rated Sloan School of Management and School of Engineering, established in 1981.

But it's really not the diploma that attracts most participants. About half of them already have master's degrees or even doctorates. They've already achieved a measure of success, having worked for an average of 10 years and having earned titles such as research engineer, senior programmer, or project manager. What they want—and what this program excels at teaching—is the skills needed to enter the senior management ranks at such technology-driven giants as IBM, Hewlett-Packard, General Motors, RCA, and AT&T. "An MBA isn't the right degree, because it doesn't build on their technical experience," says Rochelle Weichman, the program's assistant director. "They need to tap into the bigger business environment to get an international perspective on the company business and a functional perspective on the entire company. Then they can make the transition to where they're no longer doing, say, engineering work, but are managing interfaces with other parts of the company and directing others who are doing that work."

The year begins with a summer term devoted to core skill building in the disciplines normally covered in the first year of an MBA program: financial and management accounting and control, applied micro- and macroeconomic theory, probability and statistical data analysis as applied in management, strategic planning, and organizational behavior. There are also special seminars held on a variety of topics, both technical and general, presented by both MIT staffers and outside speakers; you might hear renowned Sloan School Dean Lester C. Thurow discourse on the emerging world economy, or the president of a growing high-tech company talk about his experiences as an entrepreneur. In the fall, required courses again dominate the schedule, but this time with more emphasis on technical businesses: managing technology, the strategic management of technology, the R&D process, and financial management. Every other week, a seminar in the management of technology gives participants the opportunity to meet for informal discussions with an all-star lineup of senior executives of technological or manufacturing organizations; recent guests have included Jack D. Kuehler, president of IBM; Raymond W. Smith, CEO of Bell Atlantic;

167

Kenneth Olsen, president of Digital Equipment Corp.; and Hideki Kaihatsu, director of Fuji Xerox Co.

Don't expect much of a break during the January intersession. Instead, you'll spend a week on a field trip to meet with the senior executives of companies in a variety of technology-driven fields. In 1992, the class split its time between San Francisco and Los Angeles, visiting two firms a day in a wide range of industries from biotechnology and electronics to banking and entertainment. "The idea is to expose students to as many different industries as we can, showing how each manages technology," says Weichman. "They can also take what they've been learning during the fall and see it in action." The rest of the month is filled with research for your thesis: You choose the topic by November and it's due in May. The titles are a formidable-sounding lot, with many of the topics growing out of issues that are relevant to participants' home companies so they can be applied back on the job: No other reason could explain such choices as "Development of a Business Plan for a Recombinant DNA Technology-Based Pharmaceutical Company" or "An Evaluation of Technology Transfer in the Electric Utility Industry."

The course load is kept intentionally light in spring to allow time for thesis writing, with only two courses—corporate strategies for managing research, development, and engineering and marketing management—required that term. The seminar in the management of technology continues its biweekly meetings, and participants must also complete two elective courses, which may be taken in either fall or spring and must include one course in manufacturing or process technology. (Seventeen elective choices are available.) All courses, required and elective, are, with a few exceptions, offered only to MOT participants, so you're guaranteed a small class size and plenty of personal attention from professors. The top-notch faculty, co-chaired by Edward B. Roberts and Thomas H. Lee, is drawn from both Sloan and MIT's engineering school.

For someone who's been out of school for a decade, the MOT workload can be a shock to the system. That may be one reason participants tend to form close bonds with one another. Even though the courses are graded, you won't find the cutthroat competition common in top-ranked MBA programs; after all, 80 percent of each class is company-sponsored, with jobs awaiting them after graduation. "This is a much greater collaborative environment," says Weichman. "Besides, with a 35-year-old who's looking for the next position in a career path, no one asks him what his grades are."

Since at least three-quarters of the participants bring their spouses and children with them—many moving long distances to spend the year in New England, including about half who come from overseas—there's also a tight social network that forms around the families. Many first meet during MOT's house-hunting weekend, held the spring before the program begins. (With few on-campus housing options available, most people head for the suburbs, but beware—the Boston area is one of the country's most expensive, and living expenses can easily top $20,000 for the year.) Besides the many individual get-togethers, the program sponsors a big end-of-summer picnic and a holiday party. And there's a monthly family program focusing on different countries, with native arts and crafts for the children and indigenous food and drink for the adults. Even after graduation, the bonds stay strong through the program's 300 active alumni, who are trying to form—what else?—an electronic network to keep in touch with one another.

Contact: Roger Samuel, director, 617-253-3154

Senior Executive Institute for Productivity
Through Quality
University of Tennessee

College of Business Administration
708 Stokely Management Center
Knoxville, Tennessee 37996

An Alabama-based electronics firm decided to enter into a production alliance with a potential competitor in Canada in order to satisfy the special needs of a customer. A placement officer at the University of Tennessee began holding seminars in job-hunting skills for MBA students in their first semester, instead of waiting until just before graduation to assist them in their search. General Motors' Toledo-based Powertrain Division has seen an overall boost in organizational efficiency, utilization of resources, and responsiveness to customers.

These are just three among dozens of success stories told by participants in the University of Tennessee's Senior Executive Institute for Productivity Through Quality. Started in 1981 as a spinoff of the school's Three-Week Institute, which offers an extremely detailed, technical examination of the statistical methods used to improve organizational systems, the one-week Senior Executive Institute is a more general, yet still rigorous, look at productivity, quality, and continuous improvement issues for senior-level, strategy-oriented managers, mainly of manufacturing companies. In a little more than 10 years, the course has become so popular that it is now offered five times a year—in February, April, June, August, and December—and easily fills the 35 openings in each class, often with management teams of 5 to 10 people from the same firm. "This is becoming more and more the premier management issue, not just a quality or productivity specialty," says Richard D. Sanders, a statistician who is what Tennessee's Management Development Center calls the "faculty course owner" and one of the institute's founders.

While the course content may sound forbidding to those executives whose mathematical backgrounds are limited or rusty with age, Sanders and the rest of the faculty take special care to make their material accessible to everyone. On Sunday evening, before the week begins, the class meets to review basic statistics, including current terminology and the use of a statistical calculator. As the week moves through explanations of statistical management techniques, variation, systems improvement, and the relationships among competition, quality, productivity, statistics, value, and continuous improvement, case studies, applied problems, and small-group discussions are used to show how these technical issues are relevant to the bigger picture of devising a corporate strategy for competing in a global economy. Senior executives from successful international firms like Harris Corp. are brought in to share their experiences with implementing systems management and improvement techniques. "Some people want to hear specifically about statistics, to get more competent in it, while others want to hear perspectives," says Sanders. The course aims to satisfy both.

While the institute's one-week time frame is too short to send participants back to the office with company-specific plans for quality improvement, alumni say the course does produce results back on the job—some specific, others less tangible. For Jennifer C. Grayson, the university's assistant director of business placement, attending a session in 1991 helped to crystallize ways to improve the school's placement

169

services for MBA students, which had mainly consisted of written handouts and seminars during the program's second year, when for many the interviewing process had already begun. "We found through focus groups and the Senior Executive Institute course that we could solve problems ahead of time instead of after the fact," says Grayson. "Now we have a seminar program starting in the first semester of school, covering everything from career definition, using aptitude tests, to dining etiquette"—a subject that arose when a corporate recruiter was put off during a lunch interview by a student using the wrong fork.

"The customer value concept has helped us focus our actions," agrees Bruce Ramsey, president of AVEX Electronics Inc., a contract manufacturing firm based in Huntsville, Alabama, who also attended the institute in 1991. "We had a core customer which needed products built in Canada, so we made an alliance with a Canadian company that was a potential competitor," a creative solution that Ramsey says probably wouldn't have occurred without the new perspective on meeting customer needs that grew out of the course. "Now we take a more proactive approach to what the customer needs and organize ourselves to meet those needs," he adds.

Ramsey and other participants say the faculty's extensive experience in industry was an invaluable addition to the course content. Sanders, who has been on staff at Tennessee for over 20 years, has consulted with firms in the paper and wood, pharmaceuticals, health care, and food industries. G. Harlan Carothers Jr., a consultant who regularly teaches in the institute, spent 25 years in line management at Harris Corp., ending up as corporate vice president of productivity in charge of 30 worldwide divisions. Other core faculty members include William C. Parr, who was the senior scientist in charge of statistical development for Harris Corp.'s Semiconductor Sector before joining academia, and Kenneth E. Kirby, an associate professor in Tennessee's department of industrial engineering, who spent the first 15 years of his career as a manager for ALCOA.

At $3500 for the week, the Senior Executive Institute isn't cheap. (The cost includes tuition, supplies, a room at a hotel near campus, and most meals; classes are held at the Management Development Center's William B. Stokely Center.) But it's a testament to the program's success that firms will sometimes send dozens of employees over several years' time. General Motors' Powertrain Division, for example, has enrolled four different groups of 10 to 12 workers and even hired a Tennessee professor as a consultant to the division. AVEX has sent 15 executives, including the managing directors of its foreign subsidiaries in Scotland and Singapore. (About 10 percent of each class is from overseas, usually Americans working in foreign divisions.) "To a person, every one has said it was the most useful program they've ever attended," says Bruce Ramsey.

"What I learned is that you have to get out of the fire-fighting mode," says Gary Eich, plant manager for Titleist Footjoy Co., the sports equipment manufacturer. "We have to implement systems today that will satisfy the customer tomorrow." That's a prescription that almost any company could adopt.

Contact: Richard Sanders, faculty course owner, 615-974-5001

Program for Management Development
Harvard University

Graduate School of Business Administration
Soldiers Field
Boston, Massachusetts 02163

The first clue that Harvard's Program for Management Development is going to be something different appears as soon as you arrive on campus. Instead of receiving the usual looseleaf binder containing the class directory, campus maps, and schedules, you're handed a computer card. Head back to your dorm room, pop it into the Macintosh sitting on your desk, and you'll *know* you're in for something different. On the screen, you have access to each of your 140 fellow participants' names, addresses, personal biographies, and career information. A color photo of each person is accompanied by the sound of that student's own voice, pronouncing his or her name for you. Want to know who else in your class is from California—or Japan? Just ask the computer. It will give you a list of everyone who works there, lives there, or was born there. Need to know how to get to the university bookstore, or a professor's office? Just ask the computer—a map will pop up to guide you.

Throughout the 12-week, $31,000 course, which is held in spring and fall each year, the computer will play a major role in everything you do, from electronic case studies and business simulation games to finding out your class assignments and setting up a tennis date with a classmate. And that's just what program chairman M. Colyer Crum intended in 1989 when he began setting up the unprecedented network linking student bedrooms, classrooms, faculty offices, and even professors' homes. "The computer is imbedded in the course infrastructure. No student can go through a day without using the computer," says Crum. The impact has been immeasurable. "The network has revolutionized how I interact with my colleagues and how we interact with our students," says Dennis J. Encarnation, the program's international management specialist. "I've never seen such a major shakeup in the way we do things."

Does that mean you have to be a programming genius to enroll in PMD? Far from it. From the outset, the computer was meant to be nothing more than a friendly tool for achieving what has been the program's aim since its inception in 1960: to prepare the best and brightest functional executives at the nation's leading corporations for senior management positions. You'll still find a traditional curriculum—segments in finance, marketing, systems and controls, operations, organizational behavior, strategy, the external environment, leadership, and problem solving—following Harvard's trademark format of case studies, small-group discussion, and plenary sessions. "The basic goal of training general managers has a classic simplicity to it," says Crum. "It's not a new idea, it's an old idea that remains incredibly relevant."

But when Crum, who has been on staff at Harvard B-school for more than 30 years, took over the chairmanship of the program four years ago, he felt the time was ripe to shake things up a bit. He noticed that while the students and faculty had ready access to personal computers during the program, they just weren't using them. In fact, usage was declining. At the same time, corporate general managers were telling him that, for the first time, they were beginning to use computers on the job. So Crum brought in a team from Apple Computers to design a system that anyone could learn to operate in just a day and a half of training; that would be hard-wired, so communication between units would be instantaneous; and that would accomplish the tasks that faculty and students wanted to perform.

One revolutionary result has been the electronic cases written or adapted specifically for PMD. In the "Eastern Europe and the Soviet Union" case, teams are assigned to develop analyses of the critical economic and political issues facing various countries in this fast-changing region. Students sort through hundreds of facts stored in the computer's databases, use electronic mail to contact professors with special insight into current events, and even send E-mail questions to classmates who live or work in Eastern Europe (the program draws nearly half its participants from overseas). In another case, "Corning Indonesia," teams playing the roles of Corning International, a local partner, the Indonesian government, and a World Bank subsidiary must negotiate a deal that benefits all the parties. A computerized spreadsheet is used to plug in various assumptions and calculate their outcomes, with that information forming the basis of E-mail dialogs among the teams. A third, recently completed case was based on the activities of Otis, the elevator manufacturer, in South Africa. A two-hour sound-and-image film, made on site in the corporate offices and neighboring towns there, can be called up on the computer screen through a compact disc player so participants can truly bring the case to life.

Business simulation games are another important use for the network. The "Beer Game" involves students in an imaginary beer production and distribution chain, with retailers placing orders via computer; "Kirsten's Cookies" simulates a small cookie company's manufacturing operations. The faculty has also found that the computer had an impact on their dealings with students and one another. "We created a matrix listing each day of the program on the vertical, each course across the top, and listed the topics covered by each person," Crum says. "It could be easily changed, and we found an enormous variety of ideas for sequencing, coordinating, and cross-referencing. The result has been much more coordinated, coherent, related teaching." Additionally, professors find the students are learning more from one another, without faculty involvement. "If a case is about Japan, and you want to talk to someone from Japan, you can do that very easily now," says Crum. "There's almost an infinite variety of bilateral contacts, questions, and communications, some totally among students, some between students and faculty, some managed by faculty, some not."

Crum doesn't expect the computer ever to completely replace the ink-on-paper cases and lively discussions that still make up the bulk of PMD's teaching. Currently, only about 15 of the course's 200 cases are computerized. And while PMD is serving as a model for other programs that want to integrate computer usage, the logistics can be prohibitive. In Harvard's MBA program, for example, so many students live off campus that hardwiring is not feasible, and communicating by modem would be too slow to be effective. In the school's Advanced Management Program, which is experimenting with an IBM network, the older, senior-level participants are less experienced with computer hardware and more resistant to changing their set ways. But the concept of using electronic networks as a major executive-education teaching technique is clearly the way of the future. "As the world becomes more complex, new, emerging technologies can provide richer experiences for students," says James I. Cash, Jr., who has taught in many of Harvard's executive programs since joining the faculty in 1976. Eventually, "Software will make case studies appear like Model T's." And PMD's participants will find themselves with a headstart into the future.

Contact: M. Colyer Crum, chairman, 617-495-6486

Managing Critical Resources
University of Virginia

Darden Graduate School of Business Administration
P.O. Box 6550
Charlottesville, Virginia 22906

You'd like to attend the University of Virginia's Executive Program, with its No. 1 rating by participants, but your supervisor thinks you need some more experience under your belt. Or maybe you just can't afford to spend six weeks away from the office. Then you'll want to consider Managing Critical Resources, a two-week distillation of the longer course's general management fundamentals, delivered with the same infectious enthusiasm you'll find throughout the school's executive offerings.

Held four times between March and October, the $6800 program is so popular among the faculty that four different teams, led by four different professors, teach each session. "Everybody wants to be a part of it," crows Richard Brownlee, one of the faculty leaders. "MCR epitomizes our executive programs. It's as much bang for the buck as we offer."

Intended for executives who are on the cusp of moving from functional areas into general management, MCR has, since its inception in 1968, steeped participants in the basics of the four critical management resources—finance, operations, marketing, and human resources—and their interrelationships. Cases and lectures are used as a springboard for discussion by the 40 or so participants in each session, and the faculty members happily immerse themselves in their teaching, sharing lunches, dinners, receptions, and even Saturday outings to local landmarks such as Monticello with the students. It's almost like hiring a mentor for two weeks: The professors encourage managers to meet with them individually to discuss not just course work, but any on-the-job issues on which they might need advice. "We'll go through their annual report with them in detail so they can understand the pension plan or a plant closing; we'll talk about investment analysis issues," says Brownlee. "We're there to offer advice and consultation."

The curriculum is about as straightforward an overview of general management skills as you'll find. Forget the gimmicks and novelties; you won't find any team raft-building exercises or computer games in this course. This is an academic purist's dream. You read and listen, and then talk about what you've heard and read. The pace is brisk, with the curriculum moving swiftly from the opening-day briefing on how to read a financial statement to the final segment on leadership. In between, you'll cover topics including financial statement and ratio analysis; pricing policy; cost analysis; high-performance work systems; management of quality; managing change; capital budgeting; and managing new technology. Each class of 30 to 45 is divided into small study groups that meet three times a day to digest the material; halfway through the program, the groups are rotated to help participants get to know one another.

While MCR is in a sense an abbreviated version of Darden's acclaimed Executive Program, the longer course is, of course, much broader in scope, emphasizing bigger-picture issues such as globalization, international financial management, macroeconomics, corporate strategy, and leadership. The six-week program "probably takes the lead in terms of introducing new concepts; it's more willing to innovate," says Brownlee. That doesn't mean MCR is static, however. The faculty is now looking for more concrete ways student-managers can apply what they've learned back on the job; in recent sessions, students have been asked to put together "MCR takeaways," proposals that might be implemented when they get back to the office, which are then presented to the rest of the class during a final brainstorming session on the last day of the program.

More importantly, the cases are under constant scrutiny for any signs of age; to be certain the sessions are uniform in quality and to gather ideas for new material, a faculty coordinator, Bob Landel, meets regularly with all four of the program's leaders (in addition to Brownlee, an accounting specialist who was previously affiliated with Peat, Marwick, Mitchell and Co., they include C. Ray Smith, Jim Freeland, and Robert Spekman). "This has been a very successful program, and we want to make sure the material is not outdated in any sense," says Brownlee. "There are cases that get dated very quickly, and others that don't." A case involving the Steinway piano company, taught jointly by operations and marketing faculty members, has endured since the program's inception; at the same time, professors are now trying to create cases on emerging countries such as the former Soviet Union and Brazil to keep up with world events.

Another difference between the two programs is the class makeup. The audience for the Executive Program is much more international. Only one or two executives in each session of MCR come from overseas, as opposed to 25 percent of the Executive Program's students. And the longer course's participants are a good five years further along in their general management careers. "If you were to come to a general management program that precedes the Executive Program, this is it," Brownlee says of MCR. But it is the fact that the shorter program's participants are poised at a turning point in their careers, ready to leap into the upper echelons of Corporate America, that so excites the faculty who work with them. "These people are bright, fun, they have lots of interests. They've traveled and worked around the world," says Brownlee. "This is a unique opportunity to work with quality individuals."

Trying to fit such a detailed overview into two weeks' time can make for an intense experience, so be prepared to work hard. Darden has long had a reputation for being something of a boot camp, and that's true with this program as well. Except for a two-hour break each afternoon so participants can get some exercise, you'll find yourself living and breathing the course from 7 a.m. breakfast at Sponsors Hall, the executive residence located next door to the Darden School, through the discussion-group meetings that don't even start until 8 p.m. (There's a break from Saturday noon until Monday morning during the on-campus weekend, but even the course's promotional brochure warns that "participants are expected to prepare for Monday's classes over the weekend.") And if you're lucky, in a few years' time you'll be back to do the same thing for six straight weeks—in the Executive Program.

Contact: Frank T. Morgan, director of executive education, 804-924-4847; Bob Landel, program coordinator, 804-924-4832

The Leadership Institute
Boston University

Office of Executive Programs
School of Management
685 Commonwealth Avenue
Boston, Massachusetts 02215

It's rare when an executive education program garners rave reviews for real-world practicality. Nearly everyone agrees that exec-ed is helpful, but the biggest gripe of corporate clients is that it rarely provides immediate benefits. That's not true of Boston University's unique Leadership Institute.

Here's a program in which you first sit with your boss to come up with a specific "strategy execution challenge" that you will meet as a result of the institute. Each manager arrives with a work objective that he or she works on during a pair of two-week sessions over the summer. Managers are paired with faculty mentors who act as consultants on the action plans. How's that for immediate payback?

Moreover, these aren't easy or theoretical projects. Recent examples: A Federal Express Corp. manager's challenge was to create a new division in Australia. A Bell of Pennsylvania executive had to go through a downsizing of operations. Another manager reduced the product life-cycle and time to market in a major product category. Yet another executive worked to create a culture to foster integration of racial ethnic diversity to increase creativity. Fellow classmates review your plans, often offering—in the words of one participant—"fascinating alternative approaches" unhampered by the cultural biases of your own organization.

Launched in 1989 after holding focus groups with potential customers, the program quickly won support from such big names as American Telephone & Telegraph Co. and Digital Equipment Corp. The institute is a consortium-type program to which only corporate sponsors can send executives. The latest batch of sponsors are: Federal Express, National Westminster Bank, Levi Strauss of Canada, Campbell Soup, Polaroid, Eli Lilly, John Hancock, AT&T, New York Telephone, Florida Power & Light, Bell South Communications, and BBN, a consulting firm in Cambridge.

Six weeks before managers arrive for the first module, they'll receive in the mail a strategy execution guidebook that leads them through several exercises to help them focus on a key strategic issue. Among the questions: "If you could stop doing one or two things, what would they be and why would you choose to stop them?" "If you could start doing two things, what would they be and why would you choose to start them?"

Managers also are asked to evaluate their organizations using the "7-S framework," a system of analysis developed by the consulting firm of McKinsey & Co. Thinking through the framework—which focuses on such organizational attributes as strategy, structure, systems, style, staffing, skills, and shared values—helps executives more clearly define their own projects and how best to accomplish them.

But there's a lot more to the program than that. Some graduates call it a mini-MBA, in part because the four-week program covers so much strategy and leadership material. Indeed, it's much more than a strategy program. Says Director Margaret M. Fisher, "It's a blend of strategy execution and leadership styles. That's the unique feature of the institute, because most programs usually cover leadership or have a strategic focus. This one blends both together."

The first two-week module takes place at the Cranwell Conference Center in the Berkshires in Western Massachusetts in late May. Away from the daily pressures of the job, managers move through a series of lectures, case studies, and discussions that often begin at breakfast at 7 a.m. and run throughout the day. Besides the additional work that will go into honing your strategy project, there are sessions on a wide variety of basic business issues: "Taking Action in a Global Environment," "General Manager: Managing the Change Agenda," "Competitive Marketing Strategy," "Customer-Driven Organizations," and a day-long session on "Leadership and Teams: An Experiential Approach."

When you return in mid-September for the final two weeks at the Ocean Edge resort in Brewster on Cape Cod, you'll soon discuss the implementation problems of your strategic challenge and gain valuable insights from colleagues on their projects. You'll also find plenty to debate in classroom sessions on such topics as "Managing Organization Responsiveness," "The Paradoxes of Implementation," and "Driving Strategic Change to Results." A full two and a half days is devoted to a strategic leadership simulation. And before you leave, you'll have developed a "personal leadership development plan" to improve your own management abilities.

The institute makes BUSINESS WEEK's list of the 10 most innovative programs on the basis of our surveys to corporate human resources officials, B-school program directors, and the participants themselves. Crows one participant manager: "There was a clear focus on the need to focus and act quickly and decisively to succeed. The program, and interaction among participants, surfaced many alternative techniques for instituting change and provided useful tools and examples for selecting styles appropriate to different situations. I'm more sensitive to the need to lead through persuasion and collaboration in situations in which I formerly would have been more direct. We got to test some new methods in a nonthreatening environment."

That's quite an endorsement. In 1992, Boston added a new twist to the program: It got a couple of corporate sponsors to provide two scholarships to minorities in not-for-profit organizations. Levi Strauss nominated the coordinator of Women Against Violence from the YWCA of Canada, while Federal Express footed the bill for a vice president of development affairs for LeMoyne Owen College in Tennessee. The cost, incidentally, for the four-week program is $14,500 per person.

Contact: Margaret M. Fisher, director, 617-353-4217

Global Leadership Program
University of Michigan

School of Business
700 East University
Ann Arbor, Michigan 48109

In halting English, Tamio Mori is trying to sell a small group of American and European executives on his team's strategy to enter the Indian market. The idea: to produce and sell electric-powered motorbikes to the masses in India who can't afford cars. But Mori, in a beige cardigan sweater and white sneakers, is having trouble convincing colleagues that his team's approach is worthwhile.

"You can't be serious," laughs one skeptic, reminding the Hitachi Ltd. executive of India's daily power blackouts and high electricity costs. "That's a long shot," heckles another. Undaunted, Mori presses ahead. "It will take a few years for the costs to go down," he says with a smile. "But we must plan for the next generation of technology."

That scene was recently played out in the University of Michigan's highly creative Global Leadership Program. No single program received more accolades in BUSINESS WEEK's search for the most innovative approaches to executive education than this one. Once a year, it brings together about 30 executives from the United States, Europe, and Asia for an intensive five-week course team-taught by three professors, one each from Michigan, France's INSEAD, and Hitotsubashi University in Japan. The lofty mission: to develop "global business leaders" with "the mind-set, leadership, and team-building skills to both lead their institutions and contribute to world economic growth."

To accomplish those goals, Program Director Noel M. Tichy throws executives into what he calls "compressed action learning." Rather than lecture to a classroom of executives, he engages them in a series of team-building exercises, from competitive raft-building at an Outward Bound school to creating and presenting elaborate assessments of business opportunities in such countries as India, China, and the Soviet Union. "We do real company problems, not Harvard case studies," says Tichy, who brings unbridled enthusiasm to the program. He is joined by two other exceptional professors: Hirotaka Takeuchi, a young, energetic Japanese academic with a background in marketing, and Michael Brimm, an expert in strategy from INSEAD.

The program was hatched after Robert Lundeen, chairman of Dow Chemical, told Tichy in 1983 that he had just blown a deal in Japan because of his own "cultural insensitivities." What was Michigan doing, Lundeen asked, to develop the next generation of chief executives who will have to compete in this new global environment? The light bulb went on, although it took until 1988 for Michigan to design its unusual program, sign up a bunch of corporate sponsors from the United States, Europe, and Japan, and get it off the ground. There's big league sponsorship of this program: American Express, General Electric, Procter & Gamble, Fiat, ICI, Unilever PLC, Japan Airlines, Nomura, and Sony, among others. Each sponsor pays $30,000 for every executive it sends to the program.

When the handpicked executives arrive, they typically spend the first two weeks in August building each multi-cultural team, establishing the frameworks for analyzing a given country, participating in diplomatic and economic briefings in Washing-

177

ton, D.C., and trading their pinstripes for jeans to visit homeless shelters and drug rehab clinics in the inner city. In 1990, executives from Exxon, General Motors, Sony, and Hitachi even found themselves pushing brooms and serving dinner to the homeless in Washington, D.C.—this latter part of the program is a passion of Tichy's, who wants the executives to experience first hand the world's social problems and to explore what responsibility corporations have to solve them.

But the main thrust of this program is to bring together United States, European, and Japanese executives, and mix them into teams which will travel abroad to assess business opportunities in other nations. In 1991, the teams trekked to the former Soviet Union, India, and China. Rather than simply reading or hearing about global leadership, the program forces executives to actively participate in it. They learn to view business prospects from different cultural perspectives, and they learn to work together in teams—even though they are very different from each other.

Mori's strategy for the Indian market was typical of the approach. For five weeks, he worked closely with four other executives in a team jokingly dubbed "Les Miserables" for their sobering views: two Americans from AT&T and Merck, a European from Olivetti, and a Japanese compatriot from Honda Motor. Like the other five teams, the group spent two weeks in a foreign locale to identify target markets and figure out the best way to enter them. The managers interviewed government officials, local businesspeople, and consumers. They toured factories and walked down the back streets of major cities. They gathered statistics on trade and information on tariffs.

The eye-popping trip spurred plenty of personal introspection that reached well beyond business considerations. Takeo Fukui of Honda said he couldn't eat one day because of the squalor he witnessed. James E. Clark of AT&T said the living conditions in Calcutta reminded him "of what slavery must have been like in this country for my grandparents." Hitachi's Mori recalled the cheerful faces of the children of India. "I started to wonder who they are and what I was doing there," he told his colleagues. "These questions still remain in my mind."

Back at school in Ann Arbor, each team produces written, videotaped, and oral reports for dissection by skeptical colleagues. The whirlwind process forces intense interaction with managers from diverse corners of the world. "You see how different cultures come at things differently," says James Danzeisen, a program alum from Britain's ICI Industries. "You see how the Japanese are so pragmatic and precise, yet completely gracious in groups, unwilling to criticize each other." The heckling Mori got when he made his presentation quickly taught him not to expect Japanese-style treatment from his American and European cohorts.

Contact: Robert P. Weiler, associate director, 313-936-3919

The Alfred P. Sloan Fellows Program
Massachusetts Institute of Technology

Sloan School of Management
50 Memorial Drive
Cambridge, Massachusetts 02139

The program is the precursor of all business school involvement in executive education. It got its start after a visit to MIT by Alfred P. Sloan, the legendary chairman of General Motors. Sloan, an engineering alum of MIT, mentioned the problem his company was having in moving engineers into broader management jobs. MIT Professor Erwin Schell observed that management was an entirely different field from engineering. He suggested the need for additional training that might make the transition much easier for mid-career managers. The upshot: six managers, chosen in a nationwide competition, entered an experimental year-long program in 1931.

The idea itself spurred plenty of attention. *The New York Times* devoted columns to the competition, and one Boston paper attached the odd headline, "Tech to Train Supermen," over its story. By 1938, the program was formally named in honor of Sloan, and some 60 years since its founding, about 2000 managers from more than 50 countries have become Sloan Fellows. MIT even helped initiate similar programs at Stanford, which offers a 10-month version, and the London Business School, which has a 9-month version.

MIT's early success with the program made it part of the folklore surrounding "The Organizational Man" of the 1950s. William H. Whyte Jr., author of the seminal book, even wrote a prominent magazine article on the Sloan Fellows in 1956, describing them much like the executives in his famous study. "The average Sloan Fellow," he concluded, "is a serious man of about thirty-three who has gone to engineering school, worked for one company since graduation, and risen through a series of technical line jobs to a position commanding a salary of about $11,000. His background is usually Protestant; quite likely he was born and raised in a small town, went to a large state university—where, very frequently, he met his wife. Often he is the child of a management man, often so is his wife, and both speak frequently of the word-of-mouth lessons they received from their parents about the corporate way of life."

Today, Whyte would have trouble recognizing the current crop of Fellows. For one thing, in each class of about 55 Fellows more than 12 percent are women and half hail from overseas. They arrive not only from Europe, but also from such countries as Australia, Chile, Korea, Mexico, Pakistan, Peru, Trinidad, Venezuela, and, of course, Japan. The international contingent is expected to rise further as the United States share of the world's economy continues to decline. "Years went by when we had no candidates from Singapore," says White. "This year (1991) we had 10 candidates from that country and we accepted 3 of them."

Besides the typical candidates from brand-name American firms that dominated the program in Whyte's day, Sloan Fellows are just as likely to come from nonprofit groups and government agencies these days. The Class of 1991, for example, included a manager from NASA, a hospital medical director from Israel, a U.S. Coast Guard strategic planner, a lecturer from a Singapore university, and a design head straight from the U.S. Marine Corps' Camp Lejeune in North Carolina. It's quite an eclectic bunch that leads to plenty of intriguing debate. And when Fellows graduate,

179

they do so with much confidence. "You tend to come out thinking you're an elite paratrooper," says Charles R. Grader, director of the program.

This is truly a back-to-school adventure. It begins in mid-June with a summer term and ends 12 months later in early June. The cost: $39,500, plus an extra $14,000 or so for trips and instructional materials. Every week, Fellows spend 20 to 25 hours in the classroom, while homework assignments consume up to 35 hours a week. A highlight of the program is the annual three-week-long international excursion—the longest and most extensive foreign jaunt of any general management executive program. MIT first took its Fellows abroad in 1958, long before foreign trips were in vogue. Every year—just before graduation—the group sets out to visit three countries for a series of factory tours and informal sessions with government and business leaders. No spouses are allowed on these trips, which are priced separately at a cost of between $3500 and $4000. In 1991, the Fellows traveled to Australia, Singapore, and Hong Kong. Previous groups have done study tours through the former Soviet Union, Germany, France, Japan, Korea, and the People's Republic of China.

The often exotic locales of these treks can occasionally lead to logistical nightmares. The absolute worst occurred in the mid-1970s when the entire Fellows group found itself stranded in Rome for four days after Air Italia cancelled their flight to Algeria. "We had no way to fly across the Mediterranean," recalls White. "We had to tread water until returning back to the states."

Then, there's the thesis requirement. Every Fellow must complete a major research project to gain a degree from the program. During late December and the month of January, all coursework is suspended so executives can spend a good chunk of concentrated time on their thesis projects. You can pick the topic, though, and many Fellows select subjects relevant to their own jobs. In 1989–1990, executives delved into everything from the human cost of mergers and acquisitions to the importation of nickel ore into Australia. Many managers study key topical issues. In 1989–1990, for example, there were seven thesis projects examining different aspects of competing for the Malcolm Baldrige Quality Award. One Fellow tackled the problems posed by dual-career couples in Corporate America.

It's unusual for Sloan Fellows to be self-sponsored. Most candidates are sent to the program by their companies. Indeed, a third of the sponsors have long-term relationships with the program. These "feeder companies" include AT&T, Boeing, Digital Equipment, Kodak, Caterpillar, IBM, Shell, British Petroleum, Unilever, Mitsui, and Mitsubishi. And through the years, this is a program that boasts some prestigious alums: Colby Chandler, chairman, Eastman Kodak; Robert Horton, deputy chairman of British Petroleum; Thomas Barrett, former chairman of Goodyear Tire & Rubber Co.

Alumni links are strong. Each issue of *MIT Management*, the school's alumni magazine, includes a sizable section on the doings of Sloan Fellows. Some longstanding sponsors even host informal get-togethers. When Eastman Kodak, for example, announces its Sloan candidates each year, one alum hosts a party at his or her home where all the company's Sloan Fellows gather to offer advice for the latest recruits headed for Cambridge. Every three years, MIT sponsors a "convocation" of alums. In 1989, the event saw three of MIT's Nobel Laureates deliver speeches: Franco Modigliani, Paul A. Samuelson, and Robert M. Solow.

Contact: Charles R. Grader, director, 617-253-0825

Minority Business Executive Program
Dartmouth College

The Amos Tuck School of Business Administration
Hanover, New Hampshire 03755

The black owner of an Ohio-based holding group whose success later qualified him to join the likes of Ford Motor Co. President Phil Benton and Time Warner Inc.'s Richard Munro as a Tuck executive-in-residence. A Japanese-American woman who beat the odds of surviving the Texas oil and banking collapses of the late 1980s to establish a thriving petrochemical distribution firm. A former broadcast journalist who nurtured his electrical supply start-up into a $3 million enterprise but then nearly went under for lack of other minority business owners who could share advice on strategy with him. The Hispanic owner of a Houston maintenance service who was able to cut overhead by $6000 a month. A husband and wife who in less than 10 years built their auto parts company into one of the 25 largest black-owned businesses in the United States.

These are just a few of the alumni who cite their experiences with the Minority Business Executive Program at Dartmouth's Amos Tuck School of Business Administration as seminal to their success—and the list could go on and on.

While there are any number of executive programs around that past participants recommend to their coworkers, there are few that alumni love so much that they re-enroll themselves, sometimes year after year. Over MBEP's 12 years of operation, the one-week crash course in business fundamentals for minority entrepreneurs has proven so popular that officials were obliged in 1987 to create an Advanced Minority Business Executive Program to supply fresh material to eager-to-return graduates. In 1992, the two programs, which run concurrently each August, will take in a total of 140 students and will still have to turn candidates away. The level of enthusiasm is so high that at the end of the 1991 session, participants shelled out $25,000 from their own pockets to augment a corporate scholarship fund that supports some 50 percent of first-time attendees in paying the course's $2150 tuition.

The concept is a simple one: to give minority owners of small businesses— mainly those in the $1 million to $8 million range, with fewer than 500 employees— an education in the key management issues in the various functions needed to develop and sustain a competitive advantage, according to Vijay Govindarajan (universally known as "V.G."), who has been the faculty director since 1987. Federal mandates on minority hiring may have made it easier for some entrepreneurs to get a foot in the door, says Govindarajan, "but you can't sustain that by simply saying I'm minority. If you louse up the first job, you won't get a second. You must know solid management."

Additionally, once established, minority business owners face "special problems that come partly from societal issues, values issues, perception issues. Banks may approach giving a loan to them differently," says Govindarajan. So the cases, lecture material, and guest speakers are carefully chosen to reflect this unique perspective. In 1991, for example, a case based on a former participant's firm, Grimes Oil of Boston, was written up by a Tuck professor and used for the first time. In the advanced course, which immerses managers in functional integration, strategy formulation, and implementation, much of the week is devoted to intensive computer simulation

181

games that have been devised by Tuck faculty especially for the course. Because half of each AMBEP class will be back the following year, four different simulations had to be developed and rotated over the course of four years—a manufacturing game one summer is followed by a service-industry game the next, with a retailing game the third year, and an international business game the fourth. "The fifth year we go back to manufacturing—hopefully they will have forgotten it," Govindarajan jokes. "Actually, they always learn something new, because it depends on the dynamics of the team every year."

While the specially tailored study materials are a key attraction to participants, just as important is the networking and support group that inevitably grows out of each session. For a solid week, students from both MBEP and AMBEP share meals at the campus dining hall, live in the same B-school dormitory, and attend the same cookouts, receptions, and cocktail hours, providing a rare opportunity for minority business owners from across the United States to get to know one another in person and strike up working partnerships. (While most alumni hail from big industrial states like New York and Ohio, some have come from the far reaches of Alaska, Hawaii, Montana, and North Dakota.) The program also invites executives from the largest 500 companies, many of them MBEP corporate sponsors, to meet and talk with participants who may be potential suppliers, as well as introduces participants to Tuck MBA students who may be potential employees (in 1991, four were hired by MBEP companies). Noted minority guest speakers such as Congressman Esteban Torres, former Congressman Parren Mitchell, and Undersecretary of the Treasury Sidney Jones round out the contacts managers are able to make.

"Too often, successful members of the black business community are descendants of business owners who are unwilling to share strategies, and some even discourage young people from entrepreneurship," says Burnes Ray, president of North Carolina-based BRI Supplies Inc. Ray, who first attended MBEP in 1989, nearly lost his electrical equipment distribution firm when he naively overextended himself based on the company's rapid growth and couldn't find a mentor to guide him through the crisis. "That's one of the things I liked most about MBEP," he says. "All the participants have a history of successful business management experience, and all are eager to exchange those winning strategies."

Govindarajan, one of Tuck's teaching superstars, has assembled a top-notch core faculty for MBEP, including Dennis Logue and Clyde Stickney in finance, Rohit Deshpande in marketing, Martin Davidson in human resources management, and Karla Bourland in operations management, as well as Govindarajan's own strategy segments. Their goal is to continue tailoring the course material to the participants' special requirements, eventually dealing only with minority-owned businesses in their cases, lectures, and simulations. What the staff doesn't have to work on is publicizing the program. After every August, there are over 100 satisfied customers who are more than willing to volunteer for that job.

Contact: Vijay Govindarajan, faculty director, 603-646-2156; Paula Graves, program manager, 603-646-3740

The International Forum
University of Pennsylvania

The Wharton School
255 S. 38th Street
Philadelphia, Pennsylvania 19104

As far as executive programs go, this is the top of the line. You simply won't find a more elite class of students than the 30 business leaders from Europe, Asia, and the United States who sign up each year for the International Forum's trio of four-day seminars on global issues. In the eight months between September 1991 and May 1992, the roster of top-level managers who gathered for the three sessions in Philadelphia, Bruges, Belgium, and Kyoto, Japan, included the senior managing director of Japan's Fuji Bank Ltd., two managing directors of Mitsubishi Corp., the chief operating officer of BP Oil Europe, the technology and products division president of Norsk Hydro, the president of Alcan Aluminio do Brasil, two vice presidents of Digital Equipment Corp., and the vice president and engineering systems president of Xerox Corp.

You also will find no bigger logistical nightmare than assembling such a time-starved, high-voltage group in three such farflung locations—not to mention the 50 or so additional invited guest experts for each session who are brought in to lend their views on everything from technological advances in manufacturing and political changes sweeping through Europe to medieval carillon music and the art of the Japanese tea ceremony. Nor will you find a higher price tag for a single executive course: $33,000, not including travel expenses. "It's in the stratosphere compared with any other program," acknowledges director Michael Alexander. But Alexander thrives on the pressure of measuring up to such a demanding clientele. He must be doing something right: Even in the recessionary economy of 1991–1992, with CEO time and money at a premium, the program was oversubscribed.

Alexander was tapped to develop the forum back in 1987, fresh from a career in international business (he was an executive partner at the accounting firm of Touche Ross before its merger with Deloitte, Haskins & Sells, as well as an international partner in an investment bank). "This was driven by Wharton's whole mission to make itself more international," he says. "A number of faculty, including the dean, wanted to do something unusual and new, something that wasn't being done elsewhere in the international field. The idea was to do it for the very top executives, because there were no programs at that level." It took a year and a half of market testing before the first session was held at the Wharton School in September 1989. "We went out and talked to potential participants in Asia and Europe, and in these conversations molded what became the product," says Alexander. "It very much reflected what these people felt was needed."

One thing quickly became apparent from the field research: "People wanted to see the global market from the three different perspectives of the Triad [Japan, the United States, and the European Community]," Alexander says. So it was determined that meetings should be held in each of those regions, with one-third of the executives drawn from each area. But Alexander also wanted to emphasize that "international business is not just marketing, finance, and operations, but understanding how to bridge cultures, to see the sameness and differences both in working with people and dealing with them."

To that end, the sites for the sessions were chosen not because of their status as major commercial centers, but because of the cultural and historical contexts they could provide: Philadelphia, with its rich American heritage and internationally renowned symphony orchestra and art museum; Bruges, the fifteenth-century European crucible of Flemish art and madrigal music; and Kyoto, Japan's capital for 10 centuries and one of the few traditional cultural centers largely unscathed by World War II. Cultural activities and social topics are integrated throughout the curriculum. A typical day during the Japanese session may start at 6:45 with t'ai chi exercises; move through discussions of Japan's changing conditions, trade and direct investment, relationship with the United States, and post-war recovery; then end with a demonstration of the famed tea ceremony before dinner. In Philadelphia, a day may begin with a brisk walk through the nineteenth-century University of Pennsylvania's architecture; delve into talks on equity markets and global information technology; pause for lunch and a discussion of food, mood, travel, and time zones; continue with segments on North American political issues and trade policy; and end with a tour of the American exhibits at the Philadelphia Museum of Art.

With executives of this stature—CEOs or others of the top six executives in the largest public corporations—lecturing is simply out of the question. Alexander says, "The magic time is seven minutes—top executives have an attention span of about that. We can have the most eminent philosopher-king in the world appearing, but he can only talk for seven minutes." The role of the faculty—Alexander and Wharton School colleagues Jerry Wind (marketing), Steve Coburn (management), Richard Herring (finance), and Paul Kleindorfer (operations management and manufacturing technology)—is not so much to teach but to moderate the executives' interchanges. "We don't say much, we just get people to talk—which is much harder," Alexander quips.

But participants are expected to do more than simply show up and shoot off at the mouth. Advance reading materials are sent out to prepare participants for discussing such heavy topics as managing interest and exchange rate volatility, the infrastructure of a united Germany, worldwide environmental issues, or the roles of China and Southeast Asia in the world economy. In addition, small groups of six to eight execs are assigned during each session to come up with a strategy report involving how the team would deal with specific regional business issues. It's a rare opportunity for a top-level executive in a major organization to break away from his or her usual sounding-board advisers and see things from an outside perspective.

The investment of money and time is a hefty one. CEOs simply cannot—and will not—commit to more than four consecutive days away from the office, and not infrequently, a manager who has attended one session will be unable to make the next because of a company crisis like an acquisition blowing up two days before departure. But at least two-thirds of each class holds to the commitment of attending all three sessions, and it's not just because they don't want to waste the funds they've paid in advance: This hard-to-please crowd shows a high degree of satisfaction at the end that they've gotten their money's worth. Notes Jean-Jacques Van de Berg, director of the Belgian firm Solvay & Cie: "Over the past eight months, the International Forum gave us the world, three times in four days. Excellent yield per day, I'd say."

Contact: Michael Alexander, director, 215-898-9768

CHAPTER 7

THE TOP B-SCHOOLS OFFERING MBAs FOR EXECUTIVES

For years, executives viewed the multi-week management programs at business schools as miniature versions of the MBA. But it's impossible to cram two years worth of work in just a few weeks. If you want the real thing, yet can't afford to leave your job, many of the nation's top business schools offer a solution: Executive MBA programs.

In theory, at least, these programs are like premium ice cream: All the ingredients that go into them are supposed to be richer than what you'd find in a regular MBA. They attract an older, more seasoned crowd of full-time managers who have a decade or more of experience behind them. They're taught by the schools' best professors, teachers who can withstand the challenges of executives who know better. And from the cruises to the fine wines, student-managers are often treated as if they already carry the keys to the executive suite. "The chow line has to be good," says Richard R. West, dean of New York University's Stern School. "But in the classroom, you beat the hell out of them academically."

These days some 9500 managers are taking a beating in Executive MBA programs at 102 business schools in North America—a student count that's up 27 percent from just four years ago. These programs are quite different from the more common evening MBA offerings, which are usually populated by younger people seeking the degree at their own expense. In so-called EMBA programs, most students are sponsored by their companies, which pay the steep tuition bills and allow days off from work to attend school. Classes typically meet once a week on alternating Fridays and Saturdays. There are exceptions, of course. Wharton, for example, requires a Friday night sleep-over every other week, when classes meet on both Friday and Saturday. Columbia University holds classes every Friday from 8:30 a.m. to 6:30 p.m. During each of the five semesters required to complete the program, you'll spend a full week in seclusion at the university's Arden House conference center in Harriman, N.Y. Indeed, most of these programs kick off with a live-in week during which you'll get to know your classmates and what kind of perspectives they bring to class.

In recent years, B-schools have devoted much time and energy to making the Executive MBA program as attractive and innovative as possible, developing overseas trips, business-government ties, and other luring wrinkles. At New York University, the EMBA program features five week-long residence sessions per year and a 10-day international stint at such places as INSEAD in Fontainebleau, France, or Keio University or the University of Tokyo in Japan. Washington University in St. Louis begins its two-year program in late August with a residential week at a conference center and ends the first year in June with a week in Washington, D.C., where managers meet elected officials, lobbyists, and other political players.

These are but a few of the premium ingredients commonly tossed into the mix. In many cases, the high expectations of these programs are met. But a goodly number of managers are hitting the books at programs of questionable quality, many of which were launched in the hope that they would quickly become cash cows for their schools. "Far too many programs are weakened, weekend versions of more traditional full-time programs," says Michael R. Forrest, associate dean of Pepperdine University's program.

Some of these schools, say the critics, accept virtually any paying customer who walks through the door—even those with as little as two years of work experience. The faculties are composed of too many adjunct teachers with dubious academic credentials. And the intellectual rigor of some of the programs can be suspect, requiring far fewer hours than a full-time program to gain the same MBA degree.

Graduates of even some well-regarded programs cite glaring shortcomings. An alumnus of the Loyola College program in Baltimore describes some professors as "bottom-of-the-barrel selections: find any warm body to 'teach' this class." A graduate of the University of Rochester complains that the program he enrolled in focused "too heavily on theory and quantitative analysis. I wish more creative problem solving and decision making had been included in the program," he says.

BUSINESS WEEK, in its survey of EMBA graduates and the deans who run these programs, provides some guidance on the best of the best. First, we'll share with you some of the results of a dozen key questions we asked the graduates of such programs in 1989 and 1991. Then, we'll offer up profiles on the Top 20 schools which offer programs through which you can get a master's degree in business while holding down a full-time job and trying to maintain some semblance of family life.

In our search for excellence, we surveyed 2844 graduates from 30 schools chosen on the basis of another survey sent to program directors and deans. Some 1610 graduates answered a 30-question survey, a response rate of 57 percent. The survey for program directors was sent to all 102 schools listed in the Executive MBA Council's 1991 directory. Some 76 schools responded, a response rate of 75 percent. The results are listed in the table.

BUSINESS WEEK's Top Twenty Executive MBA Programs

Overall ranking	Graduate ranking	Dean's poll rank	Total tuition	Current enrollment	Average salary of managers
1. Northwestern	2	1	$39,800	280	$ 80,000
2. Chicago	3	2	38,500	163	84,800
3. Pennsylvania	19	4	61,500	197	96,100
4. Duke	6	7	44,000	90	85,000
5. UCLA	11	5	42,700	120	92,000
6. Indiana	1	27	25,000	50	78,600
7. Columbia	25	3	59,500	225	93,300
8. Southern Calif.	7	8	38,000	118	70,000
9. Georgia State	5	12	22,500	77	65,000
10. Case Western	4	18	46,662	85	85,000
11. New York Univ.	18	6	59,600	86	104,000
12. Illinois	10	9	24,400	74	58,000
13. Purdue	8	24	28,500	70	62,300
14. Pittsburgh	9	10	27,600	81	73,200
15. Emory	12	11	37,600	91	81,700
16. Texas (Austin)	15	13	20,100	117	83,000
17. Wake Forest	13	22	29,000	100	59,000
18. Vanderbilt	14	30	40,200	52	60,100
19. Southern Methodist	17	17	29,940	95	73,100
20. Tulane	16	21	33,000	60	56,500

A glance at the list raises one obvious question: What happened to such high-powered business schools as Harvard, Stanford, Dartmouth, and the University of Michigan at Ann Arbor? The simple answer: They don't offer Executive MBA programs. Their conspicuous absence allows the emergence of a group of well-regarded B-schools that fail to make most top lists of full-time MBA programs. There's Georgia State University in Atlanta, for instance, and Tulane University in New Orleans.

Which school is best for you? Location usually plays a major role in that decision. Still, it's helpful to know how the best schools stack up against each other on key dimensions. The following graphs show some of the survey results from 24 schools: the 12 that got the best scores on a question and the dozen that received the worst.

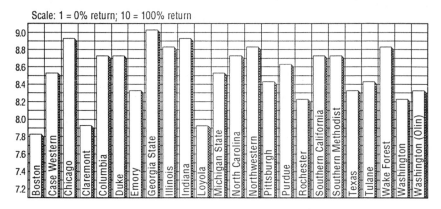

Scale: 1 = 0% return; 10 = 100% return

1. Do you believe your Executive MBA was worth its cost in time and tuition?

Even if your company foots the bill, your MBA won't come cheap. Balancing a career and a family with school is a tough and demanding game to play. By these results, most graduates of the top schools apparently think it is worth it. Grads from such schools as Georgia State, Chicago, and Indiana think they are getting the best deal. Executive MBAs from Boston University, Loyola, and Claremont are slightly less convinced the experience was worth the trouble.

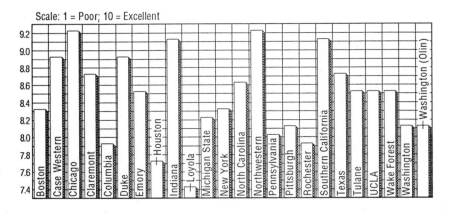

Scale: 1 = Poor; 10 = Excellent

2. How would you rate the quality of the teaching in the program?

In full-time MBA programs, it's a lot easier for schools to mix in some so-so teachers. But in these premium EMBA programs where the student-managers bring far more knowledge into the classroom, it's harder for a school to get away with that. Where to expect the absolute best teaching? Northwestern, Chicago, Indiana, and Southern California. The not-so-best? Loyola, Houston, Columbia, and Rochester.

188

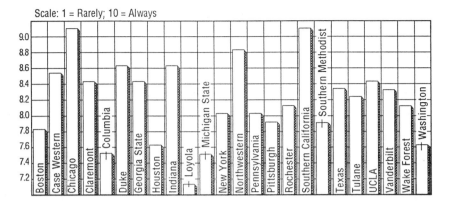

3. Did you have the feeling that your teachers were at the leading edge of knowledge in their fields?

Faculty who bring cutting-edge know-how in management, finance, marketing, and other key disciplines add great value to a program—especially when they are judged to be at the top of their fields by practicing managers who know a thing or two about management themselves. Grads were most impressed by the faculty at Chicago and Southern California. They were less impressed at Loyola, Columbia, and Michigan State.

Scale: 1 = Rarely; 10 = Always

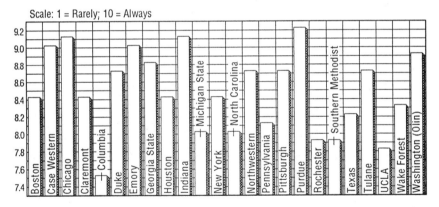

4. Was the faculty available for informal discussion when classes were not in session?

Distinguished professors at top business schools are often in high demand. They work as consultants and writers. They teach in full-time MBA programs and executive education courses. But it's important that they make time for you outside the classroom. Purdue grads thought their profs were best in this department. The teachers at Chicago, Indiana, Case Western, and Emory also did extremely well. The faculty at Columbia and UCLA didn't stack up nearly as well.

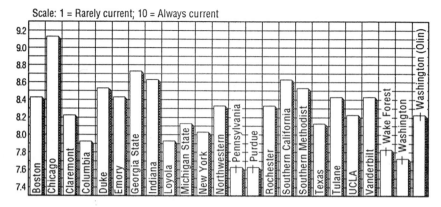

Scale: 1 = Rarely current; 10 = Always current

5. How current was the material/research presented in class for discussion and review?

While a lot of the research that goes on in academia is rather esoteric, a good deal of it is vital to a school and to American business. Professors who conduct leading-edge research, however, must be able to make it useful to managers in EMBA classrooms. By doing so, they're applying the newest ideas to the latest business problems, many of which you have to deal with on a daily basis. By far, executives believe Chicago does the best job of it. At the other end of the scale are Wharton, Purdue, and the University of Washington.

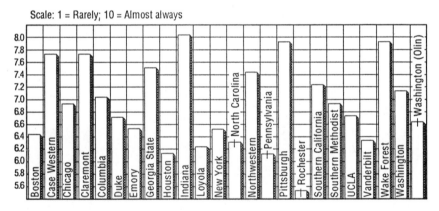

Scale: 1 = Rarely; 10 = Almost always

6. Were you given assignments or projects that had some linkage to your own full-time job?

It's nice to know whether all those hours spent at school can still help you back at the office. Some teachers make a major effort to hand out assignments and projects that link back to your duties at work and allow you to show off some of the new concepts and ideas you're learning at school. Others hardly bother. Which schools forge the best links? Indiana and Wake Forest. On the other end of the scale are Rochester and Wharton.

190

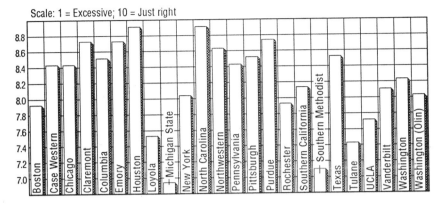

Scale: 1 = Excessive; 10 = Just right

7. Was the amount of assigned work and reading so excessive that it impeded learning?

Remember the entertainer on the old Ed Sullivan television show who ran across the stage trying to keep spinning plates atop a series of wobbling poles? That's the feeling a lot of executives have when they try to juggle an MBA with a full-time job. You often wonder when a plate will drop and crash. The schools that sense the difficulties and adjust the workload to best accommodate working students? North Carolina and Houston. That's less true at Michigan State, Southern Methodist, and Tulane.

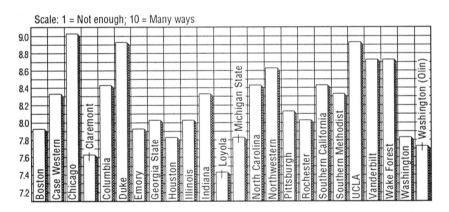

Scale: 1 = Not enough; 10 = Many ways

8. Were you given numerous ways of thinking or approaching problems that will serve you well over the long haul?

One of the most important benefits of a good Executive MBA program is learning systematic ways to solve business problems. When a manager confronts tough decisions, he or she should have a framework or way of thinking available to weigh the pros and cons. If you get anything from an MBA education, you should at least bring this home with your diploma. Graduates think that Chicago, Duke, and UCLA did the best job in this department. EMBAs were less satisfied at Loyola, Claremont, and Washington University.

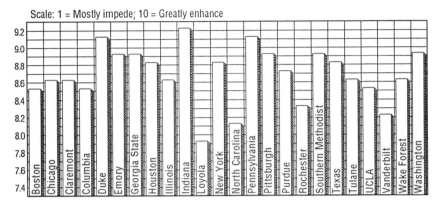

Scale: 1 = Mostly impede; 10 = Greatly enhance

9. Did the caliber of your classmates impede or enhance the learning process?

Most Executive MBA grads say they've learned as much if not more from their fellow classmates than their professors. It's not hard to understand why: Most of these elite programs require 10 or more years of work experience before you can apply. Still, some schools do a better job than others in putting the right mix of people into a classroom. Tops in this area? Indiana, Duke, and Wharton. Grads had some doubts at Loyola, North Carolina, and Vanderbilt.

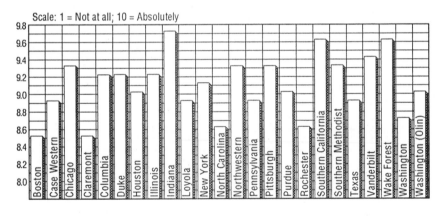

Scale: 1 = Not at all; 10 = Absolutely

10. Will you be able to shoulder greater responsibility as a direct result of the program?

For an Executive MBA program, this has got to be the bottom line. After all the time you devote to a program, you should feel much more confident back at the shop, and that confidence should translate into a feeling that you're capable of shouldering much more responsibility. Which B-school programs are best at providing that sense of confidence? Indiana, Southern California, and Wake Forest.

192

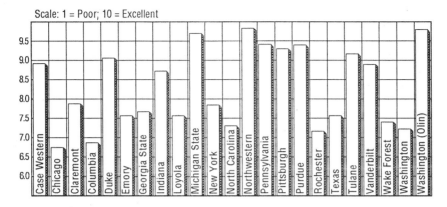

Scale: 1 = Poor; 10 = Excellent

11. How would you rate the facilities?

When a full-time manager studies for an MBA, he or she shouldn't have to put up with rundown facilities and antiquated equipment that makes an already difficult task even more difficult. Comfort is important to learning—especially when you're squeezing so much in so little time. Which schools offer the most comfortable facilities? Northwestern, Washington University, Michigan State, and Wharton. The worst? Chicago and Columbia.

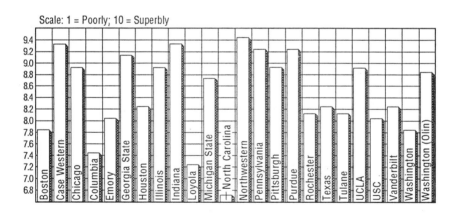

Scale: 1 = Poorly; 10 = Superbly

12. Overall, how well was the program organized?

If you're a busy, on-the-go executive, you'll greatly appreciate a school that makes it easy for you to go to school. Some programs boast superb administrators who cater to your every whim. They make getting an EMBA a hassle-free experience. Other schools—even some of the top ones—are loosely organized, adding to the tension of getting the degree itself. The schools that have their acts together? Northwestern, Indiana, and Case Western. The least organized? North Carolina, Loyola, and Columbia.

1. Northwestern University

Kellogg Graduate School of Management
2169 Sheridan Road
Evanston, Illinois 60208

Graduate ranking: 2	*Dean ranking*: 1
Enrollment: 280	*Full tuition*: $39,800
Women: 25 percent	*Minority*: 10 percent
Average GMAT score: 600 (Not req.)	*GMAT range*: 550 to 650 (mid-50 percent)
Average work exp.: 15 years	*Work exp. range*: 10 to 25 years
Average salary: $80,000	*Salary range*: $45,000 to $250,000
Advanced degrees: 35 percent	*Applicants accepted*: 40 percent

Teaching methods: Case study, 65 percent; Lecture, 35 percent; Simulations, 5 percent

Program start date: Early September

> *My boy, he ain't no dummy.*
> *You can see why he's the boss.*
> *Without Don Jacobs at the helm,*
> *We'd all be at a loss.*

Not many B-school deans become the hero of a rap song. But Donald P. Jacobs, head of Northwestern's Kellogg School of Management, is no ordinary dean. When students staged a recent follies show, one admirer rapped the tribute while jiving around a life-sized cardboard cutout of "Funky Don."

Kellogg's Executive MBAs are likely to agree with the full-timers who put on the goofy skit. Jacobs, whose school has ranked No. 1 in BUSINESS WEEK's Best B-School surveys since 1988, can now crow that the school also is at the top in offering the best degree-granting program for executives. Kellogg EMBA grads typically rave about the experience here—even those who have had to pay for it themselves. "If every business in this country was managed like Kellogg's program," gushes one grad, "we would have a booming economy."

Student-managers give Kellogg high marks not only for teaching the business basics, but also for emphasizing teamwork and collaboration. Weekly study-group sessions and team assignments form a key part of the learning experience. Kellogg assigns students to study groups, with an emphasis on diversity. One graduate noted that his study group of six included an accountant, a lawyer, a nurse, an executive vice president of marketing, and the owner of a family business. "In business discussions, we could look at problems through many different lenses, and this broad overview helped me greatly," he said.

Another executive said he left the campus of a Big 10 university to drive 300 miles a week to attend the program. He called it "the most satisfying educational experience of his career"—even though he boasted a B.A., an M.D., and postgraduate medical training. Many grads said they found much in the program that was immediately useful to them on the job. "From the first week through the final week, I took something of value to work every Monday," says a marketing manager for a major chemical company.

The program kicks off with a six-day, live-in session each year at the James L. Allen Center, the school's modern exec-ed facility on the shore of Lake Michigan. (Second-years also start out with a week in the center, playing a computer simulation

194

game among other things.) The six-day stay is hardly a vacation: You'll quickly find yourself immersed in such B-school nitty-gritty as "Operating Strategies for the General Manager" and an "Analytical Approach to Uncertainty." Then, the very next Friday, the fun really starts as the class begins its alternating-Friday-and-Saturday schedule for what seems like forever. Classes usually begin at 8:30 a.m. and continue to 11:45 a.m., with a mid-morning coffee break and informal chat. They resume after lunch at 1 p.m. and run to 4:15, with a mid-afternoon break.

Kellogg will put you through 24 required courses and give you the opportunity to select 4 out of 12 offered electives, including classes in "Negotiations," "Entre-Intrapreneurship and New Venture Formation," and "Business Marketing." The core curriculum covers the standard B-school fare, from financial reporting systems to operations management. Everyone takes two courses at a time: one verbal, one quantitative. It's marketing and accounting in the first quarter; statistics and organizational behavior in the second. And there's often some linkage with your job. In "Strategic Marketing," taught by Philip Kotler, you're required to polish off a marketing audit, usually of your own firm—an experience that lets you see how your company stacks up against the competition in marketing. To help managers suffering from math anxiety, there are two-hour evening tutorials by doctoral students on such tortuous subjects as cost accounting, microeconomics, and linear programming on Tuesdays.

One antidote to the quant material is the luncheon speaker series, which lures chief executives of such companies as Kidder, Peabody Group Inc., and Hartmarx Corp. to campus for presentations and discussions with students. Another high point is Kellogg's international trip. It's optional—whether you're a first- or second-year student—and even attracts some alums who tag along. In 1992, about 30 students traveled to Warsaw, Moscow, Vienna, and Prague for the 12-day sojourn that featured a meeting with the finance minister of Czechoslovakia and lunch at the McDonald's in Moscow. In 1991, students trekked to England, France, and Germany.

Though Jacobs is always accessible, you'll find the soft-spoken Edmund J. Wilson, an associate dean who oversees the EMBA program, the man in charge. He insures that, as one grad put it, "the easily overlooked operational aspects of the program, from lodging and meals to the curriculum, run like a well-oiled machine." That's the kind of devotion to the consumer that will encourage students to continue singing songs of tribute to Dean Jacobs for many years to come.

Organizations sending most participants: Baxter Healthcare; First Chicago Bank; Northern Trust; AT&T; Ameritech

Contact: Edmund J. Wilson, associate dean, 708-864-9270

Kellogg EMBA Graduates Sound Off

Ed Wilson told us it would be an extra 20 hours a week, excluding class day, on top of what we normally do. For me it was closer to 30 hours. Would I do it again? Absolutely!—Marketing Manager

Every Monday there was some nugget of knowledge from the last class or study group to use, discuss, or experiment with on the job. The learning was integrated into your "real" job all the time.—Manager

195

2. University of Chicago

Graduate School of Business
1101 E. 58th Street
Chicago, Illinois 60637

Graduate ranking: 3	*Dean ranking*: 2
Enrollment: 163	*Full tuition*: $38,500
Women: 21 percent	*Minority*: 6 percent
Average GMAT score: NA	*GMAT range*: NA
Average work exp.: 15 years	*Work exp. range*: 8 to 28 years
Average salary: $84,800	*Salary range*: $50,000 to $1,000,000
Advanced degrees: 20 percent	*Applicants accepted*: 70 percent

Teaching methods: Case study, 18 percent; Lecture, 60 percent; Group work and games, 22 percent

Program start date: Early September

It's the granddaddy of all Executive MBA programs. Begun in 1943 and having graduated more than 3700 executives, the University of Chicago's program was the model for them all. Indeed, for more than 20 years, it was the *only* school at which a manager could get an Executive MBA while fully employed.

Chicago's program is not only the oldest, however. For years, it has also been one of the very best in the country, luring out-of-state commuters on a regular basis to its alternating Friday-Saturday schedule. For the Class of 1993, roughly one in four student-managers drive or fly to the program from Iowa, Georgia, Michigan, Ohio, or Toronto. Nearly 10 commute from the Milwaukee area alone. Yet, Chicago offers another "Weekend Program" for managers in their late 20s with less than 10 years' experience that draws a more national audience.

What you'll get at Chicago is a solid EMBA program with few bells and whistles. Unlike other schools, Chicago offers managers no electives and no international trip. First-year students spend their first week in an on-campus residency, and second-years hole up at a rural retreat on Wisconsin's Lake Velevan for three days. Compared with other programs, that's hardly elaborate. Indeed, New York University puts its EMBAs through six one-week residencies. There's also little praise for Chicago's downtown facilities at 190 East Delaware Place where EMBA classes are held. It rated at the very bottom of 30 schools in our survey of graduates (although Chicago announced plans in May of 1992 to put up a new building).

Throughout, however, nearly everything about the Chicago experience is steeped in top quality, from a highly-regarded faculty to the emphasis on teamwork. Graduates award kudos to most of the faculty, most of the time. They also heap plenty of praise on the emphasis on group work. "There's enormous emphasis on group learning and working in study groups," says Gary Eppen, director of the EMBA program. "We want our people to meet with their study group one night a week and there are often group assignments. We think of these sessions as mini-classes that allow you to learn from your peers."

That is true from the start when managers are assigned to study groups of four or five people each. The reason Chicago offers no electives is so that each entering class is never broken up. Teams work together for two full years with only one exception, designed partly to enhance the networking value of the program. At Chicago's three-day getaway, managers work with three different study groups (one for each day). For one key exercise, groups are organized along industry backgrounds to study the impact of global competition on a business. The upshot: Manufacturing managers are aligned with other manufacturers, and the service folks are put together with service managers. On another day, differently configured study groups will tackle negotiation skills.

Many classes include special projects involving a student's company. A statistics class includes a heavy dose of total quality management, requiring each student to analyze his or her company's efforts in quality. And toward the end of the experience, managers play INTOP, a computer simulation game, in a critical strategy course. For the simulation, every study group runs a manufacturing company in competition with one another.

When the grueling experience is over, the university celebrates in style—with a black-tie dinner and dance at one of the swankier Chicago hotels. It's a fitting end for the oldest and most established Executive MBA program in the world.

Organizations sending most participants: Motorola; AT&T Bell Labs; Coopers & Lybrand; Amoco Corp.; Argonne National Laboratories

Contact: Gary Eppen, director of EMBA Program, 312-266-3430

Chicago EMBAs Sound Off

Every element of this program was first class, with the exception of the building facilities. I was surprised by the faculty's attentiveness and interest in my learning process. They demonstrated genuine excitement in the materials taught and were very solicitous for the group's inputs. Some faculty members encouraged home phone calls until late in the evening (little did I realize how often that would be).—**Senior District Sales Manager**

The entire faculty was of the first rank. The professors were more than theoreticians, each having distinguished himself in private business of some kind. They were on the cutting edge of their disciplines because of continual research and interaction with various firms on practical business issues. The support systems found at the university, particularly the libraries, were also superb. I have likened my experience to the Marine Corps' boot camp: "exquisite pain" which completely stretches one's level of experience and confidence.—**Circulation Manager**

The best learning experience I've had in my life.—**Director of New Business Planning**

It was much better than expected. I anticipated more quantitative work based on Chicago's reputation. While there was quite a bit of it, there was also conceptual problem solving, marketing, managerial training, etc. I tend to ask a lot of questions. I always felt I was given attention far beyond the minimum required to answer my inquiries.—**Associate Partner**

3. University of Pennsylvania

The Wharton School
224 Steinberg Conference Center
255 S. 38th Street
Philadelphia, Pennsylvania 19104

Graduate ranking: 19	*Dean ranking*: 4
Enrollment: 197	*Full tuition*: $61,500
Women: 25 percent	*Minority*: 12 percent
Average GMAT score: 640	*GMAT range*: 500 to 760
Average work exp.: 10 years	*Work exp. range*: 3 to 30 years
Average salary: $96,100	*Salary range*: $33,000 to $1,500,000
Advanced degrees: 40 percent	*Applicants accepted*: 33 percent

Teaching methods: Case study, 40 percent; Lecture, 40 percent; Group work and games, 20 percent

Program start date: Early June

"We laughed; we cried; we marvelled about how debits and credits always balanced; we were gracious in changing our foreign trip from Thailand to San Francisco and managed to make it the best 'foreign' trip ever. And during this whole process developed friendships we hope will last a lifetime!"

So said Grace Yabrudy in her address to Wharton's Executive MBA Class of 1993 on its first day of school. A policy officer at the World Bank in Washington, Yabrudy had only recently survived the two-year program herself. She returned to campus in June of 1991 to welcome the newcomers and reflect on her two years there, during which her class "had five weddings, eight babies, and 14 of us lost and/or had to change jobs, a telling statistic of the current tough economic times."

Tough times or not, Wharton's EMBA program is among the best in the nation, as Yabrudy can testify. The program begins in June of each year, with classes meeting all day Friday and Saturday on alternate weekends. The unusual sleepover format, as well as Wharton's great reputation, attracts students from Virginia, Washington, D.C., Delaware, Maryland, New Jersey, New York, and Connecticut.

More importantly, however, it allows students far more interaction together. On Friday evenings, Wharton invites guest speakers to campus to address the class. After those sessions, some self-styled WEMBAs (not to be confused with the WOMBAs, or Wharton Ordinary MBAs) stroll three blocks away to Smokey Joe's in dungarees and sweatshirts for a few beers and a game of pool. "We'd often come back after 1 a.m. after 'Smokes' and argue about cases after five beers," recalls Doug Anderson, a 1991 graduate. "That's when the real bonding took place."

At Wharton's modern Steinberg Conference Center, complete with a pub, accommodations are among the best of any B-school. That's also why the cost of the program is so high. At $61,500, it's the priciest EMBA of the lot. The pricetag, however, includes four full weeks of classes in residence, including a one-week international seminar. By far, nearly everyone thinks the program is worth it.

For one thing, it's hard to argue with the caliber of people drawn to Wharton. They are successful bankers and consultants, Washington policy makers, and nonprofit leaders. Ronald Reagan tapped Anne McLaughlin, a Wharton EMBA in the middle of her studies, as his Secretary of Labor. For another, they are given broad flexibility to pursue their own interests. One student-consultant, for example, recently did a detailed assessment of financial-sector reform in Czechoslovakia, Hungary, and Poland as a two-semester independent study project. Another student with interests in Third World development finished off a paper on cultural impediments to change for academic credit. That flexibility extends to an unusual array of elective courses for any EMBA program. Nine of the 19 required courses are electives students select from about 24 offerings, chosen on the basis of a class preference vote. Recent samples include "Problems in Financial Reporting," "Speculative Markets," "Strategic Planning and Control," and "Entrepreneurship and Venture Initiation." Compare that to zero electives at Chicago or just four at Northwestern.

Whether you're in a core class or an elective, it's a demanding schedule to meet. The usual drill calls for a 9 a.m. check-in at Steinberg on Friday, followed by the first three-hour class of the day at 9:30. Students often take their coffee breaks by running out to the nearby Wawa store. Lunch is served at 12:30, and an hour later you're back in class for another course. There might be a workshop from 4:45 to 6 p.m. on communications or computing. Dinner with a guest speaker is set for 7 p.m. to 8:30 p.m. Some students roll into review sessions at 9 p.m., while others head out for some fun—but not too much because breakfast is served at 7 a.m. on Saturday, before the 9 a.m. class. The final class begins at 1 p.m. and lets out three hours later.

Where can the experience fall short? No one has ever accused Wharton of boasting the best teaching. Against the top schools, in fact, Wharton has had more trouble than most in putting superb teachers in its classrooms. For decades, virtually all the awards went to academics whose narrow, esoteric research meant nearly everything. Wharton is now trying to upgrade teaching in its culture, but several grads still find too many theorists with too little practical business experience behind them.

Even so, there are few graduates who wouldn't do it again if given the chance. As Yabrudy testifies, "What other experience in your life would bring you into close personal contact with 90-something other smart, enthusiastic, motivated, successful, interesting, and crazy people?"

Organizations sending most participants: AT&T; Bankers Trust; General Electric; Manufacturers Hanover Trust; IBM

Contact: Dr. Isik Inselbag, director of EMBA program, 215-898-5887

Wharton EMBA Graduates Sound Off

*The biggest letdown in the Wharton program was the lack of effort on the part of many professors (not all) to keep courses current and relevant. Many relied on cases they had been teaching for 10 or 15 years.—**Vice President***

*I rate 40 percent of the professors as truly excellent, 30 percent as acceptable, and 30 percent as intolerable. Maybe I expected too much.—**Project Supervisor***

4. Duke University

The Fuqua School of Business
Durham, North Carolina 27706

Graduate ranking: 6
Enrollment: 90
Women: 17 percent
Average GMAT score: 563
Average work exp.: 12 years
Average salary: $85,000
Advanced degrees: 15 percent

Dean ranking: 7
Full tuition: $44,000
Minority: 17 percent
GMAT range: 350 to 710
Work exp. range: 5 to 24 years
Salary range: $30,000 to $500,000
Applicants accepted: 90 percent

Teaching methods: Case study, 55 percent; Lecture, 35 percent; Simulations, 10 percent

Program start date: January

When most people are doing their Christmas shopping, a good many of the newcomers to Duke's Weekend Executive MBA program are boning up on their math skills over a Saturday and Sunday in mid-December. That's part of the preparation you're likely to encounter before the action starts just a few weeks later with one of those team-building, executive-bonding outdoor jaunts.

The Outward Bound-like experience is the centerpiece of a three-day orientation to Duke's 20-month program. As soon as it is completed over a Tuesday-Wednesday-Thursday in January, you'll roll right into the first three classes in organizational behavior, financial accounting, and statistics. Fuqua doesn't mess around. As Deborah Horvitz, program director, explains: "It's a real boot camp mentality."

Executives tend to agree, often describing the experience as "a real grind...not for the faint of heart." Classes meet for two days at a time, every two weeks—which is one reason why more than a third of Duke's students are willing to commute to the school from outside the state. They fly in from Washington, D.C., Philadelphia, Dallas, and even Puerto Rico, to be picked up at the airport by a B-school van and whisked to the new and modern R. David Thomas Center for Executive Education. Indeed, half the class tends to arrive on Thursday evening, preferring to stay at the center for two nights instead of one—even though it costs a few bucks more for the extra night. After all, that makes it a lot easier to get to your first class at 8 a.m. on Friday. (Duke, by the way, encourages spouses to come along and stay free of charge.)

On both Friday and Saturday, you'll have a class in each of three courses. The Saturday sessions conclude at 2:30 p.m. to give you enough time to travel home for dinner. From then on, every other weekend, you'll find yourself in Durham. Of the 15 courses required to graduate, only two are electives chosen from about four offered. In the summer of 1992, Duke offered up such electives as "The Legal Environment of the Firm," "Negotiations and Bargaining," and "Advanced Marketing Strategy." The latter course pulls together concepts from earlier classes and climaxes with MarkStrat, a computer simulation game. A recent highlight was a combined course in corporate strategy, public policy, and the global environment that was team-taught by two professors and the retired chief executive of Control Data Corp.

In general, Fuqua boasts a young, bright, and aggressive faculty. Some managers complain that they could use more practical business experience, and some even maintain that a few of the teachers are intimidated by the experience executives bring to the classroom. By and large, however, managers had praise for most of the professors they encountered. What the faculty teaches on Friday and Saturday, many managers try out on Monday upon their return to work. "Their workplace becomes a living laboratory," says Horvitz. "If an idea works, it's great. If not, they come back the next weekend and try to figure out why it didn't work. So they find themselves working on live case studies almost all the time."

Those "live" cases are considerably enhanced by the wide diversity of people in the program. The Class of 1991, for example, boasted two lawyers, a heart surgeon, one Ph.D. and nearly a dozen managers with advanced engineering degrees. Among the 42 student-managers were 3 foreign nationals, 3 blacks, and 7 women. Much of the bonding occurred in self-formed study groups of 3 to 5 people. Unlike other schools, Fuqua does not assign managers to teams. Even so, one graduate noted, "Study groups were virtually a requirement, and we found out quickly how critical the 'team approach' was to surviving the transition back to 'student.'"

Other than the initial orientation, there's no residency during the 20-month program. For the first time ever in 1991, Duke made a foreign excursion optional, traveling to the former Soviet Union for two weeks in September. Managers visited factories, studied the nation's transition to a market economy, and explored doing business in the country. It was an eye-popping trip during which students saw drunken employees of a major car works stumbling out of a darkened, foul-smelling plant.

Besides the Weekend Executive MBA program, which attracts managers whose average age is 35, Duke also offers an evening program that meets Mondays and Thursdays for younger, less-experienced managers. Most business schools would call the latter program nothing more than a part-time MBA. Still, it's another option for the busy executive. But then you'll miss all that great bonding that occurs outdoors and on Friday nights at the Thomas center.

Organizations sending most participants: IBM; AT&T; Ericsson-GE; Duke University; First Union National Bank; Northern Telecom; Glaxo; GTE

Contact: Deborah Horvitz, director of EMBA programs, 919-660-7802

Duke EMBA Graduates Sound Off

The program was harder than hell sometimes, and nobody could have lasted one day more than the 20 months. Out of the 36 of us in the Class of 1989, we lost four along the way, suffered one divorce, celebrated one pregnancy, laughed a lot, bitched a lot, cried when it was over—all the richer for the experience. Would I do it again? In a heartbeat.—Director

The program did an excellent job of balancing quantitative and qualitative skills. It also did an excellent job of selecting a diverse cross section of students. We had lawyers, doctors, engineers, bankers, marketing folks, accountants, and manufacturing and service people. I learned as much from the students as I did from the lectures.—Project Leader

Some professors were excellent, but about 25 percent of them have no business in a classroom anywhere.—Manager

5. University of California at Los Angeles

John E. Anderson Graduate School of Management
405 Hilgard Avenue
Los Angeles, California 90024

Graduate ranking: 11   *Dean ranking*: 5
Enrollment: 120   *Full tuition*: $42,700
Women: 25 percent   *Minority*: 18 percent
Average GMAT score: 600   *GMAT range*: NA
Average work exp.: 14 years   *Work exp. range*: 7 to 30 years
Average salary: $92,000   *Salary range*: $55,000 to $215,000
Advanced degrees: 30 percent   *Applicants accepted*: 30 percent

Teaching methods: Case study, 40 percent; Lecture, 30 percent; Projects and games, 30 percent

Program start date: Late August

Of all the nation's Executive MBA programs, UCLA can boast what is arguably the most ambitious and intriguing management exercise of any: a six-month consulting project for a non-U.S. company. In 1992, the school's student-managers flew to Sony Corp. headquarters in Japan to finish off their study. The year earlier, managers traveled to Austria to present the findings of their strategic plan for the global expansion of an Austrian lighting concern.

Whatever the company or the assignment, the "international living case field study" is unique among top EMBA programs. Grads shower endless praise on the capstone requirement of the UCLA program, for balancing academics with the real world, and for employing teams to explore strategic issues in international business. It helps, too, that 16 percent of the EMBA class boasts non-U.S. backgrounds.

The assignment concludes an intense, 24-month program that begins every August with a one-week residency. Classes then kick in on Fridays and Saturdays of every other week, with student-managers staying overnight at the "cozy" UCLA Guest House across the street from the business school. There's nothing cozy or laid-back, however, about the program. Students immediately find themselves in the thick of "Economic Analysis for Managers," "Data Analysis and Management Decisions under Uncertainty," and "Management Information Systems"—the initial trio of courses that gobble up the first 16-week trimester.

With UCLA only a 30-minute drive from Los Angeles International Airport, many managers fly in for the program. You can even stay at the Guest House on Thursday nights for free if you're willing to share a room. Traveling executives often form mini-study groups in their locales, whether in Phoenix or the San Francisco Bay Area. Surprisingly, given the Friday/Saturday format, only 5 percent of the managers in the program are from out of state.

The routine, of course, isn't easy. Your three-hour classes begin at 9:30 a.m. on Friday. After a one-hour lunch, you're back in class until 5 p.m. Over the next hour and a half, you'll typically have a guest speaker or workshop. After dinner, most students gravitate to their study groups from 8 p.m. until the wee hours of the morning. Come Saturday, you're out of bed and in class by 8:30 a.m. so that your last course finishes up at 4 p.m. With the exception of a three-week break between each trimester, that's what life is like for the UCLA student over 24 months.

It's a rigid curriculum, too, with only one elective—in the fall of the second year. Yet, there's enough flexibility to allow much linkage between the classroom and the job. As one graduate noted, "Several term papers required that we solve a real business issue with at least one other fellow student. This allowed each student either the opportunity to learn about solving problems in another company, or the chance to have several fellow students solve a problem at one's own workplace."

Then, there's also another week-long residency in the winter of the second year, and the unusual residential week abroad at the program's end to cap off the six-month consulting project, which in past years has hooked managers up with such well-known multinationals as Unilever in Britain, Samsung in Korea, and Suntory Ltd. in Japan. (The trip is included in the tuition cost except for the air fare.) In 1991, the class was divided into six groups. Their mission: to study the possible global expansion of manufacturing and marketing operations of Austrian-based Zumtobel, a lighting company. Students spent three months examining the lighting industry in Japan, Scandinavia, the United States, Eastern Europe, and the "Golden Triangle" of Singapore, Hong Kong, Malaysia, Taiwan, Korea, and Thailand.

They dispatched videotaped mid-term reports to company officials, who then gave them written feedback on their early findings. Zumtobel top executives also visited the class to discuss the company and its objectives. Then, the student groups prepared final reports for presentation to company officials at Zumtobel headquarters in Dorbirn, Austria. "One of the fascinating aspects is to study comparative management, to learn about how we manage in the United States in contrast to Asia, Europe, and other places," says Andrea McAleenan, EMBA program director. That's a powerful sendoff from a powerful program.

Organizations sending most participants: Hughes; ARCO; TRW; Hewlett-Packard; Xerox

Contact: Andrea McAleenan, senior associate director, 213-825-2632

UCLA EMBA Graduates Sound Off

*The program provides a very powerful blend of the theoretical with the practical. The first year is devoted to quantitative methods and theory with the second year bringing it together in stimulating, "real" applications. We had our share of professors lost in space, but well over a majority were both outstanding in their fields and dynamic, stimulating teachers as well.—****Director***

*There were some exceptionally talented people in the class. However, there also were a number of managers primarily from large corporations that some of us thought were sent to the program to be fixed.—****Chief Operating Officer***

*In UCLA's Executive MBA program, you can have real executives and people with no management experience at all in the same class. At times, one wondered if it was an Executive MBA program or just another part-time MBA program.—****President***

6. Indiana University

Graduate School of Business
801 West Michigan Street
Indianapolis, Indiana 46202

Graduate ranking: 1	*Dean ranking*: 27
Enrollment: 50	*Full tuition*: $25,000
Women: 23 percent	*Minority*: 12 percent
Average GMAT score: 570	*GMAT range*: 440 to 740
Average work exp.: 14 years	*Work exp. range*: 8 to 30 years
Average salary: $70,000	*Salary range*: $45,000 to $100,000
Advanced degrees: 16 percent	*Applicants accepted*: 70 percent

Teaching methods: Case study, 30 percent; Lecture, 40 percent; Group work, 30 percent

Program start date: Late August

Like many working in Corporate America these days, Sally Hardin Lambert found her career as a corporate lawyer coming to an end as a result of a merger. Her next step, she thought, was to enter private practice in business law. But after 13 years of corporate experience, Lambert still found her overall knowledge of business wanting.

The solution for her was Indiana University's Executive MBA program. It meant that she would have to get up at 4 a.m. to drive from Louisville, Kentucky, to Indianapolis for classes on alternating Fridays and Saturdays. But after the two-year grind, she has no regrets. "The program enabled me not only to know how to organize the business side of my practice but also to effectively counsel my clients on approaches they take to solve their business problems," she says.

Ironically, the fast pace of change in the business world that led her back to school also is behind Indiana University's recent decision to suspend its own program—despite its superb ranking in the BUSINESS WEEK survey. Explains Director Pamela C. Harnett: "In our region, many of the managers interested in the program have been left with greater responsibilities after their companies have been downsized. So now they find it difficult to make the investment in time."

The business school, however, used the format of the EMBA program as a model for a new part-time MBA experience launched in 1992. Indiana also expects to offer a revised EMBA program in the fall of 1993. Judging by the high levels of customer satisfaction the business school has gotten in the past, that should be a welcome decision to many executives in the Indianapolis area. Indeed, although Indiana University's ranked only twenty-seventh among business school deans for its EMBA program, graduates were so enthusiastic about their experience that the school topped BUSINESS WEEK's graduate poll. They found Indiana's faculty to be among the best in teaching quality and accessibility outside the classroom.

That's not all. Of the graduates surveyed from 30 top EMBA programs, Indiana consistently garnered some of the top scores for the organization of its program, for putting high-caliber managers into classes, for linking class assignments to the practical workplace, and for giving its graduates the sense that they can shoulder greater responsibility as a result of the program.

What managers praised was a no-frills EMBA with a lock-step curriculum in the business basics. There were no electives—just 16 core courses over a two-year academic calendar. Small classes of students juggled four courses a semester. And each of the four semesters began with a one-week intensive residency on the Bloomington campus. Otherwise, classes met one day a week from 8 a.m. to 5 p.m. on the campus in downtown Indianapolis. Like all the other university students, you would have the entire summer off—from early May until late August.

When in class, graduates singled out as exceptional teachers such professors as Douglas Austrom, Harvey Bunke, and Harve Hagerty for the "touchy-feely" classes and George Wilson, Ashok Soni, and George Kamades for the "numbers" courses. Graduates also had good things to say about the school's support staff, which they said always came to the rescue to solve any problems or inconveniences.

Complaints? Not all of the faculty earned praise. Some came under attack for failing to be responsive to the needs of the owner-managers and entrepreneurs in the program; one or two were criticized for being poor communicators in the classroom. Overall, however, such criticism was rare. "With only one or two exceptions, the professors treated us as peers," says one graduate.

That's the kind of praise that should encourage Indiana to get a new program up and running to help future Lamberts make their career transitions.

Organizations sending most participants: General Motors (Allison Gas Turbine and Transmission Divisions); Brown Foreman; Indiana Bell Telephone; Indiana National Bank

Contact: Pamela Chambers Harnett, director of graduate programs, 317-274-4895

Indiana EMBA Graduates Sound Off

*The administration at Indiana University were very sincere in trying to adapt the program to meet individual needs and expectations. They continually monitored the students for ideas and implemented them in the program where they could. With the exception of maybe one professor, the faculty that taught the program were definitely the cream of the crop—the best any university could offer.—**Staff Engineer***

*Without exception, my experience at the Indiana University EMBA program was the best learning opportunity I have ever had. It was worth the relatively short-term disruption of social and family life and I continue to recommend the program highly to current candidates.—**President***

*The program was a grind, but well worth the effort. The participation and interaction of study groups significantly enhanced the program.—**President***

*Carrying 12 hours a semester in Indiana's Executive Program while putting in 50 to 60 hours a week at the office was a very stressful experience. What first seemed like an "Executive Boot Camp" turned out to be a rigorous educational blitz, which probably taught just as much about self-examination as economics or accounting.—**Finance Director***

7. Columbia University

Columbia Business School
310 Uris Hall
New York, New York 10027

Graduate ranking: 25	*Dean ranking*: 3
Enrollment: 225	*Full tuition*: $59,500
Women: 23 percent	*Minority*: 10 percent
Average GMAT score: 610	*GMAT range*: 440 to 750
Average work exp.: 11 years	*Work exp. range*: 5 to 30 years
Average salary: $93,300	*Salary range*: $30,000 to $200,000
Advanced degrees: 22 percent	*Applicants accepted*: NA

Teaching methods: Case study, 35 percent; Lecture, 40 percent; Group work and games, 25 percent

Program start date: Early January and early September

It was not a pleasant meeting. Indeed, one manager in Columbia's Executive MBA program termed it a "near revolt." As Program Director Tom Ference listened, participants counted down a long list of complaints on everything from the quality of the faculty, overcrowded conditions, and a curriculum deemed to be less than relevant to real business.

The hour-and-a-half session in July of 1991 was followed up by a letter to Ference signed by more than half of the second section of the Class of 1992. "Basically, Tom, this is a mid-term evaluation for the 92-II program, and it is not good," the unhappy managers wrote. "The symptoms are: faculty who appear to have insufficient time or incentive to prepare to teach the course material; faculty selected, who, even if properly prepared and motivated, are unable to communicate effectively, especially to such a large group; [a] curriculum which is not directly relevant to business challenges."

Over the years, probably every director of an Executive MBA program has heard such complaints. But it's a rare day when they surface to such visible levels at what many regard as one of the best graduate business schools in the world. Still, the disenchanted managers of the Class of 1992 were not the first to think Columbia failed to deliver the goods. BUSINESS WEEK's survey of the school's 1989 and 1991 graduates rated the school twenty-fifth out of 30 and dead last in teaching quality among the top 20 business schools. Even so, its standing among other B-school deans is so high that its Executive MBA program finished seventh in BUSINESS WEEK's rankings.

The wide disparity between the school's strong reputation among academics and the low level of satisfaction among graduates suggests that Columbia has been living off its reputation for some time. Executive grads from previous years moaned about the "sheer pomposity" and the "poor teaching skills" of some Columbia professors. Chastened by the revolt, Ference says Columbia has changed teaching assignments and launched an updated curriculum to deal with the complaints. He attributes much of the trouble to a rapid increase in enrollment, from graduating only 66 EMBAs in 1986 to 115 in 1992. "Anytime you make a change, there's going to be a period of adjustment," he says. "There was a shakedown. We had to adjust our teaching program, and we went through a bunch of changes."

Columbia, of course, can boast some exceptional faculty, including John Whitney, an expert on business turnarounds, and Donald Hambrick, who garners favorable reviews for his "Strategic Management" class. A new curriculum—also launched in Columbia's full-time MBA program—adopts a thematic structure around four major themes: globalism, ethics, human resources management, and quality. Each core course has been redesigned to fit in with the new approach.

Columbia admits two classes of up to 60 student-managers every year: one in January and one in September. Though there's no international trip, the program features five weeks in residence, some at Columbia's gracious Arden House and some at a conference center in Glen Cove, on the north shore of Long Island. A recent residence week at Glen Cove brought together 175 EMBA students, allowing a greater choice of electives than is typical in most programs. Managers pick 7 elective courses, usually chosen from up to 18 courses. If schedules permit, they also can take any classes in the full-time MBA program on Monday through Thursday.

Most managers find they just can't get the time off to take advantage of that flexibility. Regular EMBA classes begin at 8:30 a.m. every Friday on the Morningside Heights campus at Uris Hall—an overcrowded facility which rated second from the bottom after the University of Chicago's downtown location in our survey. Unlike other programs with alternating-Friday-and-Saturday schedules, therefore, Columbia requires an even greater commitment of time from your employer—a day off every week instead of every other week—plus the five solid weeks in residence.

The goal of the program, says Ference, is "to take the stuff out of the classroom and bring it to the job and then bring it back to class. We expect application and practice." That certainly occurs in the program's concluding experience, an integrating two-day workshop and residence, which serves as the finale of a two-term course in Strategic Management. The final assignment: a strategic review of your own company presented to peers.

Given the many complaints by the managers in Columbia's program, Ference probably wishes he had done his own strategic review long before the "near revolt" in 1991.

Organizations sending most participants: Nynex/New York Telephone; Time Warner; IBM; AT&T; Citibank

Contact: Thomas P. Ference, EMBA director, 212-854-2211

Columbia EMBA Graduates Sound Off

*There is not nearly enough individual work, nor sufficient feedback on written assignments. Students, at most, get an exam grade and a course grade, but no input on right or wrong answers, no critique of our case analyses or essay questions.—**Account Executive***

*Fridays on campus were about par for Columbia: crowded, overheated, dingy. But the residence weeks at Arden House were superb: great accommodations, four-star food with a respectable wine list, top-notch meeting facilities, and a great bar!—**Associate Vice President***

8. University of Southern California

Graduate School of Business
Bridge Hall
Los Angeles, California 90089

Graduate ranking: 7
Enrollment: 118
Women: 28 percent
Average GMAT score: 540
Average work exp.: 12 years
Average salary: $70,000
Advanced degrees: 20 percent

Dean ranking: 8
Full tuition: $38,000
Minority: 22 percent
GMAT range: 430 to 771
Work exp. range: 7 to 32 years
Salary range: $33,000 to $200,000
Applicants accepted: 60 percent

Teaching methods: Case study, 18 percent; Lecture, 60 percent

Program start date: Late August

A revolution of change is occurring at many graduate business schools these days. They are revamping their curriculums, requiring professors to stress the integration of narrow disciplines. They're adding leadership and ethics exercises, reemphasizing teaching and group work. And they're getting closer to the real world. But what nearly every B-school is doing today has already been common practice at this innovative Executive MBA program at the University of Southern California for years.

The surprise is that it happened by accident. In the mid-1980s, a faculty committee argued over possible changes to USC's full-time MBA program but could not agree on what to do. The upshot, says Academic Director Larry Greiner, was: "Look, you'll never change the regular program. So go design an Executive MBA program and make it different."

That is what they did. From the beginning, the school adopted what it calls "an interdisciplinary, team-taught approach." Rather than teach business in more typical discipline-related courses such as finance or marketing, the school focused its courses around 10 themes. The program starts off with a one-week residency that tackles "The Perspective of Top Management"—a course that features a case study competition among nine teams of six managers each. A CEO judges the event, which puts managers in the role of the chief executive of such companies as Corning Glass and the defunct People Express Airlines.

In "Evaluating Market Performance," managers spend seven weeks studying the stakeholders of the corporation and how each group perceives success. In "Management of Operations," student-managers focus on the internal aspects of business, including cost accounting and information systems. Other theme-related courses? "Functional Strategies and Implementation," "The Role of the Senior Executive," "Strategic Planning for Growth," "Environmental Analysis: Establishing Competitive Advantage." It's quite a different lineup from "Accounting 101" and "Organizational Behavior."

There are a lot of unusual aspects of this program. In the first week, on the second day, managers dive into another case study on the Walt Disney Co.—a team-taught exercise by three professors with backgrounds in finance, accounting, and management. Every EMBA's first assignment is to write a report that could appear in a trade journal. Every year, about half the papers get published. The idea: to encourage managers to sharpen their writing skills and to develop new ideas on business topics. Throughout the program there are what USC calls "I" days, standing for integration. Every two or three weeks, the school formally schedules team-teaching sessions to further emphasize integration of the disciplines. Team-grading also is an important part of the program. Sprinkled over the 22-month program are special seminars in such areas as real estate, entrepreneurship, and quality.

This unique approach makes USC less quantitative, as well as more applied, integrated, and differentiated. UCLA, the school's major competitor in the EMBA market, is more theory- and discipline-based. If not for an exceptional faculty, the school would be hardpressed to pull off its unusual format. In BUSINESS WEEK's survey of graduates, USC professors got among the best ratings for both the quality of their teaching and for being on the leading edge of knowledge in their fields. Of the top 30 schools, USC rated second for giving its graduates the confidence that they could shoulder greater responsibility as a direct result of the EMBA experience.

USC builds that confidence even before the first residency that kicks off the EMBA experience. For five consecutive Saturdays preceding the program's start, the school holds optional refresher courses on computer skills, algebra, and statistics—a superb way for those with math anxiety to smooth their transition back to school. And in your second year, there's an annual international excursion. In 1992, student managers travelled to Central Europe to meet with CEOs of major companies. A year earlier, the group went to Budapest and Vienna. In 1990, USC's student-managers trekked to Tokyo and Kyoto to look at the changing Japanese economy and its effect on the Pacific Rim. The class met with executives from such brand-name corporations as Fujitsu, Toshiba, and RJR Nabisco. (Air fare for the international trip is not included in the tuition fees.) In all, you'll have three off-campus, one-week residencies, including the overseas trip—a welcome break from the alternating-Friday-and-Saturday schedule of classes. Those routine sessions begin at 8:15 a.m. and end at 4:55 p.m. on the main USC campus in what is not the greatest section of L.A.

Indeed, that's about the only typical aspect of this unusually novel program: its alternating-Friday-and-Saturday class schedule.

Organizations sending most participants: Xerox; Hughes Aircraft; Northrop; IBM; First Interstate Bank

Contact: Barry D. Leskin, director of EMBA program, 213-740-6410

USC EMBA Graduates Sound Off

*We were exposed to tremendous insights and thought processes in general management. I found immediate use of this new knowledge in almost every business area. The program taught me how "not to be taken" by financial and accounting tricks.—**General Manager***

*The program far exceeded my expectations. The faculty was outstanding, the best I have ever experienced. The integrative approach to teaching is a real plus.—**Director***

209

9. Georgia State University

College of Business Administration
The Executive MBA Program
University Plaza
Atlanta, Georgia 30303

Graduate ranking: 5	*Dean ranking*: 12
Enrollment: 77	*Full tuition*: $22,500
Women: 33 percent	*Minority*: 13 percent
Average GMAT score: 566	*GMAT range*: 460 to 700
Average work exp.: 16 years	*Work exp. range*: 8 to 33 years
Average salary: $65,000	*Salary range*: $40,000 to $150,000
Advanced degrees: 16 percent	*Applicants accepted*: 37 percent

Teaching methods: Case study, 45 percent; Lecture, 38 percent; Group work and games, 17 percent

Program start date: Late August

Long before it became fashionable for business schools to bring their Executive MBAs overseas on study tours, Georgia State began its annual treks to Tokyo and Japan's industrial elite. Well before teamwork and study groups came into vogue, Georgia State focused on small-group dynamics. And today, when many schools pay little attention to their EMBA alums, Georgia State cultivates a loyal network of alumni who continue to play a key role in the program.

Those are a few of the reasons why Georgia State's business school, which fails to make lists of the nation's top 50 B-schools, fares so well with its Executive MBA program. The short answer to the school's success, however, is David C. Ewert, who as EMBA director guided the program from its inception in 1980. A former chairman of the Executive MBA Council, he wins praise from counterparts at competing schools and from student-managers for making the program his personal obsession. As one graduate from Coca-Cola Co. put it: "Dave Ewert saw and understood the growing trend in Corporate America toward using cross-functional teams to solve business problems." They also laud his and the faculty's commitment. "The faculty and the director even show up on Saturdays to have lunch with the group," says a physician who graduated from the program. "Students get plenty of personal attention."

It was Ewert, too, who began in 1982 the annual trips to Japan, building the annual business pilgrimage into a required course. "At the time, there were about 100 Japanese facilities in the state," he recalls. "Now, there are over 300 in Georgia. So we knew we were building on something. It wasn't just a fad." Not merely a fun vacation or study tour, the trip is preceded by piles of work. Study groups of five managers each put together 40-page-long strategic analyses of 8 to 10 host Japanese firms.

The Michael Porter-like studies are then shipped off to the Japanese companies a month before the 10-day trip in mid-March when student-managers meet with Japanese officials to discuss the papers. Over the years, managers have visited with the presidents of NEC, Fuji-Xerox, IBM-Japan, and Coca-Cola Japan. They've also dug deeper into the Japanese economy, routinely exploring the role of subcontractors in

Kyoto and Tokyo to Japan's giant industrial combines. The entire experience is part of a required course in "International Management Practices."

The trip is certainly the highlight of this two-year program which begins with a five-day residency at a camp on Lake Lanier in the north Georgia mountains. (Both the Japanese trip and the week-long orientation are included in the tuition fees.) In that secluded environment, managers form their own study groups and get their first dose of the initial accounting and human resources management courses. Then, the program moves into its routine: classes from 8 a.m. to 5:15 p.m. on alternating Fridays and Saturdays at Georgia State, just one block from Five Points, the center of downtown Atlanta.

The pace is intense, with one required course quickly piled on another. There are no electives. In nearly every one of the six quarters, you'll get one "soft" course and one "hard" course. "Each quarter required one or two nights," says a 1991 graduate, "where I literally did not go to bed due to studying. There were weeks on end where I averaged less than four hours of sleep per day." Much of the work is done in small study groups, and an international flavor runs throughout the program.

When it's over, you'll join an active, well-established alumni club—something of a rarity among EMBA programs. Each year, for example, they sponsor a "Return to the Madness" day when alums and current students gather to network and hear a trio of speakers offering insight and updates on important business topics. The alumni group also puts on an annual week-long trip abroad. In September of 1992, alums traveled to the Madrid Business School for a program on business and trade in the European Community.

If there's a downside to the experience, it's that Ewert has recently retired. His successor, no doubt, will have a tough time matching his stellar performance at Georgia State.

Organizations sending most participants: AT&T; Coca-Cola; Bell South & Southern Bell; IBM; Oglethorpe Power; Georgia Power

Contact: Ernest Swift, interim director of EMBA program, 404-651-3760

Georgia State EMBA Graduates Sound Off

The emphasis on oral and written communications skills was excessive. Certainly, the time spent could have been put to better use. One would expect that participants in an executive MBA program have previously mastered both oral and written communications. Regarding the faculty: Most were quite good and some truly excellent; however, a couple were atrocious.—**Operations Manager**

An excellent program and experience that has served me in both my professional and personal life. I especially liked the integration of international themes and the 10-day residency in Japan. This trip was well-balanced with visits to, and meetings with, a variety of Japanese companies and prominent Japanese leaders.—**Project Manager**

10. Case Western University

Weatherhead School of Management
500 Enterprise Hall
10900 Euclid Avenue
Cleveland, Ohio 44106

Graduate ranking: 4	*Dean ranking*: 18
Enrollment: 85	*Full tuition*: $46,662
Women: 20 percent	*Minority*: 12 percent
Average GMAT score: 520	*GMAT range*: 320 to 760
Average work exp.: 13 years	*Work exp. range*: 6 to 30 years
Average salary: $85,000	*Salary range*: $42,000 to $300,000
Advanced degrees: 20 percent	*Applicants accepted*: 20 percent

Teaching methods: Case study, 50 percent; Lecture, 30 percent; Applied research, 20 percent

Program start date: Late August

There's been a virtual revolution in management education in recent years and one of the leaders of that revolution is a business school that isn't located in Boston, fails to make any of the Top 20 lists, and has little brand identity outside of Cleveland. It's the Weatherhead School of Management at Case Western University. The school's full-time MBA program is organized around broad themes and tailored to address the strengths and weaknesses of individual· students.

Though Weatherhead's EMBA experience doesn't quite match the school's truly innovative full-time program, some of the creativity does rub off. During one residency, there's a simulation exercise in labor relations. In the marketing policy class, managers compete head-to-head in a computerized game. The operations faculty has built its course around the use of computer software. And there's also an individual project, supervised by the faculty, that links up with a current problem back at work. "We try to provide some immediate payback to the sponsor in the last year," explains Ronald Fry, the faculty director of the EMBA program. "Managers often use it to research and introduce a pilot project." Recently, for example, one manager launched a pilot training program; another began benchmarking his firm against other companies; while yet another assessed a new business opportunity for his company.

The two-year program, which meets on an alternating-Friday-and-Saturday schedule, starts in late August with a four-day residency at a conference center about an hour's commute from Cleveland. (Case Western is planning its own on-campus executive education center, which should be up by 1995.) What to expect during the first four days? "We use the residencies to build a learning community," says Fry. "They'll put together study groups of six to eight which stay intact throughout the program. They'll get all their first and sometimes second class sessions. It's a real initiation. We also have alumni come out for evening social sessions to talk with them in small groups and describe their experiences in the program."

The lockstep curriculum is composed of 21 core courses, including seminars, and a pair of electives. Though EMBAs can technically take any MBA elective (there are about 120), the school has created about five specifically for EMBAs. They include a global management course in which managers are required to write a paper on an overseas business opportunity; business law and the environment; and an advanced seminar on managing change. There are few surprises in the program: It's basic MBA fare—accounting, finance, marketing, statistics, etc. The most innovative feature of the full-time program, rigorous assessments of each person's skills and the tailoring of individualized learning plans to improve them, is not part of the EMBA program. There's also no international trip. On the other hand, alumni help to tutor student-managers having trouble in any course, and Weatherhead offers "facilitators" for the study groups—usually doctoral students—on weeknights if needed.

Every Friday, there's also an executive speaker series. In the first year, Weatherhead invites the area chief executives to come and speak to the group for an hour. In the second year, EMBAs take the responsibility for inviting the speakers. Recent guests have included Joseph T. Gorman, chairman of TRW; Morton L. Mandel, chief executive of Premier Industrial; Peter B. Lewis, chairman of Progressive Cos.; and Skip LaForge, head of General Motors' Saturn division.

In between the first two semesters, participants get together in the second of the trio of three-day residencies—and perhaps one of the most unusual because it's focused around such OB (organizational behavior) nitty gritty as leadership, motivation, working with and between groups, and designing organizations. "We spend a lot of time learning about and from their experiences in their study groups," says Fry. "We examine how to work with groups, how to manage differences, and how to build consensus. One of the takeaways is not just maintaining the cohesiveness of a study group, but learning how they work with groups in their own organization."

Common complaints: There are too many assignments; the tests overlap; and the faculty doesn't allow enough time to discuss issues or doesn't seem to want discussion in their classrooms. Some managers also think the cost of the program is quite high—particularly since the nearby Cleveland State EMBA program is about a quarter of the tuition. But it would be difficult to find another program in this area to match Weatherhead's quality and increasing reputation. "We do pamper them," says Fry. "We keep them away from all the bureaucracy." Anyone who knows anything about academia will appreciate that feature of this program.

Organizations sending most participants: BP America; General Electric; Cleveland Clinic Foundation; Centerior Energy Corp.; BF Goodrich; Ohio Bell Telephone

Contact: Ronald Fry, academic director of EMBA program, 216-368-2060

Case Western EMBA Graduates Sound Off

It was the best 20 months of my life that I never want to go through again.—**MIS Manager**

The quality of the faculty was right on in its attempt to bring in professors who could deal in real "here and now" issues rather than textbook theory.—**National Manager**

11. New York University

Stern School of Business
90 Trinity Place
New York, New York 10006

Graduate ranking: 18
Enrollment: 86
Women: 40 percent
Average GMAT score: 610
Average work exp.: 13.5 years
Average salary: $104,000
Advanced degrees: 24 percent

Dean ranking: 6
Full tuition: $59,600
Minority: 16 percent
GMAT range: 410 to 730
Work exp. range: 5 to 26 years
Salary range: $51,000 to $300,000
Applicants accepted: 24 percent

Teaching methods: Case study, 57 percent; Lecture, 35 percent; Simulations, 8 percent

Program start date: Late August

It's a balmy summer evening in New York City. More than 500 dressed-for-success executives are converging on the South Street Seaport. They're about to cruise around Manhattan on the De Witt Clinton, a replica of a turn-of-the-century steamship chartered for the night by New York University's Stern School of Business.

For the B-school, this evening is good public relations. Aboard are more than 100 corporate sponsors who send their managers to Stern's Executive MBA program at $59,600 a pop. It's also a festive alumni reunion, and it's an initiation rite for the 44 newcomers who make up the Class of 1993. But this is a party they will soon forget. Five days later, these managers from such companies as AT&T, Georgia Pacific, and Morgan Stanley begin a grueling two-year journey in pursuit of their MBAs.

For Stern's new class, the pressure begins to build in the first of six week-long residencies. On their first day at Arrowwood, a lavish resort in New York's Westchester County, they are put into study groups, assigned second-year students as mentors, and plunged into a business-simulation game. They assume executive roles, making key decisions about whether to expand abroad and where, and what product lines to sell off or extend.

Within two days, each team gets a report card on the profitability of the simulated venture, and managers are getting feedback from peers on their performance. One manager is accused of being too autocratic because he directed his teammates to close plants without asking for their ideas on how to cut expenses. Another manager concedes she was too laid-back, not wanting to fully commit herself to the exercise. Before it's all over, everyone will walk away with a cassette tape of colleagues criticizing them. Jokes an instructor: "We suggest that you don't jog with this tape near traffic."

No sooner does the week-long session end than students begin their alternating-Friday-Saturday schedule of classes. In addition to the 8 hours of class time every week, each student puts in an average of 22 hours of schoolwork. Study groups meet a minimum of once a week, though when a project deadline approaches, the pace can quicken to nightly. "You can always tell an EMBA student by the condition of his lawn and how long the storm windows stay on in the spring," laughs Shawn Feeney, a Salomon Brothers Inc. vice-president who graduated from Stern in 1991.

The Stern program is relatively new. Founded in 1982, it has graduated just a few more than 250 students. But already the school has established a top-notch program. Its eighteenth-place rating in our graduate survey fails to fully capture recent changes that have worked to strengthen the program. Indeed, more than any other school in the survey, Stern showed the most improvement in scores—its 1991 graduates were far more impressed than its 1989 grads.

What's behind the change? Only a few years earlier, alums had been describing EMBA profs here as "detached and aloof" and the support staff as "somewhat lax." Humbled by the criticism, Stern went to work to improve the deficiencies. The school attempts to put only the best 25 of its more than 160 full-time faculty into the program. That's possible because the program is not part of the faculty's normal teaching load. Instead, every teacher is there by invitation of EMBA Director Norman Berman. Even the school's pre-program workshops on calculus, personal computers, and accounting are taught by full-time faculty, two of whom have won teaching awards.

Class size is kept small: about 40 students versus the 100 at Wharton or the 60 or so at Columbia. And those small classes go through an innovative curriculum that balances more traditional courses in the basics with such novel classes as "Business and Literature," "Business History," "New Venture Management," "Communications," and "Managing a Culturally Diverse Work Force." At the end of the first year, the entire faculty conducts a two-day "Integrative Perspective" where a case is analyzed from the perspective of all first-year courses.

During the second year, students travel abroad for 10 days for an international residency in such locales as England, France, Switzerland, Germany, and Japan. Unlike other schools, which treat such trips as downtime, Stern makes the trek abroad part of its "Managing Strategy in the Global Economy" course and requires students to prepare detailed industry studies on global competition and corporate strategy. Indeed, graduates consistently praised the program's international content—a rarity for the typical EMBA program.

When it's over, most student-managers leave with a mixture of relief and sadness. "We all went through the post-partum blues," says Jeffrey Relkin, a Dun & Bradstreet Corp. manager and 1990 Stern graduate. "It's like the last performance of the school play. It's bittersweet." At least he'll be able to savor his memories as an alumnus on Stern's next cruise around Manhattan.

Organizations sending most participants: American Express; AT&T; Nynex; Bankers Trust; Citibank; IBM; Merrill Lynch; Manufacturers Hanover Trust; Chase Manhattan; Time Warner

Contact: Norman D. Berman, director of EMBA program, 212-285-6001

Stern EMBA Graduates Sound Off

*The study groups set up by the program staff were invaluable. They pushed, pulled, and carried members, whatever was necessary.—**Finance Project Manager***

This was, without a doubt, the most grueling, yet rewarding, experience in my life. After graduating this program, it felt like I was "born again." —***Director***

12. University of Illinois at Urbana – Champaign

College of Commerce and Business
1206 S. Sixth Street, Box 103
Champaign, Illinois 61820

Graduate ranking: 10
Enrollment: 74
Women: 15 percent
Average GMAT score: NA
Average work exp.: 15 years
Average salary: $58,000
Advanced degrees: 22 percent

Dean ranking: 9
Full tuition: $24,400
Minority: 4 percent
GMAT range: NA
Work exp. range: 5 to 30 years
Salary range: $38,000 to $120,000
Applicants accepted: 62 percent

Teaching methods: Case study, 35 percent; Lecture, 65 percent

Program start date: Late August

Think of this Executive MBA program as a no-frills, yet solid, experience into management education. Sure, there are a few interesting twists. But what you get here more than anything else are a lot of the old-fashioned basics of a more traditional MBA program.

Even the warm-up sessions are a harbinger of the program's emphasis on numbers. Four weeks before the program's start, there's a four-day refresher course on quantitative methods. Two weeks before you begin, there's a three-day session on financial accounting. As many as 80 to 90 percent of the participants attend the preparatory classes.

And the opening six-day, on-campus residency to this program in late August is all business. No Outward Bound excursions. No computer simulations or games. No case-study competitions. With the exception of an evening barbecue, managers immediately plunge into four heavy classes: "Financial Accounting," "Foundations of Behavioral Science," "Microeconomics," and "Statistics."

"It's not the froufrou ropes business," says Kevin Fertig, director of the EMBA program. "It's let's get to work. We get the books out and get them going." Indeed, the same is true in the second residency that kicks off the second year of this alternating-Friday-Saturday program. It's just more accelerated coursework. "It's a good way to understand what it's like to be a student again," adds Fertig.

While that may be true, some graduates of Illinois' program are critical of what they perceive to be an overemphasis on the quantitative side of business. To anyone familiar with management education, that will sound like a common complaint. Yet, it's still surprising to hear it in the 1990s in an MBA program for executives. Several managers who have gone through this EMBA experience thought Illinois didn't spend nearly enough time on leadership and people skills.

Even the program's new Management 2000 experience—a series of seminars and projects placed on top of the core curriculum—fails to completely address the critics. One novel piece requires each study group to hook up with a local community organization and provide pro bono consulting help. Managers are working with a food bank, a children's home, an occupational development center, and the local public broadcasting station. In the fall of the second year, EMBA candidates go to

Springfield, Illinois to meet on the general assembly floor of the Capitol building for a "business and government day." They hobnob with lobbyists, elected officials, and regulators to discuss the intersection of business and government.

The overlay course also includes an ethics component and seminars on working with and as management consultants and executive headhunters. "We're trying to break the students out of the mold of their own companies or their study group companies and to look at broader issues," explains Fertig. Also, for the first time, Illinois is offering a one-week international study tour to England and Germany in the spring of 1993 for second-year students.

These broadening experiences help to place more balance in the program composed of 13 core courses and three electives. Typically, a third of the coursework over the two years deals with a specific project at a manager's company or at a company chosen by the study group. One recent example: A team presented a marketing plan for a product made by the company of a group member. That kind of linkage occurs again and again throughout the program. In the school's managerial accounting class, students are asked to write reports that critique their organizations' management information systems.

Much of the focus in these and other assignments is on group work. Fertig, who interviews all candidates for the program, assigns managers to their study groups of four to six people each. In every case, the focus is on diversity. "We look for a mix of functional and industry background and personality," he says. A recent study group, for example, boasted a cost analyst from Caterpillar, a partner in a CPA consulting firm, a product design engineer for Maytag, the executive director for United Way, and a manager working in strategy and human resources for the largest credit union in Illinois. The group's project in an entrepreneurship class was to develop a business plan for a nonprofit hospice.

That's an interesting twist in a more traditional EMBA program.

Organizations sending most participants: Caterpillar; State of Illinois; Carle Hospital & Clinic; A.E. Staley Manufacturing; City Water Light & Power (Springfield, Illinois)

Contact: Kevin Fertig, director of EMBA program, 217-333-4510

Illinois EMBA Graduates Sound Off

*The program was an extremely rewarding experience, both professionally and personally. The faculty and staff at the university were some of the best in their respective fields and exhibited a strong desire for sharing that knowledge and experience with the students.—**President***

*Unfortunately, several of the tenured professors were so poor and the quality of their service to the students was such that if they were in medicine or law they would have been sued for malpractice. One instructor collected term papers on the last day, left for Europe the next day, and said he would grade the paper and fax the grades. The papers did not have a single comment on them. If this man worked for me, I would have fired him!—**Manager***

13. Purdue University

Krannert Graduate School of Management
West Lafayette, Indiana 47907

Graduate ranking: 8	*Dean ranking*: 24
Enrollment: 70	*Full tuition*: $28,500 (+ computer)
Women: 25 percent	*Minority*: 10 percent
Average GMAT score: 585	*GMAT range*: 490 to 720
Average work exp.: 15 years	*Work exp. range*: 8 to 28 years
Average salary: $62,300	*Salary range*: $35,000 to $125,000
Advanced degrees: 18 percent	*Applicants accepted*: 75 percent

Teaching methods: Case study, 65 percent; Lecture, 35 percent

Program start date: July

Congregated in Harry's Chocolate Shop like an unruly group of undergrads, executives at Krannert clearly relish their part-time role as full-time students. After a full day of lectures and study groups, they'll stream into Harry's, a State Street pub euphemistically called the Chocolate Shop, to unwind.

But Krannert students can expect to spend a minimum of their time there. Unlike conventional EMBA programs, Purdue requires its master's candidates to come to the campus for two-week-long stays. Six times during the two-year program, students travel to West Lafayette to take classes during the day, gather in six-person study groups at night, and then retire to their dorm rooms. Since the professors can get their hands on the students only during these sessions, they tend to make the most of the six. Grads describe the in-residence fortnights as both the most worthwhile and the most rigorous part of the Krannert executive program.

By housing students for 2 weeks and then sending them home for 6 to 10, Purdue made geography irrelevant. So long as managers could coax their employers to give them 2 weeks off from work and the cash to commute via plane, they could enroll in the program. Now the school and its loyal alumni body of more than 200 claim that this format, born out of necessity, has turned into a benefit.

These prolonged periods away from campus can also be viewed as a downside to the program. In between the 2-week stints in West Lafayette, executives spend up to 12 weeks without seeing a professor or classmate. They stay connected to the school through Macintosh computers and an electronic mail system that allows messages to be sent to professors and other students. Most managers use the computerized bulletin board a couple of times a week and say professors are quick to answer queries. Still, three months of being away from campus can be a long time.

Entering students attend a three-day orientation, one full day of which is devoted to teaching the ways of the Mac. Starting in 1991, Purdue added an optional fourth day, intended to teach basic computer skills. After orientation, students return home for the first of three modules, each consisting of two on-campus visits sandwiched in between lengthy at-home reading periods. In each of the first two modules, students take four classes, split fairly evenly between "soft" courses in organizational behavior and "hard" courses in accounting and statistics. Accounting, finance, and economics are all hailed for their immediate relevance back on the job. That Purdue's forte is the more number-oriented classes should come as no surprise.

If you lack an analytical background, approach the program with some caution: You'll have to do a significant amount of catch-up during the initial reading periods. Mary Sue Cavanagh, an Otis Elevator manager in the class of 1992, found that her undergraduate background in French forced her to spend chunks of time catching up to her classmates who received degrees in economics or engineering. "If someone says, 'I only spent 2 hours on something,' then I know I'll have to spend 4 or 6," she says.

In the final module, students stray from the core slightly to pick two of their four courses. But because Krannert has difficulty freeing up professors to teach electives, students have only four or five electives to choose from and the entire class must take the same two courses, determined by a class vote. This meant the class of 1991 was stuck with two finance electives, "Advanced Finance" and "Financial Risk Management," when virtually everyone wanted just one.

While on campus, students stay in Holiday Inn-like rooms in the Union Club, a university-operated hotel across the street from the Krannert Center. As part of the tuition, a dining hall in the Union serves breakfast and dinner, and lunch is offered in the Executive Center. So long as you remember that you didn't fly to West Lafayette for the food, you won't be too disappointed.

Professors contribute to the collegial atmosphere, putting in extra hours, eating dinner with students, and then hanging out with study groups to work on cases. And under the helm of Executive Education Director Dr. Wilbur Lewellen, professors conspire to ensure that the material covered in different classes shows a strong connection. Lewellen is eager to cultivate Krannert's image as a school that works its students to the bone—from 8 a.m. to 11 p.m. while on campus and up to 25 hours a week at home—without abandoning them along the way.

For those who can't get to a university every week, the school's innovative schedule may be a good option. And even those who do have a choice may think Krannert's way of doing business is better. The time spent on campus is likely to be more intense than anything a weekend program offers. If your boss gives you the time off and your marriage is strong enough, flying off to West Lafayette to play college student—Harry's beer, late-night studying, and all—might just sound like a good way to get a master's degree.

Organizations sending most participants: General Electric; United Technologies; Eli Lilly & Co.; AT&T; Eastman Kodak

Contact: Wilbur "Bill" Lewellen, director of executive education programs, 317-494-7700

Purdue Graduates Sound Off

This was definitely not a cookie-cutter type program in which the goal is simply to produce MBAs. There was a lot of individualized instruction, and the staff made certain it was available at all times.—**Branch Manager**

The students are treated like royalty. We had to work very hard, but the staff worked as hard as we did.—**Plant Engineer**

14. University of Pittsburgh

The Joseph M. Katz Graduate School of Business
301 Mervis Hall
Pittsburgh, Pennsylvania 15260

Graduate ranking: 9	*Dean ranking*: 10
Enrollment: 81	*Full tuition*: $27,600
Women: 17 percent	*Minority*: 5 percent
Average GMAT score: 571	*GMAT range*: 450 to 730
Average work exp.: 13 years	*Work exp. range*: 5 to 33 years
Average salary: $73,200	*Salary range*: $34,700 to $245,000
Advanced degrees: 22 percent	*Applicants accepted*: 67 percent

Teaching methods: Case study, 25 percent; Lecture, 65 percent; Simulations, 10 percent

Program start date: Early January

After 22 hours of travel through a dozen time zones, the group of Executive MBAs landed in Hong Kong on a late Saturday night. There's a Sunday afternoon tour and a welcoming dinner with faculty. But then, for the American managers in the University of Pittsburgh's EMBA program, it's mostly work: intensive classes at the Chinese University of Hong Kong, discussions with Asian authorities and businesspeople, and tours of local factories.

The program's annual excursion to Hong Kong every April is clearly the highlight of Pitt's EMBA experience. Formal briefing sessions precede the 10-day trip during which managers delve into global competitiveness issues and foreign business prospects. In 1991, the entourage included 39 EMBA candidates, 29 spouses (who are encouraged to attend), and a half dozen faculty and staff. The international residency also included a one-day side trip to a Digital Equipment plant in Shenzhen, China.

Of course, that's the icing on a rather heady educational cake. The two-year program begins with a three-day residency at a hotel-conference center in Monroeville, just a few miles east of Pittsburgh. Once there, EMBA Director "Skip" Gross sorts managers into study groups by home zip codes—to make it easier for them to gather on weeknights between the school's alternating-Friday-Saturday classes in the ultra-sleek and modern Mervis Hall.

This is a demanding program, with 15 core courses and three electives. Just the titles on the first term's three classes are daunting enough: "Financial Accounting," "Behavioral Science in Business" and "Computer-based Information Systems." That's a lot of work to pack in between the class hours of 8:15 a.m. and 5:15 p.m. once a week. The load hardly lightens in the second term when you'll confront "Managerial Accounting," "Organizational Analysis," and (gulp) "Probability and Statistical Analysis 1." Yes, part two follows in the next term. Pitt's electives don't kick in until your fifth and sixth terms in the second year. Recently, the trio of elective courses picked by class consensus were: "Entrepreneurship and New Venture Initiative," "The Legal Environment of Business," and an advanced marketing course.

One unusual benefit to Pittsburgh's offering is that the school will accept up to six transfer credits from other programs. Most business schools refuse to accept any. So if you were forced to quit a program because of a corporate move, you'll find

Pittsburgh more accommodating than most. That's true across the board: Graduates surveyed by BUSINESS WEEK again and again paid tribute to the EMBA staff led by Gross. Said one manager: "The administration recognizes the unique learning environment that the program creates and fosters its growth in little and big ways. Small touches like the continental breakfast and handling basic educational hassles like class registration and buying books make going back to school easy. But these amenities would be worthless if it weren't for the quality of the basic academic program."

If the Friday/Saturday EMBA program doesn't fit into your work schedule, Pitt actually boasts another way for executives to earn their MBAs. In 1991, the school launched a new Purdue-like "Flex-MBA" program that alternates fortnight stays on campus with 10-week periods spent at home. While away from campus, students stay in touch with professors and classmates by computers and fax machines. They spend roughly 20 hours a week on school work. "It's appealing to people who need flexibility in their career paths," says Gross. "It allows someone to get through an MBA and not be interrupted by a career move."

For Flex, managers have eight in-residence periods over a two-year period. Pitt's inaugural class of 22 boasted managers from AT&T, Digital Equipment, and even a U.S. Naval officer. Its second class of 19, who came aboard in February of 1992, has managers from Alcoa, Corning, General Electric, and even a local funeral director. Pitt's Flex program will set you or your company back $31,000, including a laptop. Instead of Hong Kong, Flex-MBAs spend two weeks in Europe. The first class ventured to Paris and Prague in their second year. (You have to cough up the airfare for the trip, too.)

When it's over and you graduate from either program, you'll join an active alumni group that should prove helpful to you throughout your career. The EMBA Alumni Association sponsors golf outings, career seminars, get-acquainted socials for newcomers, and two annual dinner meetings with top-level corporate speakers. The school, knowing the importance of that network these days, mails out updated alumni directories every year to graduates. Not a bad idea to encourage close contact among alums and to keep memories of that Hong Kong trip alive for years to come.

Organizations sending most participants: Westinghouse Electric; H.J. Heinz; Alcoa; PPG; Children's Hospital of Pittsburgh

Contact: A.C. "Skip" Gross, director of EMBA programs, 412-648-1600

Pittsburgh EMBA Graduates Sound Off

*Less emphasis should be given to statistics/quantitative courses and more emphasis should be placed on management, human resources, legal issues of business, and organizational behavior.—**Director***

*The program expanded my business knowledge base, which has enhanced my current job performance and helped to increase my potential career opportunities. Most importantly, the program and my classmates have forced me to put my career aspirations into perspective and to set more aggressive career goals for the future.—**Controller***

15. Emory University

Emory Business School
1602 Mizell Drive
Atlanta, Georgia 30322

Graduate ranking: 12
Enrollment: 91
Women: 22 percent
Average GMAT score: 581
Average work exp.: 14 years
Average salary: $81,700
Advanced degrees: 11 percent

Dean ranking: 11
Full tuition: $37,600
Minority: 11 percent
GMAT range: 440 to 720
Work exp. range: 6 to 26 years
Salary range: $42,000 to $220,000
Applicants accepted: 67 percent

Teaching methods: Case study, 40 percent; Lecture, 40 percent; Group work and games, 20 percent

Program start date: Early January

How's this for practical learning? A manager for John Deere came up with a distribution plan that can save his company $8 million. The medical director of an Atlanta hospital figured out a way to substantially increase payments from emergency room patients. The head of a community food bank discovered how to use planning concepts to better manage a program that distributes 10 million pounds of food a year.

In each case, a manager accomplished these on-the-job goals thanks to an unusual feature of Emory's outstanding Executive MBA program. Students worked one-on-one with professors in a required independent study project that immediately yielded direct results back at work. That's the kind of real-world applicability that graduates of Emory's program have come to expect and to receive.

This is a business school on the move, or as its dean says, one with great "upside potential." That's evident not only in Emory's full-time MBA program, but also its degree experience for executives. The fun and the grind begin in November and December with pre-program courses in math and computer skills during evenings and Saturdays. A week after you've put away the noisemakers from New Year's Eve, you'll find yourself in the first of four week-long residencies.

Two weeks later, the routine begins: classes on Fridays and Saturdays on alternate weekends. The typical schedule will have you out of bed early. There's a 7:30 a.m. continental breakfast before the 8 a.m. class. You'll keep busy until the end of the afternoon class at 4:30 p.m., although on some Fridays the school actually schedules evening sessions from 5 to 6:30 p.m. Emory puts you through 20 core courses and two electives (chosen from five that are offered by the school).

In the first term, which runs from early January to mid-April, expect to crack open the textbooks for "Financial Accounting," "Organization and Management," "Marketing Management," and "Introduction to Quantitative Managerial Decisions." The next round of courses, running from early May to early August: "Economic Analysis for Managers," "Managerial Accounting and Control," "Managerial Statistics," and "Human Resources Management."

Besides the classwork, there's also a speaker series which few business schools outside of the New York or Chicago area can match. Recent guests have included President Jimmy Carter, Coca-Cola Chairman Roberto Goizueta, Procter & Gamble

Chairman Ed Artzt, super investor Warren Buffett, and Elaine LaRoche, the first woman director of Morgan Stanley.

The professors generally get highly favorable reviews, and Emory's B-school has long had a reputation for putting strong teachers in its classrooms. Graduates surveyed by BUSINESS WEEK, however, were less impressed with Emory's quant teachers. Some groused about the excessive use of tests, including pop quizzes in, of all things, statistics. Others maintained that Emory didn't do a very good job of teaching basic computer skills to managers who fail to use computing as a management tool. On the other hand, the school offers weekly evening help sessions for managers having trouble with the "quant" material—in addition to the pre-program sessions.

The capstone course—"International Business Colloquium"—is a 10-day study trip put on by Emory in partnership with top B-schools in England, Italy, Austria, and Hungary. Including "International Perspectives" in the third term and "International Business Seminar" in the fourth term, it's actually one of a trio of courses on global business. Early in the program, managers are introduced to several companies in the host countries. Managers with these firms submit current problems which are dissected by student teams who correspond with foreign managers during the program. On the trip abroad in your fourth and final term, the teams present their findings directly to the companies. The class also meets with leading scholars, executives, and government officials in the host countries. (The airfare for this trip isn't covered in the tuition fee.)

As popular as the international excursion is, many graduates say they found the independent study project even more beneficial. Consider Earl Brinkley from John Deere Co. Working with a professor at the school, he applied just-in-time manufacturing concepts to the retail environment. His idea: Open a new hub to coordinate distribution from Deere's four divisions. Top management quickly adopted part of his proposal, and he expects the rest to gain approval soon. The upshot: savings of $8 million for the farm equipment maker. That can't be bad for his career.

Organizations sending most participants: IBM; Coca-Cola; Bell South; AT&T; Georgia-Pacific

Contact: Edgar W. Leonard, director of EMBA program, 404-727-6358

Emory EMBA Graduates Sound Off

Excellent professors: I believe they enjoyed our classes as much as we enjoyed them. There was a high level of synergy in our class, with a good mix of international students.—**Account Executive**

The professors at Emory seem genuinely interested in the experiences of the students. A large part of our learning came from those experiences and current problems of one another. I would classify Emory as a training camp for CEOs.—**Director**

As an employee who worked his way up from an entry-level position with a high school diploma, the program provided the most efficient and practical means of obtaining an advanced education.—**Marketing Director**

223

16. University of Texas at Austin

Graduate School of Business
P.O. Box 7337
Austin, Texas 78713

Graduate ranking: 15	*Dean ranking*: 13
Enrollment: 117	*Full tuition*: $20,100
Women: 25 percent	*Minority*: 6 percent
Average GMAT score: 580	*GMAT range*: 400 to 700
Average work exp.: 13 years	*Work exp. range*: 6 to 40 years
Average salary: $83,000	*Salary range*: $38,000 to $210,000
Advanced degrees: 19 percent	*Applicants accepted*: 36 percent

Teaching methods: Case study, 60 percent; Lecture, 30 percent; Simulations, 10 percent

Program start date: Late August

Bargain-hunters take note: You'd be hard-pressed to find a better deal on an Executive MBA program than the one at the University of Texas' business school. Dubbed Option II, the Executive MBA program at Texas meets on alternate weekends, on both Friday and Saturday. That schedule is one reason why Texas, over the years, has drawn commuting managers from such states as California and Colorado, New Mexico and Indiana, even Ohio and New Jersey. It also helps that Texas tuition is dirt cheap: just $24,900 for out-of-state students.

For the cash, you get great value. Included in the deal are four week-long Executive Seminars at off-campus conference centers, including one in London (airfare isn't included). The first seminar that opens the program in late August forces students to buckle down right away: It's an intensive review of basic skills in accounting, math, and microeconomics. The second one zooms in on a topical business issue (recent examples include the management of technology and international marketing). Year two of the program begins with the third seminar, which focuses on strategic planning. The final week away in mid-May ends your two-year stint in class: a five-day seminar in London to study business in Eastern and Western Europe with business and political leaders.

Founded in 1981, the Option II program is as basic as an EMBA program comes: You'll take three required courses for each of four semesters. First up are "Financial Accounting Issues in Business Decisions," "Management Science," and "Money and Capital Markets." In the second semester, you'll find yourself in the middle of "Managerial Accounting," "Managerial Microeconomics," and "Statistics." The next trio of courses in the third semester are "Advanced Marketing Management," "Case Problems in Financial Management," and "Operations Management." And the final portion of the program delves into "Corporate Strategy," "Interpersonal Behavior in Organizations," and "Topics in the Legal Environment of Business." That's a lineup of courses that is light on leadership and "soft" skills and heavy on quant courses and "hard" subjects, which tend to get more treatment in the residency sessions. "We have found that when they're in the classroom in concentrated blocks of time, theory, concepts, and analysis work well," explains Daniel G. Short, former associate dean for the program. "When we're on the retreats, we can deal with the softer areas such as leadership because we find they go off to dinner and conversations around the pool where those subjects tend to be amplified."

Besides these formal classes, managers get to select one of three final options to round out the program. You can pick two electives from the regular MBA program (there are an overwhelming 242 electives offered)—although you'll have to attend class during the weekdays. You can write a "professional report" on a business problem that will be bound and placed in the library. Or you can team up with a professor to do an independent study project on a topic of your choice. This latter option gives you the flexibility of working with the faculty on a real problem you're grappling with at work.

Two or three times each semester, the school brings to campus a leader in business or government in its Distinguished Speakers Series on Friday mornings. The sessions bring together Option II students with the school's mainstream MBA program. Recent guests have included Mary Kay Ash, the cosmetics entrepreneur; John Bookout, president of Shell Oil; Robert W. Galvin, former CEO of Motorola; and Elvis Mason, chairman of InterFirst. A novel twist to all this is the large number of Mexican business and government leaders who come to campus for both the speaker series and guest appearances in classrooms as a result of a business school partnership with Monterey Tech in Mexico.

A program strongpoint is the diversity of the managers in the Option II program. "We get students from the high-tech companies in Austin, from the oil companies in Houston, and from the banking firms in Dallas," says Short, who left the program in 1992 to become dean of Kansas State University's business school. "Sometimes these programs can get homogeneous in the types of people they draw, but we're bringing together a mixture of corporate and geographic perspectives."

From whatever perspective you look at it, Option II delivers great value for the money.

Organizations sending most participants: Motorola; Texas Instruments; IBM; La Quinta Motor Inns; 3M

Contact: Cort Huber, director of Option II program; 512-471-4487

Texas EMBA Graduates Sound Off

The program was heavily laden with quantitative coursework and little qualitative material in human resources and interpersonal skills. The majority of the students came from the computer industry and had engineering backgrounds. It was a bit of a stretch for a non-quant person, yet the use of case studies and the diversity of the study group was a great help.
—**Vice President of Sales**

For students not living in the Austin/San Antonio area, professors were always accessible by telephone and fax, but at times the program seemed ill-equipped to handle the long-distance traveler.—**Manager**

Although the majority of the professors were on the leading edge, there were a few who should have been farmed out long ago. We didn't pay $20,000 to waste our time!—**Manager**

225

17. Wake Forest University

Babcock School of Management
P.O. Box 7659
Reynolds Station
Winston-Salem, North Carolina 27109

Graduate ranking: 13	*Dean ranking*: 22
Enrollment: 100	*Full tuition*: $29,000
Women: 17 percent	*Minority*: 7 percent
Average GMAT score: Not req.	*GMAT range*: Not req.
Average work exp.: 14 years	*Work exp. range*: 7 to 32 years
Average salary: $59,000	*Salary range*: $23,000 to $270,000
Advanced degrees: 10 percent	*Applicants accepted*: 70 percent

Teaching methods: Case study, 85 percent; Lecture, 10 percent; Business games, 5 percent

Program start date: Late August

The Harvard Business School owes much of its prominence to its case method approach of teaching. Students analyze and debate brief, problem-oriented company reports or cases at the lofty general manager-CEO level. Among the top business schools offering Executive MBA programs, Wake Forest's Babcock School of Management comes closest to adopting Harvard's successful teaching formula.

Not only is case study the dominant mode of instruction at Babcock, it's a near obsession. Over the course of this 20-month EMBA program, student-managers grapple with more than 500 case studies—an often hellish, intensive ordeal that yields dynamic class debates and exchanges. As befits the case study orientation, the curriculum is more applied and practical with a general management approach. The Harvard-like emphasis also results from the school's early roots in emphasizing classroom teaching over esoteric research.

Founded in 1971, Wake Forest's executive program is the oldest in the Southeast and one of the first three in the nation. Managers begin dissecting those cases in late August with the start of the first of four equal-length semesters. Within each semester, four courses are offered, generally meeting once a week on Saturdays and occasional Fridays. Each course meets for 18 to 20 sessions for an hour and 45 minutes each. One in four of the EMBA students arrive on Friday evening and stay overnight at the local Holiday Inn and Comfort Inn—both within walking distance of the school—to make the 8 a.m. class start on Saturdays. (The tuition covers the hotel costs.)

In the second week, managers take off for a five-day residency at the Catholic Conference Center in Hickory, North Carolina for sessions on team-building—the only required residency of the program. Babcock puts managers through a full day of business simulation games during the retreat, puts on several formal classes, and holds several study group meetings in what exec-ed Director Thomas M. Brinkley calls an "intensive orientation." A four-day Outward Bound experience has been taken out of the program after the departure of a professor who was its champion, but Brinkley is reconsidering that decision in light of alumni surveys which show great appreciation for the outdoor team-building exercises.

Study groups, after all, are all-important to the Babcock program. Students are placed into groups even before the first day of class on the basis of their backgrounds and interviews with the EMBA staff. "We mix students up geographically and by function," says Brinkley. "Those teams then stay together for the entire two years and they meet at least one night a week."

This is a lockstep program of 15 core courses, with four electives. Babcock recently added a management communications course spread over the first two semesters. Given the school's bent toward the practical and applied, you'll find more emphasis on the soft skills than most EMBA programs. In the first semester, for example, you'll get the familiar dose of accounting, but the other courses are "Marketing Management," "Organization Behavior," and "The U.S. Role in a World Economy." There are also courses in "Management Information Systems," "Strategy and Environment," "Corporate Innovation and Entrepreneurship," and "Leadership and Executive Action." It's definitely a more interesting and relevant course load than most. Recent electives have been offered in total quality management and advanced marketing and finance.

Most EMBA programs now boast international trips. Babcock is unique in offering its student-managers two foreign excursions, both optional and at extra cost. There's a two-week trek to Japan in mid-May, which features a home stay with a Japanese family for three days, visits to Japanese factories, sessions with business and government leaders, and sidetrips to China and Malaysia. (Cost is about $4000, including airfare.) The other two-week study tour in early July goes to Oxford, England, for in-depth sessions on the European economy. EMBA students act as consultants to project teams of Babcock's evening and full-time MBA students who conduct studies of key industries in Europe. They stay in the dorms at St. Peter's College. (Cost is about $3000, including airfare.)

About half of Babcock's EMBAs take one of the optional trips; the rest do an "executive project" in their own organizations. Recent examples: A vice president for Sara Lee did an analysis of where to expand the company's knit outlet stores that became the guts of a strategic plan for the division; a manager with an electronics maker in Raleigh did a process project to increase assembly line production efficiency. On average, managers spend 200 hours working on these projects over the summer. It's a lot of work, but it's also a relief from all those case studies you'll have to digest over the 20 months of this program.

Organizations sending most participants: Sara Lee; Ciba-Geigy; GTE; Memorial Mission Medical Center; Lowe's Companies

Contact: Thomas M. Brinkley, director of executive education, 919-761-0707

Wake Forest EMBA Graduates Sound Off

*Students were stressed with well over 500 case studies during our 20 months. With the class time, class preparation, study groups, and travel, I never spent less than 42 hours a week on school while also holding down a full-time job. It took a toll on my family and sleep.—**Director***

18. Vanderbilt University

Owen Graduate School of Management
401 21st Avenue South
Nashville, Tennessee 37203

Graduate ranking: 14	*Dean ranking*: 30
Enrollment: 101	*Full tuition*: $40,200
Women: 27 percent	*Minority*: 6 percent
Average GMAT score: 580	*GMAT range*: 450 to 750
Average work exp.: 12 years	*Work exp. range*: 5 to 32 years
Average salary: $60,100	*Salary range*: $32,100 to $117,000
Advanced degrees: 10 percent	*Applicants accepted*: 50 percent

Teaching methods: Case study, 40 percent; Lecture, 40 percent; Project work, 20 percent

Program start date: Mid-August

Vanderbilt University's Executive MBA program makes our ranking on the basis of its scores from satisfied graduates who placed the Owen experience fourteenth in the nation. But the school still has a bit of work to do in building its reputation among deans and program directors who ranked the school thirtieth. That has been a problem for some time: Back in 1989, the graduating class of full-time MBAs left the school a unique gift—enough money to hire a public relations firm.

Yet, this is a first-class program supported by a first-class director, recruited a couple of years ago from the University of Rochester's Simon School of Business. Owen offers executives a middle-of-the-road MBA. It's a solid education without the frills of an international trip, an outdoor team-building exercise, or a corporate-sponsored consulting project. But the school pays attention to the details. No sooner than you're admitted, you're sent a test to assess your mathematical skills. If you need work, an adviser might suggest a textbook or two to read. And you'll likely get an invite to what the school calls a "Math Camp" in late July, about three weeks before the program starts. About half the class attends the three-day sessions.

Classes meet all day Friday and Saturday, every other week. Each of the two years starts with a full week in residence at a conference center in New Harmony, Indiana, a three-hour drive from Nashville. "Our objective is to get people away from their businesses and away from their families so they can concentrate on school for a week," says Thomas Hambury, director of the program. "It allows us to get into the courses and the ramp-up effect these programs tend to have."

It's a lockstep program with 20 required courses and no electives. You take five courses a semester for four semesters. The first batch: "Financial Accounting," "Microeconomics," "Organizational Behavior," "Statistics," "Management Information Systems," and "Business Law." If you return for the second semester, you'll have "Macroeconomics," "Finance," "Human Resources Management," "Marketing Management," and the first of two operations management courses. After this grueling lineup, you'll deserve the seven-week break Owen affords its students between the first and second years.

Owen is constantly updating and revising its curriculum, too. The school ditched its traditional Marketing II course a couple of years ago in favor of one on "Customer Service Marketing"—which emphasizes such things as customer satisfaction and quality. In 1993, it plans to increase by 50 percent the time devoted to international business. In "Organizational Theory and Design," the team rules. Student teams set up the structure of the course, take group tests, and receive group grades. "It tends to drive the engineers off the wall," says Hambury, "but they learn a lot about how to deal with self-managed work teams."

In the second year, student groups do a strategy project as part of a year-long integrative course. Teams of three to five managers dissect the financial history and strategic direction of a chosen company or start-up venture, from Apple Computer to mail-order entrepreneur Lands' End, to create a five-year business plan based on an in-depth analysis that takes from 80 to 150 pages. The project typically culminates in a public presentation before the senior management of the company. "You can think of it as a senior thesis with a dog-and-pony show," says Hambury. "You get to stand up before the company's executives and tell them what they're doing right and what they should be doing. You get feedback from them or others in the industry."

As is typical in most EMBA programs, there's a social side to the experience as well. In October, the school invites first-year student spouses to a Saturday of case studies to give them an idea of what their partners are going through. There's a spring dinner-dance for both first- and second-year classes at a nearby restaurant. EMBAs are always invited to the beer keg parties on Thursday and sometimes Friday nights. There's a guest speaker series, often followed by receptions. And the EMBAs have their own graduation in late June—the only Vanderbilt students with a separate graduation ceremony—followed by a champagne luncheon.

Organizations sending most participants: Bell Telephone; Northern Telecom; Ingram Industries

Contact: Thomas Hambury, director of EMBA program, 615-322-2402

Owen EMBA Graduates Sound Off

My classmates brought a wealth of experience to the program. The relationships I developed will be a valuable resource for many years to come. The Vanderbilt program is managed well. It is highly organized and run with the professionalism that I expect when dealing with any business.
—Senior Accountant

After 21 years of formal education, this experience was the most practical of any I received. Imagine a statistics professor who authored a classic textbook on the subject saying, "Don't memorize these formulas. I want you to know what's behind the numbers on a computer printout, not how to calculate them!" Or imagine an accounting professor whose favorite comment was, "That's close enough! Keep your eye on the big picture."
—President

19. Southern Methodist University

Edwin L. Cox School of Business
Executive MBA Program
Dallas, Texas 75275

Graduate ranking: 17	*Dean ranking*: 17
Enrollment: 95	*Full tuition*: $29,940
Women: 15 percent	*Minority*: 3 percent
Average GMAT score: Not req.	*GMAT range*: Not req.
Average work exp.: 17 years	*Work exp. range*: 10 to 30 years
Average salary: $90,000	*Salary range*: $60,000 to $150,000
Advanced degrees: 19 percent	*Applicants accepted*: 33 percent

Teaching methods: Case study, 70 percent; Lecture, 15 percent; Group work, etc., 15 percent

Program start date: Late August

American Airlines wanted to open a facility at an airport north of London, England. J.C. Penney sought to examine the possibility of taking their product lines to Poland, Hungary, and Czechoslovakia. Mary Kay Cosmetics considered exporting to the United Kingdom. Trammell Crow wondered how to market a management center it is building in Germany to both U.S. and European companies.

What each of these corporate projects have in common is that they were the subject of study by Executive MBAs at Southern Methodist University's Cox School of Business. Their work was part of the school's annual international trip to London in which student teams had to research and brief a real corporate objective. The assignment also is part of what makes Cox's program somewhat different from many others. As Monica Powell, program director, puts it: "We're one of the few EMBA programs that have a curricular international trip. A lot of schools offer a trip as an option. Ours is required. And a lot of them will do what we call a show-and-tell trip. They don't incorporate it into the curriculum."

That's not true at Cox. Student-managers here take a trio of international courses—in finance, marketing, and management information systems—before they depart on their 10-day European study tour in the spring of their second year. Even before they step onto the airplane, students are given binders two and a half inches thick, full of case studies and speaker bios to prepare them for class. Once in London, they stay in the spartan study bedrooms of the London Business School and spend 45 hours in its classrooms. "There's less sightseeing, but more knowledge-building," Powell says. When they return, student teams prepare comprehensive papers or group presentations for each of the three international classes. And that's all in addition to the work performed for the corporate sponsors.

It's hardly a slow-paced program. Indeed, the opening of this experience is a total immersion process, with five days of on-campus classes in late August. "Demanding is not quite the word," adds Powell. "It's basically a hell week." Incoming managers arrive for a Monday orientation dinner with their spouses—for a good reason. During the evening, spouses break off from the students for a special presentation by a psychologist who attempts to prepare them for what's to come. There's also a panel discussion with a current student and spouse, a recent graduate and spouse, and an older graduate and spouse.

Then, from Tuesday morning at 7:15 until Saturday afternoon, student-managers will find themselves in the specially designed EMBA classroom at Cox for eight hours a day. The initial intellectual gymnastics features managerial forecasting, financial accounting, and an organizational behavior course. Most students return home after these sessions, but the commuters usually stay overnight in a nearby hotel.

Classes soon kick in all day Friday and Saturday, every other week, in Room 188 of the graduate wing of the relatively new business school building. From the looks of it, managers will spend plenty of time in that room: Cox claims that executives total some 976 hours in class to earn the degree, more than any other Top 20 program. Managers will gain credit for 20 courses throughout the lockstep program. In the first year, the coursework is focused on what the school calls "the acquisition of knowledge, skills, and usable expertise" in business. In the second, the courses cover the broader, policy-level aspects of finance, management information systems, organizational behavior, and marketing. There are also a slew of "integrative" courses in industry analysis, global management and operations management, and business policy. Faculty and administrators determine the few electives offered each year.

BUSINESS WEEK's survey of graduates found several who were less than thrilled by some of the faculty (see comments below). Several managers in the program even accused some of the tenured professors of being lazy and indifferent. And one of the few criticisms of Cox's international trip was that the faculty treated the experience as a paid vacation, leaving the students to go off with their wives. Complained one 1991 graduate: "The faculty were more interested in touring the country with little involvement with the executive students while in London." (The tuition, incidentally, does not include the airfare for the overseas trip.)

In April of 1993, Cox plans to switch the locale of its international trip to Brussels, where it will hook up with companies on still more projects.

Organizations sending most participants: Dresser Industries; Arco Oil and Gas; GTE; Associates Corp. of North America; Rockwell International

Contact: Monica S. Powell, director of EMBA program, 214-692-3154

Cox EMBA Graduates Sound Off

The program is a great confidence builder and survey of the material. Some really great and some really poor professors. The interaction in our class was not always productive, because of hostility among students and the lack of teacher control.—Self-employed

The schedule of having courses staggered and ending at different times throughout the year was initially viewed as a negative by many of the younger students who preferred to have all their mid-terms and finals due at the same time. Once we got into the second semester, however, most students realized that preparing for one exam at a time was much better when you're carrying a full work load.—Vice President

20. Tulane University

A.B. Freeman School of Business
Goldring/Woldenberg Hall
New Orleans, Louisiana 70118

Graduate ranking: 16	*Dean ranking*: 21
Enrollment: 81	*Full tuition*: $33,000
Women: 29 percent	*Minority*: 13 percent
Average GMAT score: 521	*GMAT range*: 450 to 690
Average work exp.: 14 years	*Work exp. range*: 7 to 30 years
Average salary: $56,500	*Salary range*: $35,000 to $150,000
Advanced degrees: 21 percent	*Applicants accepted*: 63 percent

Teaching methods: Case study, 40 percent; Lecture, 50 percent; Simulations, 10 percent

Program start date: January

In many ways, Tulane University's Executive MBA program mirrors the major changes in this region's economy. In the program's early days, managers from the oil and gas industry tended to dominate the program. These days, as the region becomes more diversified, so has the Freeman School's EMBA experience. Today, the program is filled with physicians, attorneys, accountants, health care administrators, managers from mid-sized firms, and entrepreneurs. Only one in five participants comes from the oil and gas and manufacturing sectors.

Tulane is attempting to put that diversity in the classroom to good use—and it does so by piling on the work even before participants arrive for the 19-month-long program. The school offers preparatory courses in computer basics and quantitative methods on evenings and weekends in October and November. Just a couple of weeks before the program's start, there's a mandatory orientation in mid-December. Students get more than a tour of the library, however, because they can expect to spend the last two weeks of December preparing assignments for "Intensive Week 1."

That's a full week of on-campus instruction designed to turn managers into students. Another week-long schedule of classes is planned during the summer at the end of the second term. In the fourth and final term, EMBA students travel to France for a 10-day seminar. (The school switched to Brussels and Paris in 1992; plans to go to an Eastern and Western European capital in 1993 and perhaps a Latin American locale in 1994.) "We want to keep the program interesting and to keep it from being perceived as a bennie at the end," said Elizabeth Watson to the director of the program.

In that year, managers began the overseas trip to Hautes Écoles Commerciales outside of Paris, where the final sessions of a global strategy course are taught by faculty from the host school. After the course, students move to Paris for a series of briefings, executive lectures, and visits to multinational companies. During the semester preceding the trip, students and their spouses are offered weekly conversational French classes and briefings on the culture, business practices, and politics of France.

But that's the fun part. The regular academic grind of this 19-month program occurs in Friday and Saturday segments, every other weekend. All managers take two courses at a time so that your first class meets from 8:30 a.m. until 12:30 p.m., and your second from 1:30 p.m. to 5:30 p.m. Thursday and Friday evenings are often devoted to labs, study group exercises, and cases. Exams are scheduled on "off" weekends at the end of each course module.

Your initial two terms are, as the school puts it, "operational, focusing on the basic functional areas of management with coursework in accounting, finance, economics, marketing, and organizational behavior." The final two terms emphasize strategic problem solving and the integration of concepts learned in the first half of the program. During the summer of 1992, the school was in the midst of a major curriculum review so significant changes are possible for the 1993 entering class.

What isn't likely to change, however, is Tulane's tendency to inject special projects into many of the two dozen courses you'll take. In "Entrepreneurship," for example, managers focus on entrepreneurial or intrapreneurial ventures of their choosing. Students screen the ideas, picking the best ones to develop in teams. They then write full business plans on how to attract financial and human capital to the projects. In "Management Communications," students prepare a corporate position statement for the press and then are subjected to "hostile interviews" by media. The program's capstone project is a case analysis under which managers make and defend key decisions affecting the financial strategy of a firm. Managers spend an average of 60 to 100 hours on this project in their "Financial Strategies" course.

Tulane boasts two special classrooms for EMBA students on the first floor of Goldring/Woldenberg Hall, the relatively new, six-story B-school building. There's even a lounge for EMBA students on the second floor. Founded in 1982, the program attracts managers from the Texas border to Pensacola, Florida. In 1990, Tulane also began to offer its EMBA program at an off-site location in Alexandria, which is in central Louisiana, about a 30-minute flight from New Orleans. Managers in that program attend classes in the executive training center of Rapides Regional Medical Center.

Organizations sending most participants: Boise Cascade; AT&T; Boeing Petroleum; Ochsner Medical Institutions; Texaco

Contact: Elizabeth Watson, director of EMBA program, 504-865-5481

Tulane EMBA Graduates Sound Off

*The program enabled me to meet and work with 44 very different professionals. I can now pick up the phone and get help from each of them as needed. Perhaps the biggest thing that the EMBA program did to enhance my personal management style was to enable me to view problems from a variety of perspectives.—**Associate Director***

*The quality of the faculty varied widely—some excellent, some dismal. —**Attorney***

*Some of the faculty could have been more in touch with the "real world" of business.—**Vice President***

APPENDIX

How do corporations select the business schools they send their executives to? Who generally decides whether a manager is given an executive education experience? Do these programs enhance or undermine a company's ability to retain management talent? BUSINESS WEEK asked these and many more questions of the 346 corporations surveyed that foot the bill for business school programs. Here's how the human resources officials answered the queries.

1. **Please rank in importance the following factors in selecting an executive education program. (Answers are in order of importance, expressed as a percentage of a point scoring system.)**

   School's reputation: 18.3 percent

   Curriculum: 17.8 percent

   Past experience: 16.6 percent

   Length of program: 12.9 percent

   When executive has time to take a course: 10.3 percent

   Cost: 9.4 percent

   Boss' recommendation: 8.5 percent

   Location of school: 6.3 percent

2. **Please rank in importance the influence of the following in making decisions about who will attend an executive education program.**

   Immediate superior: 28.6 percent

   A systematic career development process: 27.5 percent

   Executive taking the course: 24.6 percent

   Human resources department: 19.2 percent

3. **Is your company sending more or less people to executive education programs at business schools?**

   More: 26.3 percent

   About the same: 45.1 percent

   Less: 28.6 percent

4. If your answer is more, why is your company sending more people to such programs at business schools?

Company has put more emphasis on management development: 50.0 percent

Payback is high: 28.5 percent

Business schools are creating excellent programs: 21.5 percent

5. If your answer is less, why is your company sending fewer people to such programs?

Prefer in-house training: 29.4 percent

Can hire the best faculty in-house: 27.7 percent

Budget cutbacks: 27.7 percent

Payback is too low: 15.2 percent

6. Do these programs in your opinion enhance or undermine your organization's ability to retain executives and managers?

Enhances retention: 64.8 percent

No effect: 33 percent

Undermines retention: 2.2 percent

7. Is your organization's investment in such programs at business schools worth it? How would you describe the payback?

Excellent: 7.0 percent

Good: 70.2 percent

Fair: 19.0 percent

Unsatisfactory: 3.9 percent

8. In general, how well are the business schools meeting the needs of business in designing and offering programs that help organizations better develop executive talent?

Excellent: 2.6 percent

Good: 63.8 percent

Fair: 25.0 percent

Unsatisfactory: 8.6 percent

9. In general, do you believe that executive education courses at business schools are too theoretical?

Yes: 50.4 percent

No: 49.6 percent

10. In general, do you believe that the material your executives learn in such courses is directly useful in their work?

Yes: 72.2 percent

No: 27.8 percent

11. Do you believe that the material your executives learn in such courses is useful for their long-term development?

Yes: 97.7 percent

No: 2.3 percent

12. To what extent do business schools care about your opinions?

Very much: 23.3 percent

Somewhat: 70.2 percent

Not at all: 6.5 percent

13. To what extent are the directors of executive education at the business schools responsive to customer needs and desires?

Very much: 24.6 percent

Somewhat: 70.0 percent

Not at all: 5.4 percent

14. In general, do you believe business schools view executive education as an important part of their overall education mission or as a way to increase revenues?

Key to educational mission: 27.5 percent

Way to raise revenues: 62.6 percent

Both: 9.9 percent

Survey Methodology

The widespread interest in BUSINESS WEEK's rankings of full-time MBA programs sparked this project to rate business schools' efforts in executive education. Like the earlier MBA ratings, the rankings examine education from the perspective of the consumer. Both the executive education rankings and the executive MBA rankings are based on a composite of two separate polls conducted during the summer and fall of 1991. Matthew Goldstein, former president of the Research Foundation of the City University of New York, consulted on the project. A well-published academic in statistics, Goldstein has co-authored four books on statistical methods and has served as a consultant to pollster Louis Harris Associates, AT&T Co., and General Foods.

Executive Education

Participant Survey

A 30-question survey was mailed to executives who attended the flagship programs of 26 top schools. Our aim was to survey both the alumni whose studies were the most recent and those who had some time to judge the subsequent payoff in the workplace. So, in nearly all cases, participants from the classes in 1989 and 1991 were asked for their views. Of the 3546 questionnaires sent out, 1567 were answered and returned by our deadline, a response rate of over 44 percent. Boston University was excluded from the final results because of the limited number of responses received.

Managers were asked to answer questions on a scale of 1 to 10. Example: "Did you have the feeling that your teachers were at the leading edge of knowledge in their fields?" If the answer was "always," the executive would check "10"; if is was "rarely," he or she would choose "1."

The executives' responses were weighted to account for how closely they related to overall satisfaction. The weighting also valued more highly the questions that showed the least variability in responses. The average raw scores for each school are shown in the tables in Chapter 3.

School Response Rates

School	Response rate	Total replies
Babson	55%	26
Boston	40	16
California, Berkeley	34	35
Carnegie Mellon	40	32
Columbia	34	43
Cornell	40	44
Dartmouth	54	74
Duke	52	118
Harvard	33	93
Indiana	41	35
INSEAD	34	56
Michigan	59	149
MIT	42	78
North Carolina	43	44
Northwestern	48	70
Pennsylvania	48	61
Penn State	55	116
Pittsburgh	49	41
Southern California	25	26
Southern Methodist	32	22
Stanford	35	131
Tennessee	47	30
Texas	56	25
UCLA	27	60
Virginia	68	116
Wisconsin	79	26

Company Survey

The survey was sent to vice presidents for human resources or directors of management development. Starting with a list of about 500 corporations, we screened out companies that either did not use university-based executive education or could not render an opinion because the company's spending was too decentralized. Some 144 of 346 companies replied, a response rate of 42 percent.

Of all the questions on the survey to corporate management development officers, the most important one for use in BUSINESS WEEK'S ranking was on customer responsiveness. The University of Michigan's Business School came out first, with slightly more than 48 percent of companies that are familiar with or have experience with Michigan believing it is doing an "excellent job" in executive education. In contrast, only about 7 percent of the companies which have experience with the University of Pittsburgh's programs believe that school is doing an excellent job.

We asked the following: "Do you know of any schools that in your opinion are doing an excellent job in meeting the needs of business in designing and offering programs that help organizations better develop executive talent?"

Each selected school received a point. The total score for a school was then divided by the number of responding companies that had experience with it. This formula became the basis for the corporate ranking. The results are presented in the following table.

Company Survey Ranking

Rank	School	Raw score
1	Michigan	.483
2	INSEAD	.449
3	Virginia	.413
4	Duke	.400
5	Harvard	.390
6	Columbia	.329
7	Northwestern	.318
8	Pennsylvania	.304
9	Stanford	.289
10	Penn State	.271
11	MIT	.240
12	USC	.216
13	Cornell	.175
14	Tennessee	.158
15	Indiana	.135
16	North Carolina	.130
17	Berkeley	.125
18	Dartmouth	.090
19	Babson	.086
20	Pittsburgh	.069

Composite Ranking

To gain an overall ranking, the raw scores from both surveys were combined, using a standard statistical approach for independent scores. The opinions of corporate officials naturally have greater weight in the overall ranking because that survey reflects a greater difference in scores between top- and bottom-ranked schools.

Executive MBA

Graduate Survey

A similar 30-question survey was mailed to 1989 and 1991 graduates of 30 schools. Out of 2844 graduates, 1610 answered the questionnaire, a response rate of 57 percent. The average raw scores for some of these questions are included in Chapter 7.

School Response Rates

School	Response rate	Total replies
Boston	28	16
Case Western	46	35
Claremont	55	37
Columbia	46	78
Chicago	60	95
Duke	56	43
Emory	60	41
Georgia State	49	40
Houston	58	53
Illinois	60	42
Indiana	67	38
Loyola	58	45
Michigan State	60	56
MIT (Sloan Fellows)	60	64
New York	72	49
North Carolina	65	53
Northwestern	61	162
Pennsylvania	60	109
Pittsburgh	48	39
Purdue	73	41
Rochester	55	40
Southern California	56	57
Southern Methodist	62	48
Texas	49	50
Tulane	57	47
UCLA	60	57
Vanderbilt	59	52
Wake Forest	59	38
Washington (Seattle)	48	40
Washington University (Olin)	48	45

B-School Survey

Because these programs serve mostly local markets, we surveyed school officials rather than corporate executives who could not render judgments on a national basis. Surveys were sent to program directors at all 102 schools listed in the Executive MBA Council's 1991 directory. Some 76 schools responded, a response rate of 75 percent. Deans were asked to list the top 10 schools, in order. A school ranked No. 1 received 10 points, while a school ranked No. 10 got 1 point. Northwestern topped the list, garnering an average score of 5.52 per respondent.

Deans' Survey Ranking

Rank	School	Raw score
1	Northwestern	5.52
2	Chicago	4.88
3	Columbia	4.55
4	Pennsylvania	4.05
5	UCLA	3.26
6	New York	2.45
7	Duke	1.84
8	Southern Calif.	1.38
9	Illinois	1.00
10	Pittsburgh	0.857
11	Emory	0.701
12	Georgia State	0.571
13	Washington U. (Olin)	0.532
	Texas*	0.532
15	Michigan State	0.506
16	Claremont	0.455
17	Southern Methodist	0.416
18	Case Western	0.390
19	Boston	0.377
20	Tulane	0.338

*Tied for rank with school above.

Composite Ranking

The scores from both surveys were combined to achieve an overall ranking.

The Best Schools in Executive Education, According to B-School Deans and Directors

Because BUSINESS WEEK sought a customers' view of executive education programs, we chose not to include in our overall ranking the results of another BW survey of the directors of B-school executive education. We gathered their views in the process of collecting more general data on their schools' involvement in the management development field. We sent these surveys to the heads of executive development at 75 top schools, mainly the members of the University Consortium for Executive Education. We received responses from 49 schools, a response rate of 65.3 percent.

Their impressions make for an interesting contrast with the corporate views collected by the magazine. Michigan, instead of coming in first, is only narrowly beaten out by Northwestern University's business school. Some 50 percent of the respondents believed Northwestern is the most customer-responsive school. Interestingly, the data shows that well over twice as many executive education directors believe that Northwestern is doing a better job in being responsive to corporate customers than the Harvard Business School.

We asked the following: "Please name five schools that in your opinion are the most responsive to their customers when it comes to executive education." The results follow.

Deans' Survey Ranking

Rank	School	Raw score
1	Northwestern	.500
2	Michigan	.475
3	Penn State	.400
	Virginia*	.400
5	Duke	.375
6	Columbia	.225
	Wharton*	.225
8	Harvard	.200
9	Babson	.175
	INSEAD*	.175
11	Indiana	.150
	Tennessee*	.150
13	MIT	.100
	Pittsburgh*	.100
	Stanford*	.100
16	North Carolina	.075
17	Carnegie Mellon	.050
	Dartmouth*	.050
	Boston*	.050
20	Cornell	.025
	UCLA	.025
	Berkeley	.025
	Texas	.025
	Southern Calif.	.025
	SMU	.025

*Tied for rank with school above.

INDEX

BEST PROGRAMS BY TOPIC

University of California, Los Angeles, Medical Marketing Program, 100

University of Pennsylvania, Advanced Industrial Marketing Strategy, 65

University of Pittsburgh, Target Marketing, 154

University of Virginia, Sales Management and Marketing Strategy, 40

University of Wisconsin:
Business-to-Business Marketing Strategy, 163
Professional Sales Skills Workshop Series, 163

Manufacturing:

Cornell University:
Managing the Next Generation of Manufacturing Technology, 115
Manufacturing Executive Program, 115–116

Dartmouth College, Effective Management of Production Program, 110

University of Michigan, Manufacturing Executive Program, 36

R&D/Technology:

Babson College, Technology Managers Program, 121

Carnegie Mellon University, Program in Engineering Design, 105

Cornell University, Managing the Next Generation of Manufacturing Technology, 115

Massachusetts Institute of Technology:
Current Issues in Managing Information Technology, 91
MIT Management of Technology Program, 91, 167–168

University of North Carolina:
Program for Technology Managers, 80
Seminar for Technology Managers, 80–81

Strategy:

Babson College, Strategic Planning and Management in Retailing, 120–121

Duke University, Competitive Strategies in the Telecommunications Industry, 50

Indiana University, Managing Business Strategies, 131

International Institute for Management Development, Seminar for Senior Executives, 148

Massachusetts Institute of Technology, MIT Executive Program in Corporate Strategy, 90–91

Northwestern University, Merger Week, 45

Pennsylvania State University, Program for Strategic Leadership, 85

University of Texas, Managing Strategy in a Changing Environment, 160

Quality:

Columbia University, Creating the Customer-Oriented Firm, 70

Harvard University, Achieving Breakthrough Service, 61

Northwestern University, Creating World-Class Quality, 45–46

University of Hawaii, Deming Procedures for the Public Sector, 142

University of Pittsburgh, Benchmarking, 154

University of Southern California, Service-Driven Organization, 157

University of Tennessee:
Executive Development Program, 93–97
Marketing and Customer Value Institute, 95
Senior Executive Institute for Productivity Through Quality, 96, 169–170

University of Texas:
Customer Service: Real Competitive Advantage, 160
Quality Excellence Forum, 160
Quality Self-Assessment Workshop, 160

Miscellaneous:

Carnegie Mellon University, Program in Engineering Design, 105

Cornell University, Purchasing Executives Institute, 116

Dartmouth College, Minority Business Executive Program, 110, 181–182

Duke University, Executive Program for Corporate Counsel, 50

Emory University, Investor Relations: Issues, Strategies, and Techniques, 136

Southern Methodist University:
Financial Planning and Control Seminar for Oil and Gas Company Managers, 125
Seminar for Senior Executives in the Oil and Gas Industry, 125

University of California, Purchasing Executive Program, 100

University of Hawaii:
Innovative Compensation Packages, 142
Self-Managing Work Teams, 140

University of Pittsburgh, How to Improve Your Negotiating Skills, 154

University of Tennessee, Executive Development for Distribution Managers, 95

BEST PROGRAMS BY GEOGRAPHIC LOCATION

California:

Claremont Graduate School (Drucker), 188–193, 239, 240

Stanford University, 2, 5, 6, 11, 14, 16–30, 32, 53–57, 58, 73, 88, 89, 134, 137, 187, 237, 238, 241

University of California, Berkeley (Haas), 16–30, 133, 137–139, 237, 238, 241
University of California, Los Angeles (John E. Anderson), 14, 16–30, 98–102, 187, 188–193, 202–203, 237, 239, 240, 241
University of Southern California, 16–30, 133, 155–157, 187, 188–193, 208–209, 237, 238, 239, 240, 241

Europe:

INSEAD, 13, 14, 16–30, 32, 73–77, 186, 237, 238, 241
International Institute for Management Development, 133, 146–148
London Business School, 149–151

Georgia:

Emory University, 134–136, 187, 188–193, 222–223, 239, 240
Georgia State University, 187, 188–193, 210–211, 239, 240

Hawaii:

University of Hawaii, 2, 6, 133, 140–142

Illinois:

Northwestern University (Kellogg), 8, 13, 16–30, 32, 43–47, 134, 187, 188–193, 194–195, 237, 238, 239, 240, 241
University of Chicago, 187, 188–193, 196–197, 239, 240
University of Illinois, Urbana-Champaign, 143–145, 187, 188, 191–193, 216–217, 239, 240

Indiana:

Indiana University, 7, 15, 16–30, 128–132, 135, 187, 188–193, 204–205, 237, 238, 239, 241
Purdue University (Krannert), 187, 188–193, 218–219, 239

Louisiana:

Tulane University (A.B. Freeman), 187, 188–193, 232–233, 239, 240

Maryland:

Loyola College, 186, 188–193

Massachusetts:

Babson College, 7, 8, 15, 16–30, 118–122, 135, 237, 238, 241
Boston University, 175–176, 188–193, 236, 237, 239, 240, 241
Harvard University, 2, 5, 6, 10, 14, 16–30, 32, 58–62, 73, 89, 98, 134, 140, 146, 152, 164, 171–172, 187, 237, 238, 241
Massachusetts Institute of Technology (Sloan), 5, 6, 14, 16–30, 32, 58, 73,

Massachusetts Institute of Technology (Sloan) (*Cont.*): 88–92, 134, 137, 152, 164, 167–168, 179–180, 238, 239, 241

Michigan:

Michigan State University, 188–191, 193, 239, 240
University of Michigan, 8, 13, 14, 16–30, 32, 33–37, 164, 177–178, 237, 238, 241

Missouri:

Washington University (Olin), 186, 188–193, 239, 240

New Hampshire:

Dartmouth College (Amos Tuck), 15, 16–30, 108–112, 164, 181–182, 187, 237, 238, 241

New York:

Columbia University, 2, 14, 16–30, 32, 68–72, 165–166, 185, 187, 188–193, 206–207, 237, 238, 239, 240, 241
Cornell University (Johnson), 5, 15, 16–30, 32, 113–117, 134, 237, 238, 241
New York University (Stern), 185, 187, 188–193, 214–215, 239, 240
University of Rochester, 186, 188–193

North Carolina:

Duke University (Fuqua), 2, 7, 8, 10, 13, 14, 16–30, 32, 48–52, 98, 99, 187, 188–193, 200–201, 237, 238, 239, 240, 241
University of North Carolina (Kenan-Flagler), 14, 16–30, 78–82, 146, 237, 238, 239, 241
Wake Forest University (Babcock), 187, 188–193, 226–227, 239

Ohio:

Case Western University (Weatherhead), 187, 188–193, 212–213, 239, 240

Pennsylvania:

Carnegie Mellon University, 5–6, 14, 16–30, 32, 103–106, 134, 153, 237, 241
Pennsylvania State University (Smeal), 14, 16–30, 32, 83–87, 237, 238, 241
University of Pennsylvania (Wharton), 1–2, 6–7, 14, 16–30, 32, 63–66, 98, 134, 164, 183–184, 185, 187, 188–193, 198–199, 237, 238, 239, 240, 241
University of Pittsburgh (Joseph M. Katz), 16–30, 152–154, 187, 188–193, 220–221, 237, 238, 239, 240, 241

Tennessee:

University of Tennessee, 6, 14, 16–30, 32, 93–97, 164, 169–170, 224–225, 237, 238, 241

CORPORATIONS AND ORGANIZATIONS

247